WITHDRAWN

SUICIDE IN AFRICAN AMERICANS

SUICIDE IN AFRICAN AMERICANS

David Lester

NOVA SCIENCE PUBLISHERS, INC.
Commack, NY
1998

Editorial Production: Susan Boriotti
Assistant Vice President/Art Director: Maria Ester Hawrys
Office Manager: Annette Hellinger
Graphics: Frank Grucci and John T'Lustachowski
Acquisitions Editor: Tatiana Shohov
Book Production: Ludmila Kwartiroff, Christine Mathosian and Tammy Sauter
Circulation: Cathy DeGregory and Maryanne Schmidt

Library of Congress Cataloging-in-Publication Data available upon request

ISBN 1-56072-562-1

Copyright © 1998 by   Nova Science Publishers, Inc.
6080 Jericho Turnpike, Suite 207
Commack, New York 11725
Tele. 516-499-3103   Fax 516-499-3146
E-Mail: Novascience@earthlink.net
Web Site: http://www.nexusworld.com/nova

Printed in the United States of America

10, 11, 12
117, 118
157 - 160
129 - 152

CONTENTS

THEORIES OF BLACK SUICIDE   129

FRUSTRATION, AGGRESSION AND THE OPPRESSED   153

CHAPTER 1

INTRODUCTION

The occurrence of suicide in African Americans has been of great concern to African Americans over the last few decades. Many articles and commentaries have appeared, and concern has been expressed over the possibility of rising suicide rates in some groups of African Americans, male youths in particular.

On the other hand, suicidology as a profession has not shown a great deal of concern over black suicide. Kirk, et al. (1992) noted that, although the American Association of Suicidology has had black members since 1971, the association has shown only a limited interest in the issue of black suicide. The authors objected to the topic being included in symposia on "minority suicide," and they noted that attendance at papers on black suicide was typically poor.

Furthermore, the research and theorizing on suicide in African Americans has not been of high quality. Research has been rare, and the majority of articles on the topic have been simple reviews of this scanty research, combined with speculative commentary. Furthermore, many of the assertions made by these commentators about black suicide have been based on myths. Some of the myths are based on erroneous facts, such as Slater's (1973) claim that suicide rates were rising alarmingly in black women -- they were not. Other myths are based on a lack of knowledge about suicidology. For example, as we shall see later, one cannot focus on the poor social and economic conditions of African Americans as explanations for their high suicide rate because black suicide rates in general are *lower* than white suicide rates -- indeed, some suicidologists theorize that suicide rates should be lower when social and economic conditions are poor, and so the poor social and economic conditions of African Americans might explain their low suicide rates.

This book will *critically* review the research that has been conducted on black suicide and the theories which have been proposed. Having done this, the book will present some correct facts about black suicide and then explore how well-established theories of suicide fare in explaining the phenomenon of black suicide and whether new theories are required to supplement these explanations.

REFERENCES

Kirk, A. R., Dennis, R. E., & Key, L. J. The role of blacks in the first 25 years of the American Association of Suicidology. In D. Lester (Ed.) *Suicide '92*, pp. 279-280. Denver, CO: American Association of Suicidology, 1992.

Slater, J. Suicide. *Ebony*, 1973, 28(11), 152-160.

CHAPTER 2

SUICIDAL BEHAVIOR IN AFRICAN AMERICAN SLAVES[1]

The National Civil Rights Museum in Memphis (Tennessee) notes in their exhibit for 1619 that "Many African Americans fought against bondage by stealing from their owners, escape, arson, even homicide. They broke tools, injured work animals, and pretended to be ill in the field or on the auction block. As a last resort, some committed suicide."

Suicide in enslaved African Americans has not been examined in any detail except for an article by Piersen (1977) documenting suicide in slaves soon after capture, during transportation to the Americas, and immediately upon arrival. The present chapter reports on suicides in enslaved African Americans more generally and seeks to understand these suicides in the context of current knowledge of suicidology.

Capture And Transportation To The Americas

As noted above, Piersen (1977) documented suicidal behavior among slaves when they were first captured in Africa and sent on their voyage to the Americas. Piersen noted that the myth was widespread in Africa that whites killed and cooked the captured Africans. As a result of this belief, some slaves decided that death in Africa was better than being eaten in the Americas. Even after they arrived in the Americas, the slaves' experiences sometimes reinforced this fear. Seeing whites drink red wine in Louisiana led some newly-arrived slaves to think that the whites were drinking blood (du Pratz, 1763).

---

[1] This chapter is based on Lester (1998).

Though the belief in white cannibalism was weaker near the Atlantic coast of Africa, the slave traders perpetuated the myth. English slave traders told slaves that the Portuguese would eat them, while Portuguese traders told slaves that the English traders would eat them (Piersen, 1977).

Slaves in the Americas sometimes teased new arrivals with the myth. In 1737, a local slave boarded the slave ship *The Prince of Orange* at St. Christopher and told the slaves that their eyes would be put out and then they would be eaten. Several hundred jumped overboard and thirty-three drowned (Pope-Hennessy, 1967; Wax, 1966).

THE NEWLY ARRIVED ENSLAVED

Suicide was reported to be common among the newly enslaved. Some slaves simply walked into the ocean and drowned, as if they were trying to walk home (Owens, 1976). Mass suicides were not uncommon. Snelgrave (1734, p. 173) reported groups of twenty or more slaves hanging themselves in the West Indies, and Henry Coor (Anon, 1790, p. 71) reported that fourteen Jamaican slaves cut their throats *en masse*.

The most common methods for suicide were hanging and drowning (Piersen, 1977). Tales were told of slaves killing themselves by holding their breath or swallowing their tongue, but these stories may possibly be false since such methods for suicide are undocumented by forensic scientists today. Eating poisonous clay or directly taking poison was not, however, unknown, though eating clay may have resulted also from malnutrition.

Piersen noted that slaves shipped with friends survived the voyage better than those more isolated. Nobility, older slaves and male slaves seemed to fare worse, and Ibo slaves from Nigeria were noted for their high rate of suicide. The association of suicidal risk with status, age and gender is found in modern times and, although well-documented (Lester, 1989a), is poorly understood.

Many African tribes believed that the soul returned home after death and suicides often announced their intention in suicide was to return home, a belief consistent with the African concept of the extended self, in which the self is extended to include all of the ancestors and those to be born in the future (Zahan, 1979), and the belief in the unification of the individual spirit with all of creation (Nobles, 1980).

Ellenberger (1960) has noted that capture and imprisonment is very traumatic. He noted that the same behavioral consequences can be observed in both psychiatric patients who are locked-up against their will and in wild animals who are captured and placed in zoos. Two common syndromes can be observed: (1) anxiety, feverish activity, stereotyped movements and self-mutilation, and (2) depression, stupor and refusal to eat. Piersen noted that slaves on board ship for the voyage across the Atlantic Ocean often lost their appetite (the food served was strange to them) and showed dissociation and depression, which may have resulted in suicidal behavior through self-starvation. The slaves' psychological state may have increased their susceptibility to illnesses, and they often refused medicines, hoping for death. Ships' crews commented on the melancholic blues-like songs of sorrow sung by the slaves.

On the Plantation

The Incidence of Suicide

Early commentators disagreed on the frequency of suicide in slaves. Hammond (1985; quoted in Elliott, 1860, pp. 230-231) said it was rare. Smith (1985) quotes an anonymous writer from 1866 with the same opinion. Homrn, a slave interviewed in 1847, also asserted that suicide was not as common in slaves as one might expect (Blassingame, 1977). He felt that the slaves continued to hope, especially for freedom, and this hope kept them alive. Genovese (1976) asserted that suicide was rare in old slaves since they had a high degree of emotional and physical security, particularly because of the support they received from their younger fellow slaves. Genovese suggested that the sense of collective responsibility for one another among the slaves reduced the risk of suicide.

In contrast, Martineau (1838, p. 178) said suicidal behavior was frequent, and many current commentators feel that suicide in slaves was underestimated (e.g., Owens, 1976). Owens (1976) felt that suicide was as common in field and unskilled slaves as in domestic and skilled slaves, despite the differences in their living conditions.

Although statistical data are lacking, others continue to make assertions about the frequency of suicide in slaves. Rose (1976) tells us that suicide was more common in slaves in Brazil and the West Indies than in the United States and more common in immigrant slaves than in native-born slaves. Meanwhile, those scholars who have statistically estimated mortality rates among the enslaved have ignored the particular issue of suicide (e.g., Steckel, 1970).

Escott (1979) analyzed interviews with former slaves collected by the Federal Writers' Project Slave Narratives and similar materials at Fisk University. His analysis documented many types of resistance by slaves. For reports of resistance by people other than those interviewed, he listed 413 incidents. Of these 28 percent were running away, 25 percent hiding in the woods, 14 percent striking their master and 11 percent stealing. Only seven incidents of fatal suicide were reported (1.2 percent).

Owens (1976) suggested that oppressed people may eventually turn their aggression inward onto themselves as well as outward on the oppressors. He was able to document many cases of self-injury: a woman who put her arm in a beehive, a man who chopped his toes off so that he would not be sold and taken from his wife and children, and a man who severed his hand with an axe (Trollope, 1832, p. 199, 1927).

In the United States today, suicide is less common among African Americans in general than in whites. For example, in 1980, the suicide rates in African American males and females were 12.3 per 100,000 per year and 2.3 respectively while the corresponding rates in white males and females were 21.4 and 4.6 (Lester, 1989a). Genovese (1976) argued that this trend is a continuation of the pattern observed in enslaved African Americans in the last several hundred years. Interestingly, however, this difference in suicide rates between blacks and whites is found today in multiracial African nations, such as Zimbabwe (Lester & Wilson, 1988) and South Africa (Lester, 1989b). Thus, explanations of the low rate of suicide in slaves, if valid, must take into account the general ethnic differences in suicide found in non-oppressive situations, such as modern Zimbabwe. The low rates of suicide in Africans in general, and African Americans in particular, may represent an African worldview which accepts suicide only as a very last resort in the face of extreme stress, an attitude consistent with the Afrocentric optimal psychology proposed by Myers (1993) and others.

EXAMPLES OF SUICIDES

It is of interest to examine historical reports of suicide in the enslaved in detail to see what can be learned about the circumstances in which the suicide occurred.

SUICIDE AFTER PUNISHMENT

Many reports can be found of slaves who killed themselves after punishment or to avoid further punishment: a young girl who hung herself to avoid a whipping (Botkin, 1945, p. 184), and a young girl who drowned herself rather than be caught and punished for running off to a dance (Botkin, 1945, p. 183).

In a footnote to a speech by Lewis Richardson in 1846, a former slave belonging to Henry Clay of Ashland, Kentucky, Blassingame (1977, p. 165) noted that Clay's shoemaker, Tom, fought with the overseer in 1844, and both Clay and the overseer flogged him so severely that Tom later killed himself.

John Homrn, a slave in Cuba and Puerto Rico, interviewed in 1847, told the story of a slave, Dominico, who was required to work in the sugar mill even though his illnesses made it impossible. He tried to persuade the overseer that he could not work, whereupon he was given twenty-five lashes. The same punishment was administered on the next two days. Dominico then went to the mill and asked the workers to stir up the fires, after which he threw himself into the machines and was crushed to death (Blassingame, 1977, p. 257).

Homrn remembered another case of suicide in a slave, Bonifacio, who was punished very severely, eventually having to wear a collar around his neck to which a heavy log was fastened by a chain. Bonifacio killed himself. In a third case, some of the food for the slaves was stolen from the store, and the overseer decided to punish someone regardless of guilt. He chose Bicente who was in charge of the oxen. He ordered Bicente to the field, but Bicente objected that he had already worked that day. Homrn felt that the real reason for Bicente's objection was that to work in the fields would lower his status in the eyes of his fellow slaves. The overseer ordered a slave to catch and bind Bicente, but Bicente persuaded the slave not to do so. The overseer decided to go to town to get support from his neighbors, but Bicente caught and murdered him as he left the estate. Bicente then hung himself from a tree.

Phillips (1909) reports the case of a slave, London, who drowned himself rather than get whipped again. His master left his body to rot on the river bank to deter suicide in other slaves.

An elderly domestic servant slit her stomach after being whipped by her mistress. A doctor advised the owner that she could continue to punish the servant, after which the servant hung herself that night (Johnston, 1852). Lewis Hayden, a slave in Kentucky, wrote in 1853, that his mother was sold to a man who wanted her sexually, but she refused to live with him and was flogged and imprisoned (Blassingame, 1977, pp. 695-696). She tried to kill herself several times, once with a knife and once by hanging, but survived.

Some runaway slaves threatened suicide perhaps to dissuade pursuers from being overly brutal (Owens, 1976), and running away with threats to commit suicide occasionally did lead owners to behave less brutally (Watson, et al., 1945, p. 199). Sometimes slaves killed themselves to avoid returning to bondage. Ticknor (1945) reported the case of runaway slave who cut his throat when he heard the owner's dogs catching up to him.

Although severe punishment often precipitated suicide, sometimes the motivation for the suicidal behavior may have been more complicated. For example, Baker (1861) told of a female slave who committed suicide after her owner whipped her, but the emotional impact of the whipping may have been exacerbated by the sexual relationship between them.

SUICIDE AFTER REBELLION

The enslaved occasionally committed suicide after unsuccessful rebellions. For example, in April 1712, in New York City, about thirty slaves set fire to a building. When some whites approached, the slaves killed nine of them and wounded others (Aptheker, 1943). Soldiers rushed to the scene and captured most of the rebels. One rebel shot his wife and then himself, and five others killed themselves by cutting their throats.

In the revolt led by Gabriel in 1800 in Virginia, after about a thousand slaves had gathered outside Richmond but abandoned their effort, scores of slaves were arrested (Aptheker, 1943). Gabriel tried to escape by ship but was arrested and executed. About thirty-five slaves were executed, and one hanged himself in prison.

In 1840, several revolts were planned in Louisiana, and two leaders committed suicide when the revolts failed (Aptheker, 1943). In Lafayette, Louisiana, six slaves were sentenced to death, but the leader, Eugene, committed suicide by drinking poison. The leader of the revolt in St. Martin, Louisiana, also committed suicide.

Suicide among those who have led rebellions is common and may be a reasonable response to the prospect of capture, torture and death. It can be documented in many situations in addition to the revolts of the enslaved in the Americas, ranging from Yakub Beg (1820-1877) in Kashgaria (now Sinkiang Province, China) to Hermann Goring (1893-1946) in Nuremburg, Germany.

OTHER PRECIPITANTS OF SUICIDE

Slave owners viewed suicide in slaves as impulsive. Chambers (1860) told of a woman who decided suddenly that she had lived long enough and hung herself "for no known cause." However, the slave owners' views cannot be given much credence since, not only were they ignorant about the motivations of human behavior, but they were ignorant about the attitudes and motivations of their slaves. Even from the brief reports of suicides among the enslaved, clear precipitants can often be documented, as in the case of severe punishment documented in the previous section.

Precipitants other than severe punishment, however, are rarely reported. Wade (1964) reported the case of suicide in a slave who saved $1500 to buy his own freedom, only to find that the person with whom he had deposited the money had spent it.

The threat of separation from their family was occasionally a precipitating cause of suicidal behavior in slaves (Owens, 1976). Ball (1837, p. 69), a slave, reported feeling suicidal after being separated from his wife and children. Catterall (1929, p. 425, 1932, p. 216) reported two cases of slaves who committed suicide because they were opposed to being sold to a new owner, and Drew (1968, p. 178) reported two similar cases. The sense of kinship, and the role of the family, was important in traditional African life (Mbiti, 1970), and the sense of belonging together, especially in families, helped the enslaved to survive the oppression of slavery (Gutman, 1977). Destruction of these bonds would have been especially traumatic.

THEORIES OF SUICIDE

The consensus of opinion is that the suicide rate in African Americans was higher immediately after capture and during transportation to the Americas than once established in bondage. This may be a general phenomenon. For example, in documenting suicide among the Jews in Austria prior to and during the Second World War, Kwiet (1984) noted that the suicide rate was high during the period of the rounding up and transportation to the concentration camps. Suicide was less common once in the concentration camps. The low rate of suicide among Jews in the concentration camps is supported by those who lived through the experience and later reviewed it (e.g., Rodin, 1982). Lester (1986) used Henry and Short's (1954) theory of suicide to explain this. Henry and Short suggested that, when people have a clear external source to blame for their misery, then they feel anger rather than depression, and this lessens the risk of suicide. In contrast, when there is no clear external source to blame for their misery, then anger is less likely and depression (and in the extreme, suicide) more likely. Those in bondage have a clear external source to blame for their anger and so, perhaps, depression and suicide are less common. This analysis may have some validity for understanding suicidal behavior among enslaved African Americans.

FATALISTIC SUICIDE

Durkheim (1897) described four types of suicide, one of which he thought applied to slaves. *Fatalistic* suicide was the type of suicide committed by those overly regulated by society, that is, those whose "futures are pitilessly blocked and passions violently choked by oppressive discipline" (Durkheim, 1951, p. 276). The notion that suicide in African Americans was and continues to be fatalistic in nature has also been proposed (Breed, 1970). Certainly, the majority of examples of suicide in slaves in bondage, reviewed above, appear to be motivated by the desire to escape from continuing oppressive and brutal conditions.

SUICIDE AND OPPRESSION

Hendin (1969), in his discussion of African American suicide in modern times, speculated that the European and white culture's rejection of the African American has been internalized by many African Americans so that some African Americans feel self-hatred. "Racial oppression institutionalized family patterns that served to make the black man feel that he deserved to be treated as he was being treated" (p. 147). This results in violence toward others, but the "feelings of impotence and self-hatred often cause his anger to turn against himself" (p. 147). Thus, past and present oppression can perhaps result in suicidal behavior. Kubacki (1992), in a discussion on the politics of self-harm, has noted that modern North American society, dominated by white, male and capitalist agendas, imposes certain norms on the majority, and those who reject those norms or who are cast out are prey to suicide, particularly suicide of the *egoistic* type described by Durkheim (1897) in which the individual has very weak social ties. Shulman (1994) saw stigmatization of members of society by others as leading to self-stigmatization, increasing the risk of self-harm, and he documented this with examples of suicide by alleged witches in both European and African societies. Thus, oppression can lead to suicidal behavior.

PSYCHIATRIC DISORDER

A common concomitant of suicidal behavior in suicidal individuals in current times is psychiatric disorder, particular affective disorders and, in particular, major depressive disorders. Thus, in seeking to understand the actions of a suicidal person, information about their psychiatric condition is critical.

In regard to the suicidal behavior of the enslaved, it has commonly been held that mental illness was less common in slaves than in freed African-Americans living in the northern states (Owens, 1976). Data from 1840 Census seemed to document this (Deutsch, 1944). The "insanity" rate for free blacks in the north was one in 144 as compared to only 1 in 1558 for slaves in the South (Postell, 1953). Scholars in the 1840s immediately criticized conclusions drawn from this Census. For example, Jarvis (1844) noted that the figure for blacks in the North were grossly wrong. Towns with no black population were listed as having "insane" blacks (for example, Dresden,

Maine). The insane blacks listed in Worcester, Massachusetts, were in fact white inmates of the state hospital there. More recently, Deutsch (1944) criticized the low reported rates of insanity of Southern slaves since Southern psychiatric hospitals refused to admit blacks. Disturbed blacks in the South ended up in jails and poorhouses.

Postell (1953) examined probate court records for localities in four southern states in the 1840s and reported that 391 of 31,170 slaves had evidence of nervous and mental disorders, giving a ratio of 1 to 86, a much higher proportion than that reported by the 1840 Census. Postell, however, failed to obtain comparison rates for other ethnic groups and other regions of America.

It must be concluded that there are no reliable and valid statistics on the rates of psychiatric disorder in the enslaved. Furthermore, the criteria for psychiatric disorder are so different today than they were in times past that meaningful statistics may never be obtained for historical times. It is, therefore, impossible to say whether suicidal behavior in the enslaved was associated with psychiatric disorder or not.

PREVENTION

Mutilation of the corpses of slaves who killed themselves became a common technique for deterring further suicides (Piersen, 1977). Since some of the slaves from Africa believed that they would return to Africa after death, one slave owner put the head of a slave dead from suicide on a stake in his yard and convinced the slaves that the deceased slave could not have possibly gone home to Africa without his head. This deterred further suicides among his slaves (Ligon, 1657).

Eventually, the impossibility of entering the Christian heaven after death replaced the impossibility of returning home to Africa after death as a deterrent to suicide. In order to reduce the incidence of suicide, suicide was labeled as a very serious sin by the slave owners. Slaves who committed suicide were branded as the worst of criminals and denied Christian burial rites (Ball, 1837; Webber, 1978). Owners sometimes tried to hide a suicide in a slave from other slaves, so as to prevent imitation, telling them that the suicidal death was really an accidental death while reporting it correctly as a suicide to the authorities (Owens, 1976).

Slave Narratives

The slave narratives are often quite brief and give little information about the person's history or current state. They were not collected, of course, with the goal of understanding the causation of suicide in the enslaved, and so usually lack the kind of information required by suicidologists for a psychological autopsy after a suicidal death (Clark and Horton-Deutsch, 1992). For example:

> Poor A'nt Nellie! De pattyrollers whipped her one day. She took an went up in the barn - hid in de hay. When night come she crawled out an' went out in the woods an' climbed top of a hill an' rolled down. We missed her but didn't think de gal wuz gwine kill herself like she had tol' me day befo': "Fannie, I don had my las' whippin. I'm gwine to God." The bread whar her old mistress had don' give her wasn't never been touched an' was found beside her. The buzzards had carried poor Nellie's head down de woods an' picked her eyes out. (Perdue, Barden & Phillips, 1976, p. 34)

Since almost all slaves were brutally treated, punishment *per se* seems insufficient as a cause of suicide. It would be useful to have more information about the lives of the slaves who committed suicide so that life experiences and personal characteristics which differentiated between those rare few who committed suicide and those who did not do so could be identified.

The Official Suicide Rate

Although writers are willing to say authoritatively that suicide was common or was rare among slaves (Elliott, 1860; Martineau, 1838), nowhere are official (or unofficial) rates of suicide reported. The present author calculated official suicide rates in the United States from data reported in the Seventh Census of the United States, conducted in 1850 (De Bow, 1855).

In the year ending June 1, 1850, there were 491 suicides recorded in the United States out of a population of 23,191,876. This gives a suicide rate for the United States of 2.12 per 100,000 per year, a rate considerably lower than the rate presently (for example, 12.4 in 1988). The rates for subgroups of the population are shown in Table 2.1. It can be seen that the suicide rates for slaves and freed slaves were lower than the suicide rates for whites. Males also had higher suicide rates than females among all groups.

There have been many criticisms of the official suicide rate even in modern times (Douglas, 1967). It has been argued that many suicidal deaths go unrecorded, and this may have been even more likely in 1850 than today. Thus, perhaps little credence should be placed in the validity of the official suicide rates in 1850. However, they are a starting point, and it is interesting to observe the higher suicide rates for whites over blacks and for men over women, differences which are still found today. It is important to note also that life expectancy was much less in 1850 than today. For example, the life expectancy in Massachusetts in 1850 was 38.3 years for men and 40.5 years for women. In 1950 the corresponding life expectancies were 66.7 and 72.1 years respectively (Census Bureau, 1975). Since suicide rates generally increase with age, the lower proportion of elderly in 1850 might be responsible in part for the low suicide rates.

The present author also calculated suicide rates for the states with more than 100,000 slaves in 1850. Alabama and Mississippi had suicide rates for slaves of 0.00, South Carolina 0.26, Tennessee 0.41, Virginia 0.42, Georgia 0.52, North Carolina 1.04, Louisiana 2.04 and Kentucky 2.37.

For the states with between 40,000 and 100,000 slaves in 1850, Arkansas and Florida had suicide rates for slaves of 0.00, Missouri 1.14, Texas 1.71 and Maryland 2.21. The two states (Delaware and New Jersey) and the District of Columbia with less than 4,000 slaves in 1850 had zero suicide rates for slaves.

DISCUSSION

• This review has shown that there have been many assertions made about suicide in enslaved African Americans, mostly based on the personal observations of slave traders, slave owners and the enslaved themselves, without the support of the statistics that modern research requires for supporting or refuting hypotheses. For example, it has been claimed that suicide was more common in newly captured slaves, during transportation to the Americas and when newly arrived than when placed in bondage or born into slavery. Although this assertion cannot be backed up with calculated suicide rates, it was noted that it is consistent with observations made about the Austrian Jews rounded-up and put into concentration camps by the Nazis.

The most common precipitants of suicide appeared to be severe punishment and after rebellions. However, suicide was apparently rather rare in these cases, and the available documentation does not enable us to discover why occasional slaves killed themselves after beatings while others did not. Did they differ in childhood experiences, personality, interpersonal situation or the conditions of slavery? To answer this, we require more detailed life histories of slaves who killed themselves to compare with the life histories of those who did not do so.

From data discovered in the 1850 Census, the present author calculated suicide rates for whites and African Americans in that year. Of course, such data are open to the criticism that they are gross undercounts. However, the rates do provide a starting point, and it is of interest to note that the sex and ethnic differences in the suicide rates parallel those in the United States today and in nations such as Zimbabwe and South Africa.

It is hoped that the facts and theories detailed in the present chapter will motivate and guide future scholars into this important topic and that lacunae in the data have been identified which others may be able to rectify.

REFERENCES

Anon. *Abridgment of the minutes of the evidence: taken before a committee of the whole House to whom it was referred to consider of the slave-trade, IV*. London: (no publisher), 1790.

Aptheker, H. *American Negro slave revolts*. New York: Columbia University, 1943.

Baker, E. G. Diary II entry for June 15th. University of North Carolina collection, 1861.

Ball, C. *Slavery in the United States*. New York: John S. Taylor, 1837. (Republished as *Fifty years in chains*. New York: Dover, 1970.)

Blassingame, J. W. (Ed.) *Slave testimony*. Baton Rouge, LA: Louisiana State University, 1977.

Botkin, B. A. (Ed.) *Lay my burden down*. Chicago: University of Chicago, 1945.

Breed, W. The Negro and fatalistic suicide. *Pacific Sociological Review*, 1970, 13, 156-162.

Catterall, H. H. *Judicial cases*. Washington, DC: Carnegie Institute, Volumes II and II, publication number 374, 1929/1932.

Census Bureau. *Historical Statistics of the United States*. Washington, DC: Census Bureau, 1975.

Chambers, R. Diary entry for June 11th. Louisiana State University collection, 1860.

Clark, D. C., & Horton-Deutsch, S. L. Assessment in absentia: The value of the psychological autopsy method for studying antecedents of suicide and predicting future suicides. In R. W. Maris, A. L. Berman, J. T. Maltsberger & R. I. Yufit (Eds.) *Assessment and prediction of suicide*, pp. 144-182. New York: Guilford, 1992.

De Bow, J. D. B. *Mortality statistics of the Seventh Census of the United States*. Washington, DC: A. O. P. Nicholson, 1855.

Deutsch, A. The first US Census of the insane and its use as pro-slavery propaganda. *Bulletin of the History of Medicine*, 1944, 15, 469-482.

Drew, B. *The refugee*. New York: Negro University Press, 1968.

Douglas, J. D. *The social meanings of suicide*. Princeton, NJ: Princeton University, 1967.

du Pratz, L. P. *The history of Louisiana*. London, UK: Becket and P. A. de Hondt, 1763. (Reprinted, Baton Rouge, LA: Louisiana State University Press, 1975).

Durkheim, E. *Le suicide*. Paris: Felix Alcan, 1897. (Translated, New York: Free Press, 1951.)

Ellenberger, H. Zoological garden and mental hospital. *Canadian Psychiatric Association Journal*, 1960, 5, 136-149.

Elliott, E. N. (Ed.) *Cotton is king and pro-slavery arguments*. Augusta, GA: Pritchard, Abbott & Loomis, 1860. (Reprinted, New York: Johnson Reprint Company, 1968.)

Escott, P. D. *Slavery remembered*. Chapel Hill, NC: University of North Carolina, 1979.

Genovese, E. D. *Roll, Jordan, roll*. New York: Vintage, 1976.

Gutman, H. G. *The black family in slavery and freedom, 1750-1925*. New York: Harper, 1976.

Hammond, J. H. *James Henry Hammond papers, 1795-1865*. Frederick, MD: University Publications of America, 1985.

Hendin, H. *Black suicide*. New York: Basic Books, 1969.

Henry, A. F., & Short, J. F. *Suicide and homicide*. New York: Free Press, 1954.

Jarvis, E. Insanity among the coloured population of the Free States. *American Journal of Medical Sciences*, 1844, 7, 71-83.

Johnston, A. M. Anna and Sarah Butler correspondence, Louisiana State University Collection, 1852.

Kubacki, A. Survival-control-dominance: The politics of self-harm. In D. Lester (Ed.) *Suicide '92*, pp. 257-258. Denver, CO: American Association of Suicidology, 1992.

Kwiet, K. The ultimate refuge: Suicide in the Jewish community under the Nazis. *Leo Baeck Institute Yearbook*, 1984, 29, 135-167.

Lester, D. Suicide, the concentration camp, and the survivors. *Israel Journal of Psychiatry & Related Sciences*, 1986, 23, 221-224.

Lester, D. *Questions and answers about suicide*. Philadelphia: Charles Press, 1989a.

Lester, D. Personal violence (suicide and homicide) in South Africa. *Acta Psychiatrica Scandinavica*, 1989b, 79, 235-237.

Lester, D. Suicidal behavior in the enslaved in America. *Omega*, 1998, in press.

Lester, D., & Wilson, C. Suicide in Zimbabwe. *Central African Journal of Medicine*, 1988, 34, 147-149.

Ligon, R. *A true and exact history of the island of Barbadoes, 1647-1650*. London, UK: H. Moseley, 1657. (Reprinted, London, UK: Frank Cass, 1970).

Martineau, H. *Retrospect of western travel, I*. London, UK: Saunders & Otley, 1838. (Reprinted, Cleveland, OH: Bell & Howell, 1960.)

Mbiti, J. *African religions and philosophy*. New York: Doubleday, 1970.

Myers, L. J. *Understanding an Afrocentric world view*. Dubuque, IA: Kendall/Hunt, 1993.

Nobles, W. *African psychology: Toward its reclamation, reascension, and revitalization*. Oakland, CA: Black Family Institute, 1980.

Owens, L. H. *This species of property*. New York: Oxford University Press, 1976.

Perdue, C. L., Barden, T. E., & Phillips, R. K. (Eds.) *Weevils in the wheat*. Charlottesville, VA: University Press of Virginia. 1976.

Phillips, U. B. (Ed.) *Plantation and frontier*. Cleveland, OH: A. H. Clark, 1909.

Piersen, W. D. White cannibals, black martyrs. *Journal of Negro History*, 1977, 62, 147-159.

Pope-Hennessy, J. *Sins of the fathers*. London, UK: Weidenfeld & Nicholson, 1967.

Postell, W. D. Mental health among the slave population on Southern plantations. *American Journal of Psychiatry*, 1953, 110, 52-54.

Rodin, R. G. Suicide and Holocaust survivors. *Israel Journal of Psychiatry & Related Sciences*, 1982, 19, 129-135.

Rose, W. L. *A documentary history of slavery in North America*. New York: Oxford University Press, 1976.

Shulman, E. Suicide by alleged witches: Death by scapegoating. In D. Lester (Ed.) *Suicide '94*, pp. 186-187. Denver, CO: American Association of Suicidology, 1994.

Smith, D. J. *An old creed for the new South*. Westport, CT: Greenwood, 1985.

Snelgrave, W. *A new account of some parts of Guinea and the slave trade*. London, UK: J. & P. Knapton, 1734. (Reprinted, London, UK: Frank Cass, 1971.)

Steckel, R. H. Slave mortality. *Social Science History*, 1970, 3, 86-144.

Ticknor, F. Letter to W. A. Nelson, April 22. F. O. Ticknor papers, University of Georgia collection, 1845.

Trollope, F. *Domestic manners of the Americans*. London: Whitaker, Treacher & Co, 1832. (Reprinted, New York: Dodd Mead, 1927.)

Wade, R. C. *Slavery in the cities*. New York: Oxford University Press, 1964.

Watson, A. P., Radin, P., & Johnson, C. S. (Eds.) (1945). *God struck me dead*. Nashville, TN: Fisk University.

Wax, D. D. Negro resistance to the early American slave trade. *Journal of Negro History*, 1966, 51, 1-15.

Webber, T. L. *Deep like the rivers*. New York: Norton, 1978.

Zahan, D. *The religion, spirituality, and thought of traditional Africa.*
Chicago: University of Chicago, 1979.

Table 2.1

Suicide Rates Calculated from the 1850 Census

	rate per 100,00	number of suicides per year
total suicide rate	2.12	491
whites	2.37	463
males	3.64	356
females	1.12	107
slaves	0.72	23
blacks	0.74	22
mulattos	0.41	1
males	1.00	16
females	0.44	7
freed slaves	1.15	5
blacks	1.45	4
mulattos	0.63	1
males	1.94	4
females	0.44	1

CHAPTER 3

AFRICAN AMERICAN SUICIDE IN MODERN TIMES

What are the differences in suicide between the ethnic groups of America? Data relevant to this was reported by Lester (1994a) for the United States in 1980. The suicide rates by ethnic group for 1980 were:

Native Americans	13.3 per 100,000 per year
whites	13.2
Japanese Americans	9.1
Chinese Americans	8.3
African Americans	6.1
Filipino Americans	3.5

It can be seen that African Americans had the second lowest suicide rate for the ethnic groups studied.

Lester reported more detailed rates (see Table 3.1). It can be seen that male suicide rates were higher than female suicide rates for African Americans, as was the case for all of the ethnic groups. For whites, Chinese Americans and Japanese Americans, suicide rates tended to increase with age; in contrast suicide rates for African Americans peaked for young adults aged 25-34. The association of suicide rates with marital status was similar in the different ethnic groups, with divorced people having the highest suicide rates, except for Native Americans. Widowhood appeared to have a less deleterious impact on African Americans than on whites, Chinese Americans and Japanese Americans.

Lester also found differences in the methods used for suicide (see Table 3.2). African Americans, whites and Native Americans preferred firearms, in contrast to the Asian Americans who preferred hanging. African Americans were less likely to use solid and liquid poisons and gas/vapors (such as car exhaust) than were whites, and a little more likely to use hanging and "other methods" than were whites.

More recent data from 1990 show similar trends (see Table 3.3). For whites, male suicide rates increased with age, peaking for those aged 85 years of age and older. The suicide rates for black males, on the other hand peaked for those aged 25 to 34. For white females, suicide rates peaked for those aged 55 to 64; for black females 35 to 44.

Looking at the methods used for suicide in 1990 (see Table 3.2), all race-by-gender groups chose firearms as their most popular methods. The major ethnic difference was that white suicides used gas/vapors more while black suicides used hanging and "other" methods more.

It is interesting to note that homicide rates are higher for African Americans than for whites. Thus, the ratio of the suicide/homicide rate is much lower for African Americans than for whites -- for example, 0.15 versus 0.74 in 1983 (Bachman, 1992).

OTHER REPORTS

McIntosh and Santos (1981) noted that African Americans and Native Americans were similar in having lower suicide rates in the elderly and higher suicide rates in young adults, unlike whites and Chinese, Japanese and Filipino Americans, and they documented this with data from 1976. They suggested that these differences must be a result of the different histories, experiences and opportunities of the groups in the United States, their original cultural characteristics and beliefs, and their present social and economic conditions. In particular, they suggested that the low suicide rate in elderly African Americans may be because they have learned to cope with their anger better than younger African Americans -- perhaps they have scaled down their aspirations and blame the system for their lack of success. It may be also that

African Americans with suicidal tendencies have already died (not necessarily from suicide, for suicidal tendencies might affect the likelihood of death from natural causes, accidents and homicide), leaving a "suicide-resistant" elderly population.

Frederick (1984) also noted the peak in suicide rates for young black adults and higher suicide rates in African Americans than in whites for males aged 15 to 24. Regarding the methods used for suicide by adolescents and youths in 1979, Frederick noted that black and white males and females all preferred firearms. However, black males used hanging, jumping and drowning for suicide more than did white males, while white males used firearms and carbon monoxide more. The differences for females were smaller, but black females used solid and liquid substances, jumping and cutting a little more often and gas and hanging a little less often than did white females.

Davis (1979) looked at black suicide rates in the United States from 1970 to 1975 and noted that the suicide rate was increasing at a faster rate for African Americans than for whites, in all regions of the nation and in states with high and low black suicide rates. However, despite the fact that some popular magazines had focused on suicide in black women, Davis documented that the increase was primarily in young black males, to such an extent that the suicide rate for black males aged 20 to 25 was higher than that for white males of the same age (27.9 versus 25.1) -- the suicide rates of young black females were still lower than those for young white females. Similar findings were reported by Saunders (1987). Like other investigators, Davis noted also that black suicide rates peaked in younger adults and that the suicide rates of African Americans were lower in states with a higher proportion of black residents (a phenomenon we will discuss in Chapter 11).

Gibbs (1988) noted that black suicide is a youth phenomenon. She noted that suicide rates peak for the ages 25-34. In recent years, the suicide rate of African Americans aged 15-24 had doubled, an increase particularly notable in black males aged 20-24. From 1960 to 1983, the suicide rate for black females aged 15-24 rose from 1.3 per 100,000 per year to 2.7, and for black males from 4.1 to 11.5, but these trends were also found for whites aged 15-24 (for white females an increase from 2.3 to 4.6 and for white males from 8.6 to 20.6). However, Gibbs noted that the suicide rates of black youths had levelled off and remained stable since 1978. She observed that the high death rate in young black males from suicide (in addition to a high death rate from homicide and accidents and a high imprisonment rate) reduced the ratio of employed black males available for marriage to marriageable black females in the 20-24 age group to only 47:100. Gibbs (1996) noted a rising suicide rate among elderly black males over the age of 75.

Although suicide rates are relatively low in African American elderly as compared to younger age groups, the suicide rate of African American elderly, especially males, rose substantially in the 1980s (Alston, 1994). Alston suggested several possible reasons for this. The family support systems in African Americans have weakened in recent times, so that the younger generations may no longer be taking care of the elderly to the same extent as they used to do. A second possibility is that poverty may be especially relevant for elderly African American men, more so than for African American women. Alston did not, however, test these hypotheses.

Gibbs (1997) has confirmed these trends: lower suicide rates in African Americans than in whites, a peaking of suicide rates in earlier age groups, and differences in choice of methods. In addition, she noted the rising black male suicide rates from 1960 to 1992, both in the youth and in the elderly, and she noted that the black youth suicide rate had risen most in the northern and western states where African Americans form a smaller percentage of the population. This latter trend had not been noticed hitherto.

McIntosh (1988) compared the white and nonwhite suicide rates from 1933 to 1985 and noted that the ratio of the white to nonwhite suicide rates was decreasing, from 3.48 in 1933 to 2.03 in 1985. This trend was found for both male and female suicide rates and when the rates were age-adjusted. He noted that this trend was due mainly to a decrease in white suicide rates rather than an increase in nonwhite suicide rates.

Rutledge (1990) noted that, while the black male youth suicide rate had risen, so had the white male youth suicide rate, and relative proportions of the two rates had remained quite stable. Rutledge argued that we should still be concerned about black youth suicide, but in doing so we should not distort the data.

Slater (1973) argued that black women were killing themselves at an increasing rate and that the phenomenon was being ignored by scholars. However, he did not document this with statistics, though he noted an epidemic of seventy suicide attempts by black females in the black community of Highland Park (with a population of about 35,000), near Detroit, in 1972.

More recently, Shaffer, et al. (1994) noted that, while the white youth suicide rate leveled off after 1988, the black youth suicide rate continued to increase. The percentage increase in the black youth suicide rate was greater than that for whites in the United States as a whole and was observed in every region except the West North Central. Similarly, the black/white youth suicide rate ratio increased in the United States as a whole and in every region except the West North Central.

Breed (1970) noted that young adult suicide rates were higher for African Americans than for whites only in northern states in the 1950s. During this period, black suicide rates declined in northern states, but rose in southern states.

MacMahon, et al. (1963) noted that the white/nonwhite differences in suicide rates were not as great in the Middle Atlantic and East North Central regions as in the South Atlantic and East South Central regions. In fact, in the first set of regions mentioned, the suicide rates were quite similar up to the age of 35. They felt that this could be a result of the different pressures in the two sets of regions or to the greater number of black migrants in the northern states. Shaffer, et al. (1981) reported that nonwhite adolescents (aged 15-19) were underrepresented in the Mid-Atlantic, South Atlantic and East South Central regions but not in the North Central region.[1]

Smith and Carter (1986), without presenting any data, asserted that black suicides peaked in the months of April and May and on Wednesdays. Greenberg and Schneider (1992) studied 22 counties in the United States with the highest proportions of African Americans and found that black and whites suicides did not differ in the day of the week for suicide, with both showing an

---

[1] Similar reviews of statistics (and theories) have appeared from Adams, et al. (1990), Anon (1975, 1981, 1983, 1987, 1989), Baker (1989, 1990, 1994, 1996), Bingham, et al. (1994), Bush (1974), Christian (1977), Comer (1973), Davis (1982), Dennis (1977), Desenclos, and Hahn (1992), Diggory (1976), Dillihay (1989), Earls, et al. (1990), Gibbs (1988, 1990, 1992), Gite (1986), Green (1977), Griffith and Bell (1989), Heacock (1990), Hendin (1982), Humphrey and Palmer (1990-1991), Jackson (1979), Jedlicka, et al. (1977), Kachur, et al. (1995), Kimmel, (1978), King (1982), Kirk (1986), Kramer, et al. (1972), Manton, et al. (1987), Marshall (1981), McGinnis (1987), Meehan, et al. (1991), Miles (1979), Moore and Buckman (1976), Palmer (1972), Parham and McDavis (1987), Prange and Vitols (1962), Rogers (1992), Rutledge (1990), Santos, et al. (1983), Seiden (1970, 1972), Shaffer, et al. (1981), Shai and Rosenwaika (1988), Staples (1975), Templer and Cappelletty (1986), Warfield (1974), Williams (1983), Woodbury, et al. (1988), Wylie (1975), Wyche, et al. (1990), and Wyche and Rotheram-Borus (1990).

excess on Mondays. Black males also had a tendency to a secondary peak on Thursdays, but this trend did not reach statistical significance.

STUDIES OF LOCAL REGIONS

Schmid and Van Arsdol (1955) calculated black and white completed and attempted suicide rates for Seattle in 1948-1952:

	completed suicide		attempted suicide	
	male	female	male	female
black	14.4	5.4	26.3	122.8
white	31.1	10.2	34.9	52.9

The completed suicide rates show the expected ethnic and gender differences, but the attempted suicide rates indicate that black females have a higher rate than white females.

Powell (1970) calculated completed and attempted suicide rates by gender for African Americans and whites in Tulsa for the period 1937-1956.

	completed suicide		attempted suicide	
	male	female	male	female
black	4.4	0.6	10.0	38.1
white	18.8	5.7	20.3	33.9

For both African Americans and whites, it can be seen that the gender difference is strong, with women having higher rates of attempted suicide and men having higher rates of completed suicide. Whites had higher rates of completed suicide, but black men attempted suicide at a higher rate than white men, while the reverse was true for women. The higher rate of attempted suicides in African Americans was especially notable in women aged 15 to 24.

Monk and Warshauer (1974) studied completed suicide in East Harlem, New York City, for 1968-1970 using Medical Examiner records and attempted suicide for 1971-1972. The rates were

	completed suicide		attempted suicide	
	male	female	male	female
black	29.6	10.7	149.8	208.0
white	31.5	32.5	175.7	220.2

Here the deviant group was white females whose completed suicide rate was higher than that for white males. Among the completed suicides, the white males and females were older than the black males and females respectively; among the attempted suicides, only the white females were older than the black females. The black completed suicides used jumping more and poisoning less often; among the attempted suicides, the African Americans used barbiturates less often and cutting more often. The African Americans were less often born in New York State and more often from the South; however, they were less likely to be new migrants to New York City (that is, in town for less than five years).

Ford, et al. (1979) studied completed suicide in whites and nonwhites in the city and the suburbs of Cleveland (OH) for 1958-1974. Ethnic and gender differences were found for both the first part of the period (1958-1962) and the later part (1969-1974), but the increases in the suicide rates were proportionately greater for the nonwhites (for example, in the city, a 12% increase for white males, 59% for white females, 137% for nonwhite males and 108% for nonwhite females). The increase was especially notable for nonwhite male youth.

In Philadelphia in 1972, the suicide rate for nonwhite males was almost as high as that for white males (16.5 versus 16.7), while the nonwhite female suicide rate was lower than the white female suicide rate (5.6 versus 9.2) (Morris, et al., 1974). The suicide rate was especially high for nonwhite males aged 15-24 (23.9 versus 14.6 for white males aged 15-24) and those aged 25-34 (48.3 versus 18.4). The nonwhite suicides used firearms and jumping more often and drugs and drowning less often, and they were more often separated and less often single, married or widowed. The nonwhite suicides had lower suicidal intent scores on an objective scale of intent.

Allen (1973) reported data for California for 1960-1970. White suicide rates were higher than black suicide rates. Her aged-adjusted rates were:

	1960	1970
whites	16.9	20.0
blacks	5.3	11.2

Calculating suicide rates by age indicated that black suicide rates peaked for those aged 20-24 for both black men and women, whereas while male suicide rates peaked for those aged 75+ and white female suicide rates for those aged 55-64.

The African American and white differences in completed suicide rates for men and women were also reported for three New Jersey cities for 1985-1990 by Greenberg and Schneider (1994): black males 10.9, white males 23.4, black females 2.7 and white females 3.9. Tunakan and Bartholow (1972) found black suicide rates to be lower than white suicide rates in Omaha-Douglas County, Nebraska, in 1955-1964, as did Gowitt and Hanzlick (1986) for Fulton County, Georgia, in 1975-1984. Gowitt and Hanzlick found that black suicides were younger than white suicides: the average ages were black males 31, white males 38, black females 31 and white females 45.

Alexander, et al. (1982) reported on suicide rates in South Carolina for 1970-1978, where white suicide rates were higher than nonwhite suicide rates (14.0 versus 4.1 in 1970 and 14.6 versus 4.5 in 1978). The difference was less for younger males (under the age of 40) and younger females (under the age of 25). Whites used firearms more for suicide while the nonwhites used hanging more.

Prange and Vitols (1962) noted that African Americans in the South had especially low suicide rates and they suggested several reasons for this: (1) in the South, the African Americans feel less in competition with whites and so do not experience reduced prestige, (2) African Americans in the South do not have as low self-esteem as African Americans in other regions, and (3) since African Americans in the South have so little in the way of material goods, they have less to lose in hard times. Prange and Vitols did not think and African Americans in the South differed in the frequency of the loss of love objects. Prange and Vitols also felt that there were protective factors for southern African Americans: (1) different attitudes, such as lower aspirations and "quiet defiance," (2) religion played a more important role in their lives, (3) their extended families were larger, and (4) the oppression and racism was more palpable. However, Prange and Vitols did not produce any evidence for or against their hypotheses.

Hatcher and Hatcher (1975) studied suicide in El Paso (Texas) for 1963-1965 and 1970-1972 and found that the median suicide rate was 17.5 for Anglos over the two periods, 12.1 for African Americans and 7.6 for Mexican-Americans. The population of African Americans was too small for changes over the two periods to be meaningful, but Hatcher and Hatcher noted that, while the suicide rates of Anglos and Mexican-Americans declined from the first to the second period, the black suicide rate increased.

In Denver, Colorado, Loya (1973) calculated a white suicide rate of 25.0 for 1965-1969, a Chicano suicide rate of 10.1 and a black suicide rate of 10.3. For the period 1970-1972, the white suicide rate rose to 28.4, the Chicano suicide rate rose to 14.3, and the black suicide rate rose to 12.1. Most of the black and Chicano suicides were under the age of 40, whereas most of the white suicides were over the age of 40.

Taylor and Wicks (1980) looked at suicides by African Americans in Cleveland, Dayton, and Detroit for 1969-1971. They noted that black females used firearms for suicide more than white females in all three cities, and the same was true for black versus white males in two of the cities (Dayton and Detroit).

Frazer (1985) looked at suicides in Cuyahoga County, Ohio (which contains Cleveland) and found that black females had a lower suicide rate than white females in 1963 to 1983. The black female suicide rate rose during the period from 1.2 to 7.6, while the white female suicide rate rose from 7.8 to 12.4.

Copeland (1989) examined suicide rates in Dade County, Florida, from 1982 to 1986 and found that the suicide rate for African Americans differed for the different ethnic groups: the suicide rates were 3.1 per 100,000 per year for Haitians, 3.9 for American blacks, and 13.9 for Hispanic blacks.

More recently, Rigsbee, et al. (1993) noted a rise in suicide rates among young black adolescents in Chicago, so that the white-to-black ratio of suicide rates was approaching the value of one. They compared samples of white and black adolescent suicides and found that, although firearms were the most common method for suicide in both groups, black adolescents used firearms more for suicide (79% versus 41%). The black adolescent suicides were more likely to shoot themselves in the presence of others, and 61 percent of these were playing Russian roulette, a practice which was rare in the white adolescents and the black female adolescents. Whereas the white adolescents most often used guns owned by parents, the black adolescents who used guns rarely did. (The researchers had difficulty determining the source of the guns used by the black adolescent suicides.) There appeared to be a trend for the white adolescents to have had more experience of violent death by motor vehicle accidents in their friends whereas the black adolescents had more friends die from homicide. Rigsbee also found that the black adolescents came from poorer homes, were less often attending school regularly, and had less often received any psychiatric care, but of course these differences may be true also for nonsuicidal white and black adolescents.

Hendin (1969a, 1969b) found that the black suicide rate in New York City in 1960 was 7.8 while the white suicide rate was 10.8. However, this racial difference was reversed for those aged 20-35 for whom the black suicide rate exceeded the white suicide, for both men and women. This difference was also found in 1920, and so appeared to be a stable phenomenon. The group showing the largest and most consistent tendency for black suicide rates to exceed white suicide rates was aged 20-24; the difference was present, although less consistent, for those aged 15-19 and 25-34.

METHOD

McIntosh and Santos (1982) looked at the methods used for suicide by whites, African Americans and other ethnic groups in America from 1929 to 1978.[2] They noted that firearms had increased in popularity for both black males and white males during this period, from 50 percent of the suicides to 60 percent for black males and from 40 percent to 60 percent for white males. A similar trend was found for black and white females. The use of poisons declined over the period for both black and white males and, to a lesser extent, for black and white females. The other major trend was a decline found only for black males, whose use of hanging for suicide declined over the period. Whites used gas for suicide more than African Americans did throughout the period. McIntosh and Santos also included data from Asian Americans in their

---

[2] Mortality statistics for the whole United States were not reported until 1933. Statistics from earlier years omit the data from some states.

report, and they noted that each ethnic group displayed its own unique pattern and history of methods chosen for suicide.

In New Orleans from 1966-1970, Swanson and Breed (1976) found that whites used firearms more for suicide (both men and women), and poison and jumping less (more so for women).

French and Wailes (1980) examined suicides in Mississippi and Nebraska for 1969-1976, but did not calculate suicide rates, although they noted that African Americans were underrepresented among the suicides as compared to their proportion in the population of the two states. African Americans used more violent methods for suicide than whites (94% versus 87%) which, to French and Wailes, suggested a greater level of violence among the African Americans.

In New York City in 1960, Hendin (1969b) found that jumping was a much more popular method for suicide than in the United States as a whole, especially among African Americans. Jumping was used by 30 percent of white male suicides, 56 percent of black male suicides, 34 percent of white female suicides and 63 percent of black female suicides. Jumping is a more popular methods in cities with high buildings, such as Singapore and Hong Kong (Lester, 1994b), but the racial difference in New York City is notable. Hendin attributed the greater use of jumping by African Americans as a symbolic search for an escape from tenement life in African Americans.

It should be noted, however, that since the age of black and white suicides differs (and probably there are differences in other characteristics such as social class, etc.), differences in the methods used for suicide may be a result of these other differences. A good study would control for these other confounding variables.

SUICIDE IN THE LAST CENTURY

Lane (1979) examined violent death in Philadelphia in the period 1839 to 1901. In general, the suicide rate rose in the city, from 5.0 per 100,000 per year in 1839-1845 to 11.8 for 1895-1901. Lester (1987) noted that the suicide rate in Philadelphia in 1972 was 12.1 (Morris, et. al., 1974).

Lane did not calculate rates for African Americans. However, Lester (1987) calculated rough rates from the data provided by Lane: 12.6 for whites for 1899 to 1901 and 2.3 for African Americans for 1885 to 1900. Morris, et al. (1974) reported suicide rates for Philadelphia in 1972 of 12.8 for whites and 10.7 for nonwhites, who in Philadelphia are primarily African Americans. Thus, while the white suicide rate had remained relatively unchanged, the current black suicide rate was much higher than at the end of the 19th Century.

Lester (1995) compared suicide rates in the United States in 1890 and 1980. The suicide rates of African Americans and whites for both genders increased:

	1890	1990
black males	1.4	10.4
black females	0.8	4.9
white males	8.0	20.6
white females	2.1	6.1

However, the suicide rates of some groups (Chinese American males and Native American females) decreased over the same period.

SUICIDE IN THE MILITARY

Datel and Johnson (1979) noted that the suicide rate among Army personnel in 1975-1976 was 18.9 for white males and 9.9 for black males, a ratio of 1.9:1. Hayes and Johnson (1979) noted that the white/black suicide rate ratio for the United States Air Force for 1974-1975 was 1.2:1. On the other hand, Rothberg, et al. (1990) reported that standard mortality ratios for suicide in Army personnel were low (roughly in the 60s where 100 is average) for both white and black men.

Koshes and Rothberg (1992) found no racial differences in psychiatric referrals among Army personnel for attempted suicide versus other reasons.

SUICIDE IN PARTICULAR OCCUPATIONS

Delzell and Grufferman (1985) found high proportional suicide mortality ratios for both white and nonwhite farmers in North Carolina. Blair, et al. (1983), however, found high proportional suicide mortality ratios only for white male workers in the tobacco industry.

DISCUSSION

There is agreement in the reports reviewed here that black suicide rates are lower than white suicide rates in the United States, although reports from some cities occasionally claim to find a reversal in this ethnic difference for some age groups.

It has been reported that the two ethnic groups use different methods for suicide. This phenomenon, however, has never been adequately tested, that is, after controlling for all of the social and economic differences between African Americans and whites.

Many commentators argue that black male youth suicide rates have been rising, but one dissenting voice claimed that white male youth suicide rates have been rising too. Perhaps, however, black male youth suicide rates have been rising proportionally faster? There are reports that black elderly suicide rates have been rising recently, and one report claimed that black female suicide rates had risen alarmingly. This latter report is demonstrably false, as we shall see in Chapter 5, and in that chapter we will also examine the validity of the other conclusions from this review of the literature.

REFERENCES

Adams, G. R., Bennion, L. D., Openshaw, D. K., & Bingham, C. R. Windows of vulnerability. *Journal of Primary Prevention*, 1990, 10, 223-240.

Alexander, G. R., Gibbs, T., Massey, R. M., & Alterkruse, J. M. South Carolina's mortality in the 1970s. *Public Health Reports*, 1982, 97, 476-482.

Allen, N. H. *Suicide in California 1960-1970*. Sacramento, CA: Department of Public Health, 1973.

Alston, M. H. Suicide in African-American elderly. In D. Lester (Ed.) *Suicide '94*, pp. 145-146. Denver, CO: American Association of Suicidology, 1994.

Anon. Suicide and depression. In Anon, *Miniconsultations on the mental and physical health problems of black women*, pp. 27-48. Washington, DC: Black Women's Community Development Foundation, 1975.

Anon. Suicide taking its toll on blacks. *The Crisis*, 1981, 88(October), 401.

Anon. Violent deaths among persons 15-21 years of age. *Mortality & Morbidity Weekly Report*, 1983, 32(35), 435-437.

Anon. Youth suicide. *Mortality & Morbidity Weekly Report*, 1987, 36(6), 87-89.

Anon. Suicide among blacks. In Anon, *Suicide and ethnicity in the United States*, pp. 11-29. New York: Brunner/Mazel, 1989.

Bachman, R. *Death and violence on the reservation*. New York: Auburn House, 1992.

Baker, F. M. Black youth suicide. In M. R. Feinleib (Ed.) *Report of the Secretary's Task Force on Youth Suicide, Volume 3*, pp. 177-195. Washington, DC: United States Government Printing Office, 1989.

Baker, F. M. Black youth suicide. *Journal of the National Medical Association*, 1990, 82, 495-507.

Baker, F. M. Suicide among ethnic minority elderly. *Journal of Geriatric Psychiatry*, 1994, 27, 241-264.

Baker, F. M. Suicide among ethnic elders. In G. T. Kennedy (Ed.) *Suicide and depression in late life*, pp. 51-79. New York: Wiley, 1996.

Bingham, C. R., Bennion, L. D., Openshaw, D. K., & Adams, G. R. An analysis of age, gender and racial differences in recent national trends of youth suicide. *Journal of Adolescence*, 1994, 17, 53-71.

Blair, A., Berney, B. W., Heid, M. F., & White, D. W. Causes of death among workers in the tobacco industry. *Archives of Environmental Health*, 1983, 38, 223-228.

Breed, W. The Negro and fatalistic suicide. *Pacific Sociological Review*, 1970, 13, 156-162.

Bush, J. A. *Suicide and blacks*. Los Angeles: Charles R. Drew Postgraduate Medical School, 1974.

Christian, E. R. Black suicide. In C. L. Hatton, S. M. Valente & A. Rink (Eds.) *Suicide*, pp. 143-159. New York: Appleton-Century-Crofts, 1977.

Comer, J. P. Black suicide. *Urban Health*, 1973, 2, 41-43, 47.

Copeland, A. R. Suicide among nonwhites. *American Journal of Forensic Medicine and Pathology*, 1989, 10, 10-13.

Datel, W. E., & Johnson, A. W. Suicide in United States Army personnel, 1975-1976. *Military Medicine*, 1979, 144, 239-244.

Davis, R. Black suicide in the Seventies. *Suicide and Life-Threatening Behavior*, 1979, 9, 131-140.

Davis, R. Black suicide and social support systems. *Phylon*, 1982, 43, 307-314.

Delzell, E., & Grufferman, S. Mortality among white and nonwhite farmers in North Carolina, 1976-1978. *American Journal of Epidemiology*, 1985, 121, 391-402.

Dennis, R. E. Social stress and mortality among nonwhite males. *Phylon*, 1977, 38, 315-328.

Desenclos, J. C. A., & Hahn, R. A. Years of potential life lost before age 65. *CDC Surveillance Summary*, 1992, 41, SS6, 13-23.

Diggory, J. C. United States suicide rates, 1933-1968. In E. S. Shneidman (Ed.) *Suicidology*, pp. 25-69. New York: Grune & Stratton, 1976.

Dillihay, T. C. Suicide in black children. *Psychiatric Forum*, 1989, 15(1), 24-27.

Earls, F., Escobar, J., & Manson, S. M. Suicide in minority groups. In S. J. Blumenthal & D. J. Kupfer (Eds.) *Suicide over the life cycle*, pp. 571-598. Washington, DC: American Psychiatric Press, 1990.

Ford, A. B., Rushforth, N. B., Rushforth, N., Hirsch, C. S., & Adelson, L. Violent death in a metropolitan county. *American Journal of Public Health*, 1979, 69, 459-464.

Frazer, M. The female suicide victim. *American Journal of Forensic Medicine & Pathology*, 1986, 6, 305-311.

Frederick, C. J. Suicide in young minority group persons. In H. S. Sudak, A. B. Ford & N. B. Rushforth (Eds.) *Suicide in the young*, pp. 31-44. Littleton, MA: PSG, 1984.

French, L. A., & Wailes, S. N. Regional comparisons of suicidal aggression. *Corrective & Social Psychiatry*, 1980, 26, 180-192.

Gibbs, J. T. (Ed.) *Young, black, and male in America*. Dover, MA: Auburn House, 1988.

Gibbs, J. T. Conceptual, methodological, and sociocultural issues in black youth suicide. *Suicide & Life-Threatening Behavior*, 1988, 18, 73-89.

Gibbs, J. T. Mental health issues of black adolescents. In A. R. Stiffman & L. E. Davis (Eds.) *Ethnic issues in adolescent mental health*, pp. 21-52. Newbury Park, CA: Sage, 1990.

Gibbs, J. T. Homicide and suicide in young black males. In C. D. Llewellyn & R. J. Brown (Eds.) *The African American male*, pp. 15-26. New York: National Urban League, 1992.

Gibbs, J. T. African-American suicide. In J. L. McIntosh (Ed.) *Suicide '96*, pp. 8-9. Washington, DC: American Association of Suicidology, 1996.

Gibbs, J. T. African-American suicide. *Suicide & Life-Threatening Behavior*, 1997, 27, 68-79.

Gite, L. Black men and suicide. *Essence*, 1986, 17(7), 64, 66, 134.

Gowitt, G. T., & Hanzlick, R. L. Suicide in Fulton County, Georgia (1975-1984). *Journal of Forensic Sciences*, 1986, 31, 1029-1038.

Green, J. Ethnic aspects of suicide statistics. In C. L. Hatton, S. M. Valente & A. Rink (Eds.) *Suicide*, pp, 139-143. New York: Appleton-Century-Crofts, 1977.

Greenberg, M., & Schneider, D. Blue Thursday? *Public Health Reports*, 1992, 107, 264-268.

Greenberg, M., & Schneider, D. Violence in American cities. *Social Science & Medicine*, 1994, 39, 179-187.

Griffith, E. E., & Bell, C. C. Recent trends in suicide and homicide among blacks. *Journal of the American Medical Association*, 1989, 262, 2265-2269.

Hatcher, C., & Hatcher, D. Ethnic group suicide. *Crisis Intervention*, 1975, 6(1), 2-9.

Hayes, F. W., & Johnson, M. L. Blacks, suicide and the military. *Military Medicine*, 1979, 144, 811-813.

Heacock, D. R. Suicidal behavior in black and Hispanic youth. *Psychiatric Annals*, 1990, 20, 134-142.

Hendin, H. Black suicide. *Archives of General Psychiatry*, 1969a, 21, 407-422.

Hendin, H. *Black suicide*. New York: Basic Books, 1969b.

Hendin, H. *Suicide in America*. New York: Norton, 1982.

Humphrey, J. A., & Palmer, S. The effects of race, gender, and marital status on suicides among young adults, middle-aged adults, and older adults. *Omega*, 1990-1991, 22, 277-285.

Jackson, J. J. Epidemiological aspects of mental illness among aged black women and men. *Journal of Minority Aging*, 1979, 4, 76-87.

Jedlicka, D., Shin, Y., & Lee, E. S. Suicide among blacks. *Phylon*, 1977, 38, 448-455.

Kachur, S. P., Potter, L. B., James, S. P., & Powell, K. E. *Suicide in the United States 1980-1992*. Atlanta: National Center for Injury Prevention & Control, 1995.

Kimmel, R. Black suicide. *Focus* (University of Wisconsin), 1978, 3(1), 6-7.

King, L. M. Suicide from a "black reality" perspective. In B. A. Bass, G. E. Wyatt & G. J. Powell (Eds.) *The Afro-American family*, pp. 221-236. New York: Grune & Stratton, 1982.

Kirk, A. R. Destructive behaviors among members of the black community. *Journal of Multicultural Counseling & Development*, 1986, 14, 3-9.

Koshes, R. J., & Rothberg, J. M. Parasuicidal behavior on an active duty Army training post. *Military Medicine*, 1992, 157, 350-353.

Kramer, M., Pollack, E. S., Redick, R. W., & Locke, B. Z. *Mental disorders/suicide*. Cambridge, MA: Harvard University, 1972.

Lane, R. *Violent death in the city*. Cambridge, MA: Harvard University, 1979.

Lester, D. Suicide in Philadelphia over the last 150 years. *Philadelphia Medicine*, 1987, 83, 477.

Lester, D., Economic status of African-Americans and suicide rates. *Perceptual & Motor Skills*, 1993, 77, 1150.

Lester, D. Differences in the epidemiology of suicide in Asian Americans by nation of origin. *Omega*, 1994a, 29, 89-93.

Lester, D. Suicide by jumping in Singapore as a function of high-rise apartment availability. *Perceptual & Motor Skills*, 1994b, 79, 74.

Lester, D. Suicide rates among Native Americans in 1890. *Perceptual & Motor Skills*, 1995, 80, 830.

Loya, F. Suicide rates among Chicano youths in Denver, Colorado. Paper presented at the annual meeting of the American Association of Suicidology, Houston, TX, 1973.

MacMahon, B., Johnson, S., & Pugh, T. Relation of suicide rates to social conditions. *Public Health Reports*, 1963, 78, 285-293.

Manton, K. G., Blazer, D. G., & Woodbury, M. A. Suicide in middle age and later life. *Journal of Gerontology*, 1987, 42, 219-227.

Marshall, M. Why our children are killing themselves. *Ebony*, 1981, 36(11), 36-38.

McGinnis, J. M. Suicide in America. *Suicide & Life-Threatening Behavior*, 1987, 17, 18-32.

McIntosh, J. L. Trends in racial differences in US suicide statistics. *Death Studies*, 1988, 13, 275-286.

McIntosh, J. L., & Santos, J. R. Suicide among minority elderly. *Suicide & Life-Threatening Behavior*, 1981, 11, 151-166.

McIntosh, J. L., & Santos, J. R. Changing patterns in methods of suicide by race and sex. *Suicide & Life-Threatening Behavior*, 1982, 12, 221-233.

Meehan, P. J., Saltzman, L. E., & Sattin, R. W. Suicides among older United States residents. *American Journal of Public Health*, 1991, 81, 1198-1120.

Miles, D. E. The growth of suicide among black Americans. *The Crisis*, 1979, 86, 430-433.

Monk, M., & Warshauer, M. E. Completed and attempted suicide in three ethnic groups. *American Journal of Epidemiology*, 1974, 100, 333-345.

Moore, G., & Buckman, J. Epidemiologic observations on suicides in Virginia. *Virginia Medical Monthly*, 1976, 103, 371-377.

Morris, J. B., Kovacs, M., Beck, A. T., & Wolfe, A. Notes toward an epidemiology of urban suicide. *Comprehensive Psychiatry*, 1974, 15, 537-547.

Palmer, S. *The violent society*. New Haven, CT: College & University Press, 1972.

Parham, T. A., & McDavis, R. J. Black men, an endangered species. *Journal of Counseling & Development*, 1987, 66, 24-27.

Powell, E. H. *The design of discord.* New York: Oxford University Press, 1970.

Prange, A. J., & Vitols, M. M. Cultural aspects of the relatively low incidence of depression in Southern Negroes. *International Journal of Social Psychiatry,* 1962, 8, 104-112.

Rigsbee, S. S., Goebel, A. E., Di Canio, P. T., & Clark, D. C. Trends in adolescent suicide by firearms. In D. Lester (Ed.) *Suicide '93,* pp. 82-84. Denver, CO: American Association for Suicidology, 1993.

Rogers, R. G. Living and dying in the U.S.A. *Demography,* 1992, 29, 287-303.

Rothberg, J. M., Bartone, P. T., Holloway, H. C., & Marlowe, D. H. Life and death in the US Army. *Journal of the American Medical Association,* 1990, 264, 2241-2244.

Rutledge, E. M. Suicide among black adolescents and young adults. In A. R. Stiffman & L. E. Davis (Eds.) *Ethnic issues in adolescent mental health,* pp. 339-351. Newbury Park, CA: Sage, 1990.

Santos, J. F., Hubbard, R. W., & McIntosh, J. L. Mental health and the minority elderly. In L. D. Breslau & M. R. Haug (Eds.) *Depression and aging,* pp. 51-70. New York: Springer, 1983.

Saunders, C. O. Blacks and Hispanics. In P. Muehrer (Ed.) *Research perspectives on depression and suicide in minorities,* pp. 21-29. Washington, DC: Public Health Service, 1987.

Schmid, C. F., & Van Arsdol, M. D. Completed and attempted suicides. *American Sociological Review,* 1955, 20, 273-283.

Seiden, R. H. We're driving young blacks to suicide. *Psychology Today,* 1970, 4(3), 24-28.

Seiden, R. H. Why are suicides of young blacks increasing? *HSMHA Health Reports,* 1972, 87, 3-8.

Shaffer, D., & Fisher, P. The epidemiology of suicide in children and young adolescents. *Journal of the American Academy of Child Psychiatry,* 1981, 20, 545-565.

Shaffer, D., Gould, M., & Hicks, R. C. Worsening suicide rate in black teenagers. *American Journal of Psychiatry,* 1994, 151, 1810-1812.

Shai, D., & Rosenwaika, I. Violent deaths among Mexican-American, Puerto Rican and Cuban-born migrants to the United States. *Social Science & Medicine,* 1988, 26, 269-276.

Slater, J. Suicide. *Ebony,* 1973, 28(11), 152-160.

Smith, J. A., & Carter, J. H. Suicide and black adolescents. *Journal of the National Medical Association*, 1986, 78, 1061-1064.

Staples, R. To be young, black and oppressed. *Black Scholar*, 1975, 7(4), 2-9.

Swanson, W. C., & Breed, W. Black suicide in New Orleans. In E. S. Shneidman (Ed.) *Suicidology*, pp. 99-128. New York: Grune & Stratton, 1976.

Taylor, M. C., & Wicks, J. W. The choice of weapons. *Suicide & Life-Threatening Behavior*, 1980, 10, 142-149.

Templer, D. I., & Cappelletty, G. G. Suicide in the elderly. *Clinical Gerontologist*, 1986, 5, 475-487.

Tunakan, B., & Bartholow, G. W. A ten year survey of suicide in Omaha-Douglas County, Nebraska. *Nebraska Medical Journal*, 1972, 57, 265-269.

Warfield, J. L. Black people and suicide. *Journal of Black Health Perspectives*, 1974, August/September, 11-28.

Williams, J. Why are blacks less suicide prone than whites? *The Crisis*, 1983, 90(10), 29.

Woodbury, M. A., Manton, K. G., & Blazer, D. Trends in US suicide mortality rates 1968 to 1982. *International Journal of Epidemiology*, 1988, 17, 356-362.

Wylie, F. Suicide among black females. In Anon, *Miniconsultations on the mental and physical health problems of black women*, pp. 121-125. Washington, DC: Black Women's Community Development Foundation, 1975.

Wyche, K. F., Obolensky, N., & Glood, E. American Indian, black American, and Hispanic American youth. In M. J. Rotheram-Borus, J. Bradley & N. Obolensky (Eds.) *Planning to live*, pp. 355-389. Norman, OK: National Research Center for Youth Services, 1990.

Wyche, K. F., & Rotheram-Borus, M. J. Suicidal behavior among minority youth in the United States. In A. R. Stiffman & L. E. Davis (Eds.) *Ethnic issues in adolescent mental health*, pp. 323-338. Newbury Park, CA: Sage, 1990.

Table 3.1

Suicide Rates By Age, Sex And Marital Status, 1980

	Whites	African Americans	Native Americans	Chinese Americans	Japanese Americans	Filipino Americans
Gender:						
male	20.6	10.4	22.0	9.1	13.4	5.3
female	6.1	2.2	4.9	7.5	5.5	1.7
Age:						
15-24	13.7	7.3	26.5	6.8	8.3	5.6
25-34	17.3	12.5	24.7	8.8	10.6	5.0
35-44	16.8	9.6	17.6	5.8	9.8	1.7
45-54	17.4	7.0	11.4	16.6	10.9	6.4
55-64	17.2	6.5	7.9	9.7	11.2	7.1
65+	19.1	5.5	2.8	25.9	18.9	5.2
Marital Status:						
single	19.1	9.4	31.9	10.5	12.7	6.9
married	12.7	7.1	10.5	7.4	8.5	3.3
widowed	20.4	6.5	8.9	34.0	19.2	4.2
divorced	41.8	12.5	24.3	32.8	15.8	5.0

Table 3.2

Methods Used For Suicide, 1980 and 1990

	solids/ liquids	gas/vapors	hanging	firearm	other
1980					
whites	11.5%	9.5%	13.3%	57.5%	8.1%
African Americans	7.6%	1.8%	16.4%	58.8%	15.4%
Native Americans	7.7%	1.6%	26.4%	57.1%	7.1%
Chinese Americans	10.4%	4.5%	43.3%	10.4%	31.3%
Japanese Americans	7.8%	3.1%	37.5%	23.4%	28.1%
Filipino Americans	11.1%	7.4%	29.6%	29.6%	22.2%
1990					
whites	10.3%	7.9%	13.6%	61.8%	6.4%
males	6.1%	7.6%	14.1%	66.6%	5.7%
females	27.2%	9.3%	11.5%	42.5%	4.1%
African Americans	8.6%	1.4%	17.7%	59.8%	12.5%
males	4.8%	1.2%	18.9%	63.4%	11.6%
females	25.9%	2.4%	12.0%	43.0%	16.6%

Table 3.3
Suicide Rates, 1990

	whites		blacks	
	male	female	male	female
age:				
5-14	1.1	0.4	0.8	*
15-24	23.2	4.2	15.1	2.3
25-34	25.6	6.0	21.9	3.7
35-44	25.3	7.4	16.9	4.0
45-54	24.8	7.5	14.8	3.2
55-64	27.5	8.0	10.8	2.6
65-74	34.2	7.2	14.7	2.6
75-84	60.2	6.7	14.4	*
85+	70.3	5.4	*	*
total	22.0	5.3	12.0	2.3

* less than 20 suicides and so the rates are unreliable

CHAPTER 4

OFFICIAL STATISTICS: ARE THEY RELIABLE?

B efore discussing any ethnic differences in suicidal behavior, we ought to ask whether the official statistics on suicide are reliable and whether they are equally reliable for all ethnic groups.

Douglas (1967) argued forcefully that coroners' (or medical examiners') decisions to certify a death as suicide will depend both on their own biases and on the information they receive from the investigating officers and informants. Douglas suggested that a suicidal death is more likely to be "covered up" and miscertified if, for example, the deceased is a Roman Catholic rather than a Protestant since the negative ramifications of suicide for a Roman Catholic are greater than for a Protestant. Suicides are more likely to be covered up if the deceased is socially integrated, for there is a stigma associated with suicide and the significant others may be motivated to avoid having the deceased (and themselves) stigmatized. Because of their greater ability to manipulate the societal agencies and processes, Douglas suggested that the middle classes will be more likely to successfully conceal suicides.

In these situations, not only will significant others attempt more often to conceal a suicide, but the local officers involved in the certification of death will be more likely to be favorably influenced by the wishes of the significant others. Interestingly, Douglas's thesis is widely cited and given great weight although he presented no methodologically sound research to back up his argument. His argument remains purely speculative.

These factors could clearly influence the certification of suicide in African Americans versus whites, especially given the negative attitude toward suicide of the African American church and community. Many commentators have suggested that black suicide rates are underestimated (Alston and Anderson, 1995; Peck, 1983), though some commentators have suggested that the biases may work in the opposite direction to make African Americans more likely to be labeled as suicides, when they are in fact not, had a more thorough investigation been carried out by the medical examiner's office (Peck, 1983). Christian (1977) felt that the suicides of lower class individuals are less likely to be covered up by medical examiners, and she thought that black suicides may be more accurately counted than those of whites.

Whether these biases in certifying deaths have influenced the officially reported rates of suicide has never been explored. This is a serious omission since the issue has been explored with regard to Native American suicide rates (Lester, 1997). For Native Americans, investigators have searched medical examiner files in order to see how many suicides they can identify, and then they have compared this number with those reported by the medical examiner to the government agencies responsible for collecting mortality rates. Typically, these investigators identify more suicides than are officially recorded.

A report which provides a little support for this possibility is the subjective opinion from Peck (1983) that the medical examiner files for black suicides in the one city he studied were much "thinner" than the files for white suicides, suggesting a more cursory investigation for the black suicides. This opinion was shared by Breed (1970) in his study of suicide in New Orleans in 1954-1963. He commented that the quality of the police and coroner data was worse for the black suicides than for the white suicides.

DISGUISED SUICIDES

Wolfgang (1957), in his discussion of murder, noted that victims often played a role in precipitating their own murder. For example, in these *victim-precipitated murders*, the victim may be the first to use physical force against his or her subsequent murderer or be the first to display a weapon.

In his study of 588 criminal homicides in Philadelphia in 1948 to 1952, Wolfgang found that the victim played a role in his or her own death in 26 percent of the incidents. There was a significant ethnic difference here, with 28 percent of the black victims playing a role in their own murder versus only 19 percent of the white victims. Black murderers were more common in victim-precipitated homicides than were white murderers, possibly because the majority of the homicides were interracial.[1] The ethnic difference in victim-precipitated murder may mean that suicidal African Americans, especially black males, are more likely than whites to choose this method (consciously or unconsciously) for committing suicide.

Many commentators have suggested that victim-precipitated homicide may be common in African Americans, both in black men and in black women (Alston and Anderson, 1995; Blake, 1971; Gibbs, 1988; Howze, 1977). Gibbs (1988) and Howze (1977) have noted that some black males set up violent confrontations with law enforcement officers in order to provoke a lethal response. Several Black Panther members were killed in confrontations with the police, as were member of the Symbionese Liberation Army in 1974 and members of MOVE in Philadelphia in 1986. However, some commentators do not see such behaviors as suicidal, but rather as self-defensive (e.g., Valentine and Valentine, 1972).

Both Blake and Gibbs noted, in addition, the large numbers of unintentional accidents among black males, including car accidents, especially when drunk. The large numbers of drug overdoses may also include deaths with suicidal motivation. For example, in a study of 103 methadone patients (whose ethnic affiliation was not mentioned), thirteen admitted to 33 heroin overdoses (Friedman, et al., 1973). Six percent of these were clear attempts at suicide while 73 percent were judged by the authors to be "covert" suicide attempts.

CAUSES OF POSSIBLE STATISTICAL INACCURACIES

Linden and Breed (1976) noted three problems which can affect official suicide rates by ethnicity. First, accurate biological descriptions of race are not

---

[1] Other common characteristics of victim-precipitated homicides were male victims, female murderers, stabbings, mate slayings, alcohol intoxication in the victim, and prior arrest record in the victim.

used when registering deaths or in census counts. Racial designations are usually those in common usage and based on self-report.

Second, suicide rates are based on populations determined in census counts. Certain groups are typically under-represented in such counts, particularly the young and the poor. Linden and Breed (1976) used correction factors for the census count in New York State in 1960 and found that the suicide rate for metropolitan nonwhite males aged 25-34 dropped from 16.1 to 13.5 after the correction, whereas the white suicide rate for the same age group dropped only from 10.5 to 10.3.

Third, the numerator for suicide rates by age and gender, for example, can be quite small for a rare event such as suicide (Davis, 1979). Thus, calculated rates can fluctuate widely from year to year. Averaging rates over several years can reduce the magnitude of this problem, a process used in the present book for black suicide rates by state in Chapter 6.

Fourth, and most important of all, many scholars have used nonwhite suicide rates rather than calculating black suicide rates. Although African Americans comprise almost 90 percent of the nonwhites in the United States according to Linden and Breed (1976), it is important that serious scholars of *black* suicide obtain *black* suicide rates for their research.

One of the few scholars to have done this is Davis (1979) who used mortality records to calculate black suicide rates in 1970 and 1975 for major urban areas of the nation. In 1970, Pittsburgh and Los Angeles-Long Beach had the highest black suicides rates (21.5 and 21.4 respectively). Black suicide rates tended to be highest in the West and lowest in the South. Black suicide rates were lowest in the least populous urban areas and in the both the oldest and the youngest urban areas. From 1970 to 1975, suicide rates rose most in the non-Southern regions and in the most populous urban areas.

A final point here is that black suicides tend to be more often from the lower social classes and urban areas than white suicides, and to differ in marital status, age and, indeed, in many respects. Thus, it may not be meaningful to compare crude black and white suicides rates without correcting for these differences in demographic characteristics. Indeed, Wyche and Rotheram-Borus (1990) thought that black and white suicide rates might not differ once such differences were taken into account.

RESEARCH ON THESE ISSUES

MEDICAL EXAMINERS

Warshauer and Monk (1978) examined deaths in four districts in New York City in 1968-1970. They found that the medical examiner's office considered many deaths to be suicides, yet they did not sign-off on these deaths as definite suicides. The suicide rate based on their statistics would have been greater if they had called all of these deaths suicides: the white male rate of 25.6 would have increased to 37.1 (an increase of 45%), the white female suicide rate from 14.4 to 19.6 (a 36% increase), the black male suicide rate from 11.9 to 21.7 (an 82% increase), and the black female suicide rate from 5.0 to 8.8 (a 76% increase). Thus, the undercounting was more pronounced for African Americans than for whites. It was especially large for black males over the age of 25 and black females aged 18-24. The undercounting appeared to greatest for those completing suicide by jumping and "other" methods, and African Americans tended to use these methods more than whites. Thus, the undercounting could have resulted from race or from the method chosen for suicide.

Warshauer and Monk noted also that the change in the International Classification of Disease system from the 7th version to the 8th version permitted an undetermined category. As a result, the New York City health department official suicide rates dropped dramatically for both whites and African Americans since many of these deaths were now classified as undetermined. The white suicide rate dropped by 45% after the change in the classification system, while the black suicide rate dropped 80%. (Incidentally, the change in classification system did not appear to affect the Medical examiner statistics.)

BLACK VERSUS NONWHITE SUICIDE RATES

It has been common to use nonwhite suicide rates in research on black suicide since the United States Government did not calculate black suicide rates prior to 1979. To see whether this is a valid procedure, I calculated suicide rates for African Americans for the period 1960 to 1978, based on the absolute number of black suicides reported in *Vital Statistics of the United States* and the estimated black population from *Current Population Reports, Series P-25*, and combined these rates with the official black suicide rates reported in *Vital Statistics of the United States* for the period 1979-1992 -- see Table 4.1.

It can be seen that the discrepancy between the nonwhite and black suicide rates was greater in the 1960s (the difference was as large as 0.8) than in the 1980s (the difference was no greater than 0.5). Furthermore, the rates do not always change in the same direction. From 1963 to 1964, the nonwhite suicide rate dropped from 5.0 to 4.7, whereas the black suicide rate rose from 4.2 to 4.3.

The mean black suicide rate over the 33 years was 5.67 (standard deviation 1.02) whereas the mean nonwhite suicide rate was 6.12 (standard deviation 0.90). The two rates were, however, highly correlated (Pearson r = 0.98).

The United States population which is neither white nor black is changing constantly as new immigrants arrive. The proportion of immigrants from different regions (Asia, the Middle East, Central and South America, etc.) changes over time. Since these immigrant have different suicide rates, their inclusion in the nonwhite suicide rate can have large effects, effects which have not been consistent over time since the source of immigrants has changed over time.

Thus, in order to make definite conclusions about black suicide rates we must use *black* suicide rates. Even if the estimates prepared for this volume turn out to be somewhat inaccurate, they will hopefully spur scholars to improve on the estimates in future studies.

AGE-ADJUSTED SUICIDE RATES

Crude suicide rates may not accurately portray differences between groups if the groups differ in age. Age-adjusted suicide rates are available from Anon (1993) and are shown in Table 4.2. It can be seen that the differences in trends are quite small.

DISCUSSION

There is only tentative evidence so far that medical examiner practices affect the official black suicide rate, and less evidence that it affects the black suicide rate differentially from the white suicide rate. However, there is no excuse today for using nonwhite suicide rates instead of black suicide rates in research on black suicide. Researchers must build upon the efforts made in this book to calculate accurate black suicide rates for the period prior to 1979.

REFERENCES

Alston, M H., & Anderson, S. E. Suicidal behavior in African-American women. In S. S. Canetto & D. Lester (Eds.) *Women and suicidal behavior*, pp. 133-143. New York: Springer, 1995.

Anon. *Health United States 1992*. Hyattsville, MD: Public Health Service, 1993, #93-1232.

Blake, C. Suicide among black Americans. In D. B. Anderson & L. J. McClean (Eds.) *Identifying suicide potential*, pp. 25-28. New York: Behavioral Publications, 1971.

Breed, W. The Negro and fatalistic suicide. *Pacific Sociological Review*, 1970, 13, 156-162.

Christian, E. R. Black suicide. In C. L. Hatton, S. M. Valente & A. Rink (Eds.) *Suicide*, pp 143-159. New York: Appleton-Century-Crofts, 1977.

Davis, R. *Metropolitan black suicide*. Madison, WI: University of Wisconsin Institute for Research on Poverty, 1979.

Douglas, J. D. *The social meanings of suicide*. Princeton: Princeton University, 1967.

Friedman, R. C., Friedman, J. G., & Ramirez, T. The heroin overdose as a method of attempted suicide. *British Journal of Addiction*, 1973, 68, 137-143.

Gibbs, J. T. Conceptual, methodological, and sociocultural issues in black youth suicide. *Suicide & Life-Threatening Behavior*, 1988, 18, 73-89.

Howze, B. Suicide. *Journal of Non-White Concerns*, 1977, 5, 65-72.

Lester, D. *Suicide in American Indians*. Commack, NY: Nova Science, 1997.

Linden, L. L., & Breed, W. The demographic epidemiology of suicide. In E. S. Shneidman (Ed.) *Suicidology*, pp. 71-98. New York: Grune & Stratton, 1976.

Peck, D. L. "Official documentation" of the black suicide experience. *Omega*, 1983, 14, 21-31.

Valentine, C. A., & Valentine, B. L. The man and the panthers. *Politics & Society*, 1972, 2, 273-286.

Warshauer, M. E., & Monk, M. Problems in suicide statistics for whites and blacks. *American Journal of Public Health*, 1978, 68, 383-388.

Wolfgang, M. E. Victim-precipitated criminal homicide. *Journal of Criminal Law, Criminology & Police Science*, 1957, 48, 1-11.

Wyche, K. F., & Rotheram-Borus, M. J. Suicidal behavior among minority youth in the United States. In A. R. Stiffman & L. E. Davis (Eds.) *Ethnic issues in adolescent minority mental health*, pp. 323-338. Newbury Park, CA: Sage, 1990.

Table 4.1
Black And Nonwhite Suicide Rates, 1960-1992

year	nonwhite	black	year	nonwhite	black
1960	4.6	3.9	1977	7.3	6.5
1961	4.8	4.0	1978	6.9	6.5
1962	4.7	4.0	1979	7.5	7.0
1963	5.0	4.2	1980	6.4	6.0
1964	4.7	4.3	1981	6.6	6.1
1965	5.1	4.5	1982	6.2	5.9
1966	5.1	4.5	1983	6.2	5.8
1967	5.1	4.5	1984	6.5	6.2
1968	4.7	4.3	1985	6.6	6.2
1969	5.3	4.9	1986	6.7	6.5
1970	5.6	5.1	1987	6.9	6.6
1971	5.8	5.2	1988	6.8	6.7
1972	6.6	6.0	1989	7.1	7.0
1973	6.4	5.8	1990	7.0	6.9
1974	6.5	5.9	1991	6.8	6.7
1975	6.8	6.1	1992	6.8	6.8
1976	7.0	6.4			

Table 4.2
Crude And Age-Adjusted Suicide Rates
(based on the population in 1940)

	white males		white females		black males		black females	
	adj.	crude	adj.	crude	adj.	crude	adj.	crude
1950	18.1	19.0	5.3	5.5	7.0	6.3	1.7	1.5
1960	17.5	17.6	5.3	5.3	7.8	6.4	1.9	1.6
1970	18.2	18.0	7.2	7.1	9.9	8.0	2.9	2.6
1980	18.9	19.9	5.7	5.9	11.1	10.3	2.4	2.2
1990	20.1	22.0	4.8	5.3	12.4	12.0	2.4	2.3

CHAPTER 5

FACTS ABOUT BLACK SUICIDE

It is surprising that black suicide rates have been published by the National Center for Health Statistics only since 1979. Prior to that, suicide rates were available only for nonwhites as a whole. Since, as we have seen in Chapter 3, suicide rates show very different epidemiological patterns for the different groups of nonwhites, the data for nonwhite suicide rates as a whole are useless.

Numbers of black suicides were published for the period 1933 (the first year that all states reported mortality statistics to the federal government) to 1978, but published estimates of the black population are not available prior to 1960. My requests to the Census Bureau failed to obtain any unpublished estimates. Again, the lack of these data is surprising.

For the period 1960-1978, I calculated black suicide rates based on published estimates of the black population by age and gender. For the period 1933-1959, I calculated black suicide rates based on my own estimates of the black population. To do this, I used the census data for 1930, 1940[1], 1950 and 1960 and simple linear interpolation since I was unable to fit any accurate curvilinear regression lines to the census-year population data points -- I tried both quadratic and cubic equations.[2]

The results are shown in Table 5.1 through Table 5.6.

---

[1] The 1940 Census did not report the population by age for African Americans aged 75-84 and 85+, rendering the estimated suicide rates for these age groups less reliable.

[2] I also had to calculate white suicide rates by 10-year age groups for 1933-1939 in Table 5.3.

THE MODERN PERIOD: 1960-1992

The mean suicide rates for the 33-year period from 1960-1992 are:

black: total	5.67	white: total	12.74
black: male	9.37	white: male	19.55
black: female	2.30	white: female	6.24

It can be seen that black suicide rates were lower than white suicide rates during this period, and female suicide rates were lower than male suicide rates for both groups.

The Pearson correlation coefficients between the black and white suicide rates for this same period were:

total	0.92
male	0.93
female	0.75

Thus, the black and white suicide rates appeared to change in the same direction over this period and, therefore, be strongly associated.

The correlations of the suicide rates with the year during this same period were:

black: total	0.91	white: total	0.83
black: male	0.95	white: male	0.93
black: female	0.18	white: female	-0.38

Thus, male suicide rates, both black and white, appeared to increase over the period, while black female suicide rates did not appear to change much at all and white female suicide rates declined slightly. Claims that there has been a large increase in black female suicide rates (Slater, 1973), therefore, appear to be unfounded.

Table 5.2 shows the ratios of black/white suicide rates and male/female suicide rates. The correlations of these rates with the year during this same period (1960-1992) were:

black/white: total   0.90
black/white: male   0.89
black/white: female   0.70

male/female: black   0.82
male/female: white   0.79

It is clear that the ratio of black/white suicide rates increased over the years, indicating that black suicide rates increased proportionately more than white suicide rates. This was true for both men and women. It is also clear that male suicide rates increased proportionately more then female suicide rates, both for African Americans and for whites.

SUICIDE RATES BY AGE

In the 1960s, the age distribution of black male suicide rates was not pronounced, save that the suicide rate was somewhat lower for those aged 15-24 and over 85 (see Table 5.3). However, from 1970 on, the suicide rate of black males aged 25-34 was somewhat higher than the rates for other age groups.

This is intriguing given what has been written about black suicide. First, the peak in suicide rates for black males aged 25-34 is not tremendous. Suicide rates above 15.0 are found in some years for those aged 15-24, 35-44, 65-74, 75-84 and over 85. Second, while commentators have written about the alarming increase in "youth" suicide (which is typically taken to mean those aged 15-24), the age group at highest risk for suicide rate has been black males aged 25-34 -- young adults. One suspects that the commentators used the term "youth" because that term might spur public and official concern more. It is also noteworthy that black male suicide rates have risen during the period studied with perhaps the exception of those aged 45-54 and 55-64.

White suicide rates, on the other hand, have shown a different pattern, with the elderly males consistently having the highest suicide rate. However, the suicide rate of white males aged 15-24 has risen as has that of black males aged 15-24.

There has been little change in black female suicide rates over the years, whereas the suicide rates of middle-aged white females have declined substantially in recent years.

These results are illustrated by the data in Table 5.4. It can be seen that black male and female suicide rates peaked during the period 1960-1992 in those aged 25-34, whereas white male suicide rates peaked for those aged over 85 and white female suicide rates peaked for those aged 45-54.

Furthermore, black male suicide rates increased during the period only for those aged 15-44 and over 65. Black female suicide rates did not change significantly during the period. A similar phenomenon was found for white suicide rates, except that the suicide rates for middle-aged white males decreased during the period. White female suicide rates decreased during the period except for those aged 15-24.

To explore the peak in black suicide rates more precisely, suicide rates for five-year age groups were calculated -- see Table 5.5. For black males, the peak is clearly for those aged 25-34. Black male teenagers have lower suicide rates, although they are increasing in recent years. A parallel phenomenon is found for white male suicide rates.

METHOD

For method (see Tables 5.6 and 5.7), both black and white males prefer firearms for suicide. Black males use hanging relatively more often and poisons less often than do white males. For females, again both black and white females prefer firearms for suicide; black females use poisons more often and hanging less often than do white females.

OLDER TRENDS

Looking at trends back to 1933, it can be seen that black suicide rates did not seem to rise as much during the Great Depression as did white suicide rates. However, all of the suicide rates appear to have declined during the Second World War.

COMMENT

This chapter has presented suicide rates for African Americans back to 1933, rates which have not been available hitherto. It is hoped that scholars will improve upon the accuracy of these estimates and use them for future research.

Some trends were identified which modify the conclusions of commentators presented in Chapter 3. It is young black male adults (not black youth) who have had the highest suicide rates. This is an important distinction for theoretical explanations.

While the suicide rates of black middle-aged men have remained steady in recent years, the suicide rates of white middle-aged men have declined. Similarly, while black female suicide rates are lower than white female suicide rates, they have remained steady over the last thirty years, whereas white female suicide rates have, on the whole, declined (with the exception of white females aged 15-24). It is important to explain this failure of some black suicide rates to decline.

REFERENCE

Slater, J. Suicide. *Ebony*, 1973, 28(11), 152-160.

Table 5.1
Suicide Rates By Gender For African Americans And Whites (from
government data for 1979-1992 and calculated by the present author for other
years)

	African American			White		
	total	male	female	total	male	female
1992	6.8	12.0	2.0	13.0	21.2	5.1
1991	6.7	12.1	1.9	13.3	21.7	5.2
1990	6.9	12.0	2.3	13.5	22.0	5.3
1989	7.0	12.2	2.4	13.1	21.4	5.2
1988	6.7	11.5	2.4	13.4	21.7	5.5
1987	6.6	11.6	2.1	13.7	22.1	5.7
1986	6.5	11.1	2.3	13.9	22.3	5.9
1985	6.2	10.8	2.1	13.4	21.5	5.6
1984	6.2	10.6	2.2	13.4	21.3	5.9
1983	5.8	9.9	2.0	13.1	20.6	5.9
1982	5.9	10.1	2.1	13.2	20.7	6.1
1981	6.1	10.2	2.4	12.9	20.9	6.2
1980	6.0	10.3	2.2	12.7	19.9	5.9
1979	7.0	11.6	2.8	13.1	20.0	6.6
1978	6.5	10.6	2.7	13.4	20.2	6.9
1977	6.5	10.5	3.0	14.2	21.4	7.3
1976	6.4	10.3	2.9	13.3	19.8	7.2
1975	6.1	9.9	2.7	13.6	20.1	7.4
1974	5.9	9.6	2.5	13.0	19.2	7.1
1973	5.8	9.4	2.5	12.8	18.8	7.0
1972	6.0	9.4	2.9	12.8	18.5	7.3
1971	5.2	7.7	3.0	12.5	17.9	7.3
1970	5.1	7.9	2.6	12.4	19.0	7.1
1969	4.9	7.5	2.4	11.9	17.2	6.8
1968	4.3	6.8	2.0	11.6	16.9	6.3
1967	4.5	6.8	2.4	11.7	16.8	6.5

1966	4.5	7.1	2.0	11.8	17.2	6.3
1965	4.5	7.2	2.1	12.1	17.4	6.6
1964	4.3	6.7	2.0	11.8	17.2	6.1
1963	4.2	6.7	1.8	11.7	17.8	6.3
1962	4.0	6.2	1.9	11.5	17.8	5.9
1961	4.0	6.6	1.6	11.2	17.1	5.3
1960	3.9	6.3	1.6	11.4	17.6	5.3
1959	4.2	6.8	1.8	11.4	17.7	5.0
1958	3.8	6.2	1.5	11.5	18.0	5.1
1957	3.5	5.9	1.2	10.5	16.5	4.6
1956	3.3	5.3	1.4	10.8	16.9	4.8
1955	3.3	5.4	1.3	11.0	17.2	4.9
1954	3.6	6.0	1.4	10.9	17.5	4.5
1953	3.2	5.4	1.1	10.8	17.2	4.6
1952	3.2	5.4	1.2	10.7	16.9	4.7
1951	3.6	5.9	1.5	11.1	17.3	5.0
1950	3.8	6.3	1.5	12.2	19.2	5.5
1949	3.7	6.2	1.4	12.3	19.2	5.5
1948	3.7	6.1	1.4	12.0	18.4	5.6
1947	3.5	5.7	1.5	12.3	18.8	5.9
1946	3.4	5.3	1.7	12.2	18.3	6.1
1945	2.9	4.5	1.4	11.3	16.5	6.2
1944	2.5	3.8	1.3	10.3	14.7	5.8
1943	2.6	4.0	1.2	10.8	15.7	5.9
1942	3.4	4.9	1.9	12.8	19.4	6.3
1941	3.5	5.6	1.5	13.8	20.7	6.8
1940	4.0	6.2	2.0	15.6	23.5	7.3
1939	3.6	5.4	1.8	15.3	23.4	7.1
1938	4.3	6.4	2.4	16.4	25.4	7.4
1937	4.3	6.4	2.3	16.1	24.5	7.5
1936	4.0	5.8	2.3	15.4	23.3	7.3
1935	4.4	6.4	2.5	15.4	23.3	7.2
1934	3.9	5.5	2.4	16.0	24.6	7.3
1933	4.3	6.5	2.1	17.1	26.8	7.3

Table 5.2
Suicide Rate Ratios

| | African-American/white | | | male/female | |
	total	male	female	African-American	white
1992	0.52	0.57	0.39	6.00	4.16
1991	0.50	0.56	0.37	6.37	4.17
1990	0.51	0.55	0.43	5.22	4.14
1989	0.53	0.57	0.46	5.08	4.12
1988	0.50	0.53	0.44	4.79	3.95
1987	0.48	0.52	0.37	5.52	3.88
1986	0.47	0.50	0.39	4.83	3.78
1985	0.46	0.50	0.37	5.14	3.84
1984	0.46	0.50	0.37	4.82	3.61
1983	0.44	0.48	0.34	4.95	3.49
1982	0.45	0.49	0.34	4.81	3.39
1981	0.47	0.49	0.39	4.25	3.37
1980	0.47	0.52	0.37	4.68	3.37
1979	0.53	0.58	0.42	4.14	3.03
1978	0.49	0.52	0.39	3.93	2.93
1977	0.46	0.49	0.41	3.50	2.93
1976	0.48	0.52	0.40	3.55	2.75
1975	0.45	0.49	0.36	3.67	2.72
1974	0.45	0.50	0.35	3.84	2.70
1973	0.45	0.50	0.36	3.76	2.69
1972	0.47	0.51	0.40	3.24	2.53
1971	0.42	0.43	0.41	2.57	2.45
1970	0.41	0.42	0.37	3.04	2.68
1969	0.41	0.44	0.35	3.12	2.53
1968	0.37	0.40	0.32	3.40	2.68
1967	0.38	0.40	0.37	2.83	2.58
1966	0.38	0.41	0.32	3.55	2.73

1965	0.37	0.41	0.32	3.43	2.64
1964	0.36	0.39	0.33	3.35	2.82
1963	0.36	0.38	0.29	3.72	2.83
1962	0.35	0.35	0.32	3.26	3.02
1961	0.36	0.39	0.30	4.12	3.23
1960	0.34	0.36	0.30	3.94	3.32
1959	0.37	0.38	0.36	3.78	3.54
1958	0.33	0.34	0.29	4.13	3.53
1957	0.33	0.36	0.26	4.92	3.59
1956	0.31	0.31	0.29	3.79	3.52
1955	0.30	0.31	0.27	4.15	3.51
1954	0.33	0.34	0.31	4.29	3.89
1953	0.30	0.31	0.24	4.91	3.74
1952	0.30	0.32	0.26	4.50	3.60
1951	0.32	0.34	0.30	3.93	3.46
1950	0.31	0.33	0.27	4.20	3.49
1949	0.30	0.32	0.25	4.43	3.49
1948	0.31	0.33	0.25	4.36	3.29
1947	0.28	0.30	0.25	3.80	3.19
1946	0.28	0.29	0.28	3.11	3.00
1945	0.26	0.27	0.23	3.21	2.66
1944	0.24	0.26	0.22	2.92	2.53
1943	0.24	0.25	0.20	3.33	2.66
1942	0.27	0.25	0.30	2.58	3.08
1941	0.25	0.27	0.22	3.73	3.04
1940	0.26	0.26	0.27	3.10	3.22
1939	0.24	0.23	0.25	3.00	3.30
1938	0.26	0.25	0.32	2.67	3.43
1937	0.27	0.26	0.31	2.78	3.27
1936	0.26	0.25	0.32	2.52	3.19
1935	0.29	0.27	0.35	2.56	3.24
1934	0.24	0.22	0.33	2.29	3.37
1933	0.25	0.24	0.29	3.10	3.67

Table 5.3
Suicide Rates By 10-Year Age Groups

	15-24	25-34	35-44	45-54	55-64	65-74	75-84	85+
Black Males								
1933	4.5	8.5	14.8	13.1	9.3	12.8	7.7	8.3
1934	4.6	9.8	14.0	9.3	11.2	5.7	11.0	0.0
1935	5.0	9.7	11.1	11.9	14.9	8.7	7.0	7.9
1936	4.9	7.9	11.3	8.9	14.4	9.2	5.0	0.0
1937	4.0	9.9	12.1	10.9	13.6	9.7	8.0	7.6
1938	4.8	9.3	11.5	12.3	13.4	6.5	15.4	7.4
1939	3.7	8.7	9.8	10.0	9.5	8.0	13.3	0.0
1940	4.2	10.1	9.9	12.4	11.3	9.3	4.3	14.2
1941	4.2	9.1	8.8	11.3	10.0	7.8	9.6	7.0
1942	4.4	8.8	8.2	5.8	9.7	8.4	4.0	0.0
1943	4.3	6.6	5.0	5.5	9.0	5.1	5.1	6.7
1944	3.0	5.5	6.1	6.7	9.2	5.0	6.2	0.0
1945	4.0	7.0	8.0	7.4	6.6	7.5	9.6	12.9
1946	4.3	9.3	7.5	8.7	11.9	6.9	10.5	6.4
1947	4.4	8.8	9.6	8.7	11.6	10.7	14.8	6.2
1948	4.7	9.1	11.9	12.1	9.3	8.7	8.8	6.1
1949	4.3	9.2	10.6	10.3	14.9	10.6	10.7	6.0
1950	4.9	9.4	10.4	10.4	16.5	10.0	5.2	11.9
1951	4.5	10.1	9.7	10.1	10.1	8.8	13.1	5.6
1952	3.6	11.0	8.1	7.9	12.2	8.9	6.8	16.0
1953	3.1	9.7	9.1	10.8	9.8	8.3	14.0	10.2
1954	4.4	12.4	10.2	10.7	10.5	10.5	9.9	4.8
1955	5.4	8.9	9.2	8.9	11.1	8.5	12.2	18.5
1956	4.4	9.7	9.8	9.2	11.3	7.2	5.9	4.4
1957	4.7	11.5	10.0	10.3	10.3	14.6	11.4	4.3
1958	4.7	11.6	12.2	10.8	13.0	10.4	7.1	12.3
1959	5.5	13.4	10.8	13.0	13.7	12.6	16.1	0.0
1960	4.0	12.3	12.7	10.7	16.2	11.1	6.5	7.1
1961	6.7	13.9	10.2	13.6	13.2	9.5	10.3	3.7
1962	5.9	11.5	11.9	11.7	11.3	11.7	10.1	3.7

1963	5.5	13.8	13.8	11.6	10.6	13.8	10.6	7.4
1964	7.4	14.5	12.2	11.3	11.5	10.9	9.7	3.6
1965	8.0	13.2	14.3	12.9	12.8	11.4	13.4	10.0
1966	7.6	16.7	10.6	13.6	12.0	10.3	11.9	18.7
1967	6.9	15.8	13.7	10.8	10.6	10.5	10.4	5.9
1968	6.9	14.9	11.6	12.1	11.5	11.7	12.1	2.9
1969	8.8	16.2	15.6	11.0	9.5	11.2	12.6	5.4
1970	10.0	18.6	12.5	13.7	10.5	8.6	8.7	10.3
1971	9.5	16.3	14.5	10.0	10.8	16.9	7.0	7.5
1972 '	14.4	20.0	14.9	12.8	11.1	11.1	8.1	5.0
1973	12.4	21.6	13.5	13.4	11.4	11.2	12.3	9.8
1974	10.9	22.5	15.9	12.7	11.7	13.2	12.9	7.0
1975	12.5	23.1	15.8	12.4	10.7	11.6	11.7	4.3
1976	12.8	21.8	16.3	14.0	11.1	13.5	9.4	29.8
1977	12.8	24.7	14.7	12.0	12.5	10.8	10.6	14.3
1978	12.8	22.8	16.8	14.5	10.1	11.6	11.7	9.8
1979	14.4	26.3	16.9	13.0	12.9	12.9	13.4	11.4
1980	12.3	21.8	15.6	12.0	11.7	11.1	10.5	18.9
1981	11.1	21.8	15.5	12.3	12.5	9.7	18.0	12.7
1982	11.0	20.3	15.6	11.8	11.9	12.1	12.2	16.1
1983	11.5	19.1	14.0	12.1	11.6	13.6	15.8	12.7
1984	11.2	20.7	16.5	11.6	13.4	13.8	15.1	11.1
1985	13.3	19.6	14.9	13.5	11.5	15.8	15.6	7.7
1986	11.5	21.3	17.5	12.8	9.9	16.1	16.0	17.9
1987	12.9	21.1	17.9	13.0	10.3	17.6	20.9	13.0
1988	14.5	22.1	16.4	11.7	10.6	12.9	17.6	10.0
1989	16.7	22.0	18.1	10.9	10.4	15.4	14.7	24.2
1990	15.1	21.9	16.9	14.8	10.8	14.7	14.4	19.4
1991	16.4	21.1	15.2	14.3	13.0	13.8	21.6	17.4
1992	18.0	20.7	16.9	12.4	10.1	11.8	18.5	16.9

	15-24	25-34	35-44	45-54	55-64	65-74	75-84	85+
Black								
Females								
1933	3.0	3.9	3.0	3.2	2.6	0.7	1.8	0.0
1934	3.4	4.3	3.6	2.5	2.5	1.9	3.4	5.8
1935	3.3	6.0	3.7	0.9	2.1	1.2	4.9	0.0
1936	2.9	4.7	2.6	2.6	2.4	1.6	7.9	0.0
1937	3.0	4.4	2.9	3.4	2.6	1.6	1.5	0.0
1938	2.6	5.0	3.1	2.7	3.8	2.5	0.0	5.1
1939	2.2	3.0	2.2	3.0	1.5	2.3	4.2	0.0
1940	2.8	3.2	2.8	2.8	1.5	2.2	1.4	4.8
1941	2.1	2.4	1.8	2.2	2.6	1.7	1.3	4.7
1942	2.7	3.9	2.8	1.8	1.4	0.8	0.0	0.0
1943	1.5	1.6	2.5	1.2	2.2	0.8	3.7	0.0
1944	1.9	2.1	2.0	1.6	1.1	2.3	2.4	0.0
1945	2.1	2.7	2.2	1.3	1.3	0.4	2.3	0.0
1946	2.0	2.7	2.7	2.9	2.3	1.4	0.0	0.0
1947	2.6	2.9	2.3	1.3	0.7	0.7	0.0	0.0
1948	1.7	2.8	2.2	1.8	1.0	1.3	0.0	0.0
1949	1.5	2.3	2.5	1.8	2.3	0.6	2.0	0.0
1950	1.8	2.6	2.0	3.5	1.1	1.8	3.0	0.0
1951	2.0	2.4	2.4	2.0	2.4	2.1	1.9	0.0
1952	1.0	2.6	2.1	1.6	1.6	0.3	0.9	3.5
1953	1.8	1.7	1.3	1.9	1.6	2.0	0.8	0.0
1954	1.2	2.8	1.8	2.5	2.2	2.4	0.8	3.3
1955	1.5	2.7	1.5	2.5	2.0	2.4	1.5	0.0
1956	1.2	2.4	2.7	2.5	2.4	2.6	0.7	0.0
1957	1.1	2.5	2.2	1.0	3.6	1.2	0.7	9.0
1958	1.5	3.0	2.6	2.7	2.5	1.5	2.7	2.9
1959	1.9	3.7	2.4	2.8	3.9	2.6	2.0	2.8
1960	1.3	3.0	3.0	3.1	3.0	2.3	1.2	0.0
1961	1.6	3.0	3.3	2.5	2.6	1.5	0.6	2.6
1962	2.8	3.8	3.5	2.8	3.0	1.5	1.1	0.0
1963	2.5	3.7	3.4	2.5	2.4	2.6	0.5	2.5
1964	1.9	4.1	4.0	3.3	3.5	2.1	1.0	0.0

1965	2.7	5.1	3.1	4.2	2.0	0.9	2.0	2.2
1966	2.3	5.4	2.6	3.3	2.8	2.2	1.0	2.0
1967	3.8	5.1	4.1	3.2	2.6	2.0	1.4	1.9
1968	2.9	4.0	3.7	3.2	2.4	2.0	1.4	0.0
1969	4.1	4.8	4.2	3.5	1.6	1.7	1.8	1.7
1970	3.8	5.7	3.7	3.7	1.9	2.9	1.7	3.1
1971	4.8	6.0	5.1	3.6	2.8	2.4	1.5	1.5
1972	4.7	5.5	4.7	4.1	3.3	1.0	1.4	0.0
1973	3.3	5.0	4.5	3.2	3.2	1.6	0.7	1.4
1974	3.4	5.4	3.8	3.4	3.1	2.0	0.6	1.3
1975	3.2	5.4	4.0	4.0	3.4	3.0	1.2	0.0
1976	3.7	5.9	4.1	4.0	2.7	3.5	0.9	1.1
1977	3.7	6.0	4.8	4.0	3.4	1.5	1.7	1.1
1978	2.6	5.4	4.6	4.2	3.0	2.3	2.5	1.0
1979	3.4	5.7	4.1	2.9	4.0	2.6	3.3	0.7
1980	2.3	4.1	4.6	2.8	2.3	1.7	1.4	0.0
1981	2.4	4.6	4.2	2.5	2.9	3.0	1.0	1.8
1982	2.2	3.7	4.0	3.1	2.2	2.1	1.3	0.9
1983	2.7	2.9	3.5	3.0	1.7	1.3	1.3	2.3
1984	2.4	3.5	3.2	3.5	3.1	2.5	0.5	0.8
1985	2.0	3.0	3.6	3.2	2.2	2.0	4.5	1.4
1986	2.3	3.8	2.8	3.2	4.2	2.8	2.6	0.0
1987	2.5	4.0	2.9	2.2	1.8	2.5	2.3	0.0
1988	2.6	3.8	3.5	3.8	2.5	2.0	1.3	0.0
1989	2.8	3.7	3.9	3.0	2.5	2.2	1.6	0.7
1990	2.3	3.7	4.0	3.2	2.6	2.6	0.6	2.5
1991	1.6	3.3	2.9	3.0	2.1	2.4	1.4	1.2
1992	2.2	3.3	3.3	3.0	2.0	2.1	1.0	3.0

	15-24	25-34	35-44	45-54	55-64	65-74	75-84	85+
White Males								
1933	9.1	20.4	33.2	56.3	74.7	84.1	88.2	70.9
1934	9.6	21.3	31.0	48.1	63.6	74.8	78.1	56.2
1935	9.5	20.7	29.0	47.0	58.5	63.6	75.8	62.6
1936	9.1	21.0	30.7	44.9	57.3	61.6	73.0	59.9
1937	9.5	21.5	32.2	48.5	59.2	61.6	73.8	62.6
1938	9.4	22.2	33.1	50.1	63.6	61.9	68.5	59.9
1939	8.5	19.8	29.3	44.8	58.2	60.2	70.4	52.9
1940	8.8	19.9	30.1	44.1	58.8	58.2	65.9	60.1
1941	7.8	18.3	26.4	35.8	49.2	55.2	65.7	66.9
1942	7.2	17.4	25.3	33.0	46.8	49.9	61.1	59.5
1943	6.5	13.5	19.9	26.2	37.1	44.0	60.2	65.9
1944	6.2	14.0	20.1	25.8	33.8	40.0	57.4	56.2
1945	7.7	16.7	23.3	29.0	38.6	44.7	58.4	57.6
1946	7.7	14.7	23.4	32.4	42.8	45.7	56.4	72.0
1947	6.8	13.8	23.3	32.6	45.5	48.3	67.6	68.4
1948	6.8	13.3	21.8	33.3	44.7	48.8	58.1	68.2
1949	6.9	13.3	24.0	33.6	46.6	51.2	59.6	73.7
1950	6.6	13.8	22.4	34.1	45.9	53.2	61.9	61.9
1951	6.8	12.8	20.5	30.3	39.7	50.3	53.8	70.9
1952	6.9	12.6	19.6	29.8	38.4	47.2	56.7	70.0
1953	6.8	13.0	20.5	31.0	38.7	48.1	56.6	63.7
1954	6.8	13.6	19.9	33.0	41.8	47.1	53.3	53.9
1955	6.1	12.7	19.8	31.7	43.1	46.9	55.5	61.2
1956	6.3	13.0	19.1	30.1	41.8	48.0	59.0	53.9
1957	6.4	12.7	20.2	30.2	38.3	45.5	56.3	62.7
1958	7.5	14.4	22.2	33.9	42.1	48.4	59.3	58.9
1959	7.8	14.5	21.7	32.6	42.0	47.9	57.8	65.2
1960	8.6	14.9	21.9	33.7	40.2	42.0	55.7	61.3
1961	7.9	14.7	22.4	32.8	39.7	39.9	53.2	60.3
1962	8.7	16.5	22.9	33.4	40.5	41.3	57.1	61.5
1963	9.2	16.9	23.6	33.0	40.2	40.3	52.6	59.5
1964	9.3	17.0	22.2	31.8	38.5	39.0	50.6	65.6

1965	9.6	17.7	23.4	30.8	39.7	39.3	49.5	57.7
1966	9.9	17.2	22.7	30.1	38.4	38.8	51.1	59.0
1967	10.8	17.2	23.8	29.2	36.5	34.6	43.8	56.3
1968	11.3	17.2	23.2	28.8	36.1	36.2	44.2	56.8
1969	12.6	18.3	22.4	28.6	34.9	37.0	46.7	52.2
1970	13.9	19.9	23.3	29.5	35.0	38.7	45.5	45.8
1971	14.5	19.2	23.2	28.5	34.8	38.0	46.3	50.1
1972	15.5	20.9	23.0	29.7	33.5	38.4	48.0	54.5
1973	17.4	21.8	22.8	28.4	32.4	37.0	46.3	54.6
1974	17.8	23.3	23.8	28.3	32.1	34.9	46.0	48.5
1975	19.6	24.4	24.5	29.7	32.1	36.1	44.8	50.3
1976	19.2	23.7	23.6	27.7	31.6	36.2	45.6	49.9
1977	22.9	26.7	24.7	27.3	30.9	37.5	48.4	49.9
1978	20.8	25.8	22.5	24.7	29.3	35.5	50.9	53.1
1979	21.0	26.2	22.5	23.9	26.6	33.5	51.0	48.7
1980	21.4	25.6	23.5	24.2	25.8	32.5	45.5	52.8
1981	21.1	26.2	24.3	23.9	26.3	30.3	43.8	53.6
1982	21.2	26.1	23.6	25.8	27.9	33.1	48.5	53.9
1983	20.6	26.2	23.2	25.5	27.4	33.2	52.9	56.8
1984	22.0	25.8	23.7	25.3	28.8	35.6	52.0	55.8
1985	22.7	25.4	23.5	25.1	28.6	35.3	57.1	60.3
1986	23.6	26.4	23.9	26.3	28.7	37.6	58.9	66.3
1987	22.7	25.6	23.9	25.4	28.7	36.8	60.9	71.9
1988	23.4	25.7	24.1	23.2	27.0	35.4	61.5	65.8
1989	23.2	24.9	23.8	24.2	26.6	35.1	55.3	71.9
1990	23.2	25.6	25.3	24.8	27.5	34.2	60.2	70.3
1991	23.0	26.1	24.7	25.3	26.8	32.6	56.1	75.1
1992	22.7	25.1	25.2	24.0	26.0	32.0	53.0	67.6

	15-24	25-34	35-44	45-54	55-64	65-74	75-84	85+
White								
Females								
1933	5.9	9.0	11.3	12.9	14.6	12.1	9.1	7.8
1934	5.7	9.2	11.1	13.8	13.3	10.9	9.9	5.7
1935	5.4	9.4	10.9	13.0	13.8	11.9	7.9	5.5
1936	5.0	9.8	10.9	13.3	13.4	11.6	9.0	7.1
1937	5.1	9.4	11.6	14.6	14.4	11.5	9.8	6.3
1938	4.6	8.5	11.7	14.3	14.0	11.4	9.0	7.8
1939	3.9	7.6	11.0	14.3	13.7	12.4	7.5	7.0
1940	3.9	8.6	11.5	14.0	13.1	12.9	9.0	6.4
1941	4.1	8.1	10.3	12.8	12.5	10.7	8.3	5.5
1942	3.2	7.1	9.3	11.8	12.0	9.7	12.2	5.2
1943	3.2	6.1	8.4	10.8	12.4	11.2	9.1	5.0
1944	3.3	6.1	9.0	10.5	11.5	9.6	10.4	4.9
1945	3.0	6.8	9.5	12.0	11.4	10.9	9.9	5.5
1946	3.4	6.3	9.4	11.7	11.9	10.3	8.7	9.2
1947	2.7	6.0	8.9	11.8	10.9	11.5	8.8	8.7
1948	3.1	5.5	9.0	10.7	10.6	9.4	9.7	7.6
1949	2.6	5.1	8.2	10.4	11.5	10.0	7.6	7.7
1950	2.7	5.2	8.2	10.5	10.7	10.6	8.4	8.9
1951	2.3	5.0	7.7	9.8	9.2	9.1	8.3	8.2
1952	2.1	5.0	6.9	9.4	9.2	9.0	7.0	6.3
1953	2.3	4.8	6.5	9.0	9.3	8.4	7.7	5.3
1954	1.8	4.4	6.8	8.2	9.5	8.9	6.4	6.9
1955	2.0	4.9	6.6	10.2	10.4	9.7	8.5	7.2
1956	2.0	4.7	6.6	9.6	10.5	9.7	6.9	4.7
1957	1.8	5.0	7.1	8.7	10.0	8.7	6.3	4.1
1958	2.4	5.9	7.1	10.3	9.9	10.1	6.6	7.2
1959	2.1	5.7	7.5	9.3	10.5	10.4	7.5	4.2
1960	2.3	5.8	8.1	10.9	10.9	8.8	9.2	6.1
1961	2.3	6.1	8.3	10.8	10.4	9.1	7.6	4.9
1962	2.9	7.2	9.5	12.4	11.1	8.8	7.6	7.6
1963	3.1	7.5	10.9	12.9	11.6	9.5	7.7	5.1
1964	2.9	7.3	10.9	12.5	10.9	10.4	6.7	4.4

1965	3.0	7.6	12.0	13.6	12.3	10.0	7.9	6.7
1966	3.2	7.8	11.3	12.9	11.5	9.7	7.4	4.3
1967	3.4	7.9	11.5	13.0	12.3	9.9	6.9	5.7
1968	3.4	7.5	11.5	13.4	11.6	8.1	6.5	4.9
1969	3.8	8.1	12.7	13.3	11.8	9.8	7.5	4.5
1970	4.2	9.0	13.0	13.5	12.3	9.6	7.2	5.8
1971	4.6	8.8	13.1	14.5	12.6	10.5	7.2	4.0
1972	4.6	9.2	12.6	13.4	13.3	9.2	7.8	5.9
1973	4.3	8.5	12.2	13.7	12.0	9.1	7.7	4.4
1974	4.8	8.7	12.1	14.1	11.0	8.5	7.3	4.0
1975	4.9	8.9	12.6	13.8	11.7	9.5	7.8	4.7
1976	4.9	8.6	11.0	13.8	12.1	8.9	7.8	5.8
1977	5.5	9.3	11.2	13.6	11.6	9.4	7.5	4.4
1978	5.0	8.5	10.9	12.1	10.3	8.4	7.7	5.2
1979	5.1	8.0	10.1	11.7	10.2	7.9	7.2	4.9
1980	4.6	7.5	9.1	10.2	9.1	7.0	5.7	5.8
1981	4.9	7.7	9.5	11.1	9.4	7.3	5.5	3.7
1982	4.5	7.5	9.2	10.4	9.5	7.4	6.1	3.9
1983	4.6	7.2	8.2	9.9	9.1	7.9	6.6	5.3
1984	4.7	6.6	8.4	10.0	9.1	7.8	6.8	5.1
1985	4.7	6.4	7.7	9.0	8.4	7.3	7.0	4.7
1986	4.7	6.2	8.3	9.6	9.0	7.7	8.0	5.0
1987	4.6	6.3	7.9	9.4	8.4	7.6	7.5	4.8
1988	4.6	6.1	7.4	8.6	7.9	7.3	7.4	5.3
1989	4.4	5.9	7.1	8.0	7.9	6.4	6.3	6.2
1990	4.2	6.0	7.4	7.5	8.0	7.2	6.7	5.4
1991	4.2	5.8	7.2	8.3	7.1	6.4	6.0	6.6
1992	3.8	5.4	7.2	7.9	7.2	6.3	6.6	6.3

Table 5.4
Correlations of Suicide Rates by Age with Year, 1960-1992

	black males	black females	white males	white females
15-24	0.88*	-0.17	0.95*	0.67*
25-34	0.75*	-0.26	0.90*	-0.40*
35-44	0.79*	-0.05	0.68*	-0.62*
45-54	0.27	-0.08	-0.91*	-0.74*
55-64	-0.27	-0.13	-0.94*	-0.81*
65-74	0.53*	0.26	-0.75*	-0.83*
75-84	0.76*	0.24	0.40*	-0.49*
85+	0.59*	-0.04	0.40*	-0.01

Mean Suicide Rates, 1960-1992:

	black males	black females	white males	white females
15-24	11.08	2.81	17.31	4.14
25-34	19.21	4.41	22.25	7.42
35-44	14.83	3.78	23.49	10.00
45-54	12.45	3.28	27.66	11.51
55-64	11.51	2.69	32.09	10.35
65-74	12.48	2.14	36.30	8.44
75-84	12.86	1.46	51.00	7.16
85+	11.38	1.17	58.11	5.19

* significant at the 5% level or better

Table 5.5
Suicide Rates by 5-Year Age Groups

	10-14	15-19	20-24	25-29	30-34
Black Males					
1933	0.2	1.5	7.8	7.5	9.7
1934	0.2	3.0	6.5	8.6	11.2
1935	0.5	2.1	8.2	10.5	8.8
1936	0.5	3.4	6.5	8.1	7.6
1937	0.6	2.7	5.4	8.6	11.3
1938	0.3	2.9	6.9	8.4	10.3
1939	0.0	1.6	6.2	9.1	8.2
1940	0.8	2.2	6.5	9.1	11.3
1941	0.2	1.0	7.8	9.4	8.9
1942	0.5	1.6	7.6	8.2	9.4
1943	0.6	2.1	6.9	6.1	7.3
1944	0.2	1.1	5.0	5.5	5.6
1945	0.0	1.8	6.5	5.0	9.2
1946	0.3	1.5	7.3	8.8	9.9
1947	0.6	2.3	6.6	8.5	9.0
1948	0.0	1.7	8.0	8.8	9.6
1949	0.1	2.2	6.6	8.7	9.7
1950	0.0	2.4	7.6	8.6	10.4
1951	0.7	1.5	7.8	10.9	9.1
1952	0.7	1.9	5.5	11.5	10.4
1953	0.3	0.8	5.7	9.3	10.1
1954	0.0	1.1	8.3	12.3	12.4
1955	0.1	3.0	8.1	7.1	10.8
1956	0.1	1.9	7.4	9.3	10.1
1957	0.1	2.9	6.9	9.7	13.3
1958	0.4	1.4	8.8	9.6	13.7
1959	0.4	3.0	8.6	13.8	13.1
1960	0.2	2.8	5.8	12.8	12.2

1961	0.1	3.6	10.6	14.2	13.6
1962	0.2	3.0	9.6	9.7	13.2
1963	0.5	2.1	9.7	12.8	14.7
1964	0.3	3.5	12.4	15.3	13.7
1965	0.4	5.1	11.8	14.2	12.2
1966	0.2	4.2	12.3	16.3	17.2
1967	0.2	2.1	12.2	16.1	15.5
1968	0.4	3.7	11.3	15.7	14.0
1969	0.2	4.4	14.8	15.0	17.5
1970	0.3	4.7	17.1	18.6	18.7
1971	0.8	5.0	15.3	16.5	16.1
1972	0.0	8.0	22.7	21.6	18.2
1973	0.5	5.6	21.2	24.5	18.0
1974	0.8	4.9	18.5	23.0	21.9
1975	0.2	6.1	20.5	25.5	20.1
1976	0.4	7.0	20.0	22.8	20.4
1977	0.6	5.9	20.9	27.0	21.7
1978	0.5	5.5	21.2	24.3	20.8
1979	0.3	6.9	23.2	27.5	24.8
1980	0.5	5.6	20.0	21.5	22.1
1981	0.3	5.5	17.1	22.8	20.5
1982	1.5	6.2	16.0	21.6	18.7
1983	0.9	6.5	16.7	18.7	19.5
1984	1.0	5.9	16.7	21.4	20.0
1985	1.3	8.2	18.5	19.5	19.7
1986	1.5	7.1	16.0	21.4	21.1
1987	1.6	8.9	17.2	21.4	20.8
1988	1.3	9.7	19.8	20.1	24.2
1989	1.7	10.3	23.7	21.2	22.8
1990	1.6	11.5	19.0	22.7	21.0
1991	2.0	12.2	20.7	21.6	20.6
1992	2.0	14.8	21.2	20.4	20.9

	10-14	15-19	20-24	25-29	30-34
Black Females					
1933	0.0	2.3	3.7	3.6	4.2
1934	0.0	2.0	4.9	3.9	4.8
1935	0.3	1.7	4.9	5.7	6.4
1936	0.6	2.7	3.1	5.2	4.0
1937	0.3	1.3	4.8	5.6	3.0
1938	0.3	1.6	3.6	4.4	5.7
1939	0.3	1.3	3.1	2.8	3.3
1940	0.0	1.9	3.7	2.6	4.0
1941	0.3	1.8	2.5	1.9	3.0
1942	0.3	2.3	3.1	4.6	3.0
1943	0.0	0.9	2.1	1.3	2.0
1944	0.1	1.1	2.8	1.4	2.9
1945	0.0	0.3	3.8	1.6	3.9
1946	0.0	1.4	2.6	1.9	3.7
1947	0.1	2.3	2.9	2.4	3.5
1948	0.1	1.7	1.7	2.7	2.9
1049	0.3	0.9	2.0	2.0	2.7
1950	0.0	1.6	1.9	1.9	3.4
1951	0.0	1.5	2.4	2.0	2.8
1952	0.3	0.8	1.2	2.4	2.8
1953	0.4	1.3	2.3	2.0	1.5
1954	0.0	1.3	1.1	3.4	2.3
1955	0.0	0.9	2.1	2.8	2.5
1956	0.0	1.7	0.6	2.3	2.5
1957	0.0	0.7	1.5	2.2	2.8
1958	0.1	0.5	2.5	3.0	3.1
1959	0.2	1.5	2.5	4.1	3.4
1960	0.0	1.1	1.6	2.9	3.2
1961	0.4	1.2	2.1	2.4	3.6
1962	0.1	1.7	4.0	3.9	3.6
1963	0.1	2.1	2.9	3.9	3.5
1964	0.1	1.9	2.0	4.5	3.8

1965	0.2	2.2	3.5	4.7	5.5
1966	0.3	1.9	2.9	5.3	5.5
1967	0.3	3.3	4.4	4.6	5.7
1968	0.1	1.8	4.2	3.8	4.1
1969	0.4	3.0	5.6	5.7	3.9
1970	0.4	2.9	4.9	5.8	5.5
1971	0.2	3.4	6.5	5.9	6.0
1972	0.3	3.0	6.7	6.7	4.1
1973	0.1	1.7	4.7	5.9	3.9
1974	0.3	2.5	4.5	5.2	5.7
1975	0.3	1.5	5.2	6.4	4.3
1976	0.6	2.5	5.1	6.0	5.6
1977	0.4	2.4	5.3	6.7	5.1
1978	0.4	1.3	4.1	5.4	5.3
1979	0.2	2.2	4.7	5.7	5.6
1980	0.1	1.6	3.1	3.5	5.0
1981	0.2	1.6	3.2	4.3	5.0
1982	0.2	1.5	2.9	3.3	4.2
1983	1.1	1.7	3.6	3.0	2.8
1984	0.4	1.7	3.0	3.4	3.5
1985	0.4	1.5	2.4	2.8	3.2
1986	0.4	2.1	2.4	3.3	4.4
1987	0.3	2.7	2.4	3.7	4.2
1988	0.9	2.2	2.9	3.7	3.9
1989	0.7	2.3	3.4	3.7	3.8
1990	0.6	1.9	2.6	3.9	3.5
1991	0.3	1.5	1.8	4.2	2.4
1992	0.4	1.9	2.4	2.7	3.8

	10-14	15-19	20-24	25-29	30-34
White Males					
1933	0.5	4.7	14.0	18.3	22.5
1934	0.6	5.0	14.8	19.4	23.1
1935	0.7	4.8	14.7	19.2	22.2
1936	0.8	5.4	13.4	18.5	23.4
1937	1.0	5.0	14.5	19.1	24.1
1938	0.6	5.2	14.0	19.8	24.8
1939	1.1	4.9	12.5	17.8	22.1
1940	0.8	4.3	13.6	18.0	22.0
1941	0.6	4.3	11.7	16.7	20.0
1942	0.8	4.0	10.5	14.2	19.9
1943	0.8	4.0	7.9	10.6	14.5
1944	0.7	3.3	6.7	10.3	12.8
1945	0.8	3.7	7.3	10.1	14.5
1946	1.0	3.7	10.7	13.5	15.8
1947	0.9	4.1	9.4	12.0	15.9
1948	0.8	3.7	9.9	12.0	14.9
1949	0.8	3.7	10.0	12.2	14.8
1950	0.6	3.7	9.5	12.0	15.9
1951	0.7	3.8	9.7	11.9	13.7
1952	0.5	4.7	9.2	11.9	13.3
1953	0.8	4.2	9.9	12.9	13.1
1954	0.5	3.8	10.3	13.0	14.1
1955	0.4	4.0	8.7	12.5	12.8
1956	0.7	3.5	9.6	11.3	14.4
1957	0.8	4.1	9.4	10.9	14.3
1958	0.8	4.7	11.2	13.6	15.0
1959	1.0	5.4	11.0	12.8	15.9
1960	1.0	5.9	11.9	13.8	15.9
1961	0.7	5.5	11.0	13.0	16.2
1962	1.1	5.8	12.6	14.5	18.4
1963	1.0	6.3	12.9	16.2	17.7
1964	1.0	6.6	12.8	15.2	18.9

1965	1.0	6.3	13.9	16.5	18.9
1966	1.1	6.7	14.2	16.1	18.4
1967	1.0	7.5	14.9	16.9	17.5
1968	1.0	8.3	15.0	16.3	18.3
1969	1.0	9.0	17.0	18.4	18.2
1970	1.1	9.4	19.3	19.8	20.0
1971	1.0	10.4	19.2	19.7	18.5
1972	0.9	11.1	20.5	21.0	20.7
1973	1.2	11.4	24.3	22.1	21.4
1974	1.5	11.9	24.5	23.8	22.8
1975	1.4	13.0	26.8	25.1	23.5
1976	1.3	11.9	27.0	24.1	23.1
1977	1.8	15.3	30.8	28.8	24.3
1978	1.4	13.8	28.1	27.6	23.8
1979	1.2	14.6	27.5	28.5	23.5
1980	1.4	15.0	27.8	27.5	23.5
1981	1.4	14.9	26.8	27.6	24.7
1982	1.7	15.5	26.4	27.5	24.5
1983	1.7	15.1	25.5	26.7	25.7
1984	2.1	15.8	27.5	26.5	25.1
1985	2.5	17.3	27.4	26.3	24.3
1986	2.4	18.2	28.4	26.4	26.4
1987	2.5	17.6	27.5	26.0	25.3
1988	2.1	19.6	27.0	26.4	24.9
1989	2.2	19.4	26.8	25.9	24.0
1990	2.3	19.3	26.8	25.5	25.7
1991	2.4	19.1	26.5	25.4	26.7
1992	2.6	18.4	26.6	25.1	25.1

	10-14	15-19	20-24	25-29	30-34
White Females					
1933	0.2	3.9	8.1	8.7	9.1
1934	0.3	4.3	7.2	9.0	9.3
1935	0.3	4.2	6.8	8.3	10.5
1936	0.4	3.4	6.8	9.2	10.5
1937	0.3	3.3	7.0	8.4	9.6
1938	0.1	3.5	5.8	8.0	8.9
1939	0.2	3.0	5.0	6.3	9.0
1940	0.1	3.0	4.9	7.8	9.5
1941	0.3	3.0	5.3	7.3	9.1
1942	0.2	2.4	4.1	6.3	8.0
1943	0.3	2.3	4.1	5.3	7.0
1944	0.2	2.4	4.2	5.2	7.1
1945	0.2	1.9	4.1	5.5	8.2
1946	0.2	2.4	4.4	5.1	7.5
1947	0.1	1.9	3.6	5.0	7.0
1948	0.1	2.2	3.9	4.3	6.7
1949	0.2	1.5	3.7	4.2	6.0
1950	0.1	1.9	3.5	5.1	5.4
1951	0.2	1.7	2.9	4.6	5.5
1952	0.1	1.4	2.7	4.4	5.5
1953	0.1	1.8	2.9	4.6	5.0
1954	0.1	1.2	2.4	4.2	4.7
1955	0.2	1.4	2.6	3.9	5.8
1956	0.1	1.2	2.8	4.2	5.3
1957	0.2	1.0	2.7	4.5	5.6
1958	0.2	1.8	3.1	5.3	6.3
1959	0.1	1.6	2.8	5.4	5.9
1960	0.2	1.6	3.1	4.8	6.7
1961	0.2	1.6	3.2	5.3	7.0
1962	0.2	2.0	4.1	6.3	8.1
1963	0.2	1.9	4.6	6.6	8.4
1964	0.1	1.7	4.5	6.2	8.3

1965	0.1	1.8	4.3	6.6	8.7
1966	0.2	2.1	4.5	6.8	8.8
1967	0.3	2.2	4.8	7.0	8.9
1968	0.2	2.2	4.8	7.0	8.1
1969	0.4	2.6	5.0	7.3	8.9
1970	0.3	2.9	5.7	8.6	9.5
1971	0.3	3.0	6.3	8.2	9.5
1972	0.4	2.7	6.6	8.8	9.9
1973	0.4	3.2	5.5	8.0	9.1
1974	0.4	3.3	6.4	8.4	9.0
1975	0.4	3.1	6.9	8.0	10.0
1976	0.3	3.3	6.6	7.8	9.7
1977	0.3	3.5	7.5	8.7	10.0
1978	0.4	3.4	6.7	8.3	8.7
1979	0.6	3.4	6.7	7.7	8.4
1980	0.3	3.3	5.9	6.9	8.1
1981	0.6	3.8	5.9	8.0	7.4
1982	0.5	3.4	5.4	7.3	7.7
1983	0.4	3.5	5.5	7.1	7.2
1984	0.6	3.8	5.5	6.1	7.1
1985	.0.9	4.1	5.2	6.1	6.7
1986	0.7	4.1	5.3	5.8	6.7
1987	0.7	4.4	4.7	5.7	7.0
1988	0.8	4.8	4.4	5.5	6.6
1989	0.7	4.5	4.3	5.3	6.5
1990	0.9	4.0	4.4	5.2	6.7
1991	0.8	4.2	4.3	5.2	6.3
1992	1.1	3.7	4.0	4.5	6.1

Table 5.6
Methods for Suicide
(percentages shown)

	poison	hanging	firearms	other
Black Males				
1933	16	9	53	22
1934	18	15	48	19
1935	18	8	47	27
1936	14	9	50	27
1937	14	12	51	23
1938	15	10	49	26
1939-1948	no data			
1949	12	12	56	20
1950	9	12	60	20
1951	15	16	49	19
1952	8	15	58	19
1953	11	15	54	21
1954	7	16	56	21
1955	8	14	61	16
1956	10	15	59	17
1957	8	16	62	14
1958	9	15	57	20
1959	8	13	59	20
1960	9	12	55	24
1961	12	12	56	19
1962	9	13	57	21
1963	12	12	53	23
1964	8	16	56	20
1965	11	16	52	21
1966	8	11	61	20
1967	11	13	57	19
1968	8	17	59	15
1969	9	13	61	13

1970	10	16	59	15
1971	10	16	62	12
1972	9	15	65	11
1973	8	17	64	12
1974	7	16	65	12
1975	7	17	63	13
1976	8	17	61	13
1977	8	17	61	14
1978	7	15	62	16
1979	8	17	61	14
1980	6	18	63	13
1981	6	18	61	15
1982	7	20	57	16
1983	6	21	60	13
1984	8	20	59	13
1985	7	21	60	13
1986	8	20	60	12
1987	9	19	61	11
1988	7	21	62	10
1989	7	21	61	11
1990	6	19	64	12
1991	7	19	63	11
1992	7	19	64	10

	poison	hanging	firearms	other
Black Females				
1933	49	4	17	30
1934	49	3	22	26
1935	48	5	20	27
1936	47	5	26	22
1937	54	6	19	21
1938	46	8	15	31
1939-1948	no data			
1949	30	12	30	28
1950	27	11	31	31
1951	36	13	30	21
1952	31	10	32	26
1953	25	22	30	23
1954	28	15	29	28
1955	26	15	32	27
1956	20	15	37	28
1957	19	13	36	31
1958	28	8	33	31
1959	29	8	26	37
1960	25	15	28	32
1961	23	5	29	43
1962	23	13	31	34
1963	31	6	37	26
1964	29	9	32	30
1965	31	8	30	32
1966	25	6	34	35
1967	29	8	39	24
1968	37	6	39	18
1969	36	7	41	17
1970	37	9	38	15
1971	35	7	41	17
1972	37	6	44	14
1973	30	6	44	19

1974	26	10	48	17
1975	29	9	46	16
1976	30	11	40	19
1977	31	7	40	21
1978	32	6	40	22
1979	24	7	48	20
1980	24	11	43	23
1981	25	7	47	22
1982	26	9	41	23
1983	32	12	40	17
1984	24	10	47	19
1985	26	8	48	17
1986	25	10	46	19
1987	30	12	43	15
1988	30	8	45	17
1989	29	11	43	18
1990	28	12	43	17
1991	26	12	41	20
1992	29	9	40	22

	poison	hanging	firearms	other
White Males				
1933	24	19	45	12
1934	22	20	45	13
1935	23	20	44	13
1936	23	21	43	13
1937	23	21	43	13
1938	24	20	43	13
1939-1948	no data			
1949	18	22	49	12
1950	19	21	49	11
1951	19	21	49	11
1952	17	21	51	11
1953	17	21	52	10
1954	18	20	52	10
1955	17	21	52	10
1956	17	21	53	9
1957	17	21	53	9
1958	18	19	54	9
1959	18	19	54	9
1960	19	18	54	9
1961	19	17	55	9
1962	20	16	55	9
1963	21	15	55	9
1964	21	15	56	9
1965	21	16	55	8
1966	20	14	57	9
1967	20	14	58	8
1968	20	14	59	7
1969	20	14	59	6
1970	20	14	59	7
1971	19	15	59	6
1972	19	14	60	6
1973	18	14	61	6
1974	16	14	64	6

1975	18	14	62	6
1976	16	14	62	7
1977	16	14	64	6
1978	16	13	64	7
1979	15	13	64	7
1980	15	14	63	7
1981	15	14	65	6
1982	14	15	65	6
1983	15	14	65	6
1984	15	15	65	6
1985	15	14	65	6
1986	15	15	65	5
1987	16	14	65	6
1988	15	14	66	6
1989	14	15	66	6
1990	14	14	67	6
1991	14	14	66	6
1992	14	15	65	6

	poison	hanging	firearms	other
White Females				
1933	50	14	17	19
1934	49	15	18	18
1935	49	15	17	19
1936	47	16	18	19
1937	48	17	16	19
1938	47	16	18	19
1939-1948	no data			
1949	40	21	20	18
1950	40	22	21	18
1951	38	22	23	17
1952	34	23	24	18
1953	34	24	23	19
1954	35	24	23	18
1955	33	24	25	18
1956	34	26	24	17
1957	34	24	25	17
1958	35	21	25	18
1959	37	19	25	19
1960	38	17	25	19
1961	39	16	25	19
1962	44	13	25	18
1963	48	12	24	16
1964	47	13	25	15
1965	48	12	24	16
1966	46	11	28	16
1967	45	11	29	15
1968	46	14	30	10
1969	47	13	29	10
1970	49	12	30	9
1971	46	12	32	10
1972	45	11	34	10
1973	45	13	32	10

1974	44	11	35	9
1975	43	11	36	10
1976	43	11	35	11
1977	42	11	36	10
1978	42	11	36	12
1979	41	11	38	11
1980	40	10	39	11
1981	38	10	41	11
1982	37	11	41	11
1983	38	10	41	10
1984	37	13	40	10
1985	39	11	41	10
1986	39	12	39	9
1987	40	11	40	9
1988	39	12	40	14
1989	37	12	41	9
1990	37	12	42	9
1991	38	13	40	9
1992	38	14	40	8

Table 5.7

Suicides by Method

(percentages shown: the percentages for 951 were all zero after 1979)

	950	951 952	953	954	955	956	957	958
Black Males								
1933	10	6	9	7	53	7	6	2
1934	13	5	15	8	48	6	5	0
1935	13	5	8	11	47	7	6	3
1936	19	4	9	10	50	7	7	3
1937	8	5	12	10	51	6	5	3
1938	11	4	10	12	49	5	6	3
1939-1978	no data							
1979	6	2	17	4	61	1	5	4
1980	4	2	18	5	63	1	5	2
1981	4	2	18	5	61	2	5	3
1982	5	2	20	5	57	2	6	3
1983	4	2	21	5	60	1	4	3
1984	5	3	20	4	59	2	4	4
1985	5	2	21	4	60	1	5	3
1986	4	3	20	4	60	1	4	2
1987	6	3	19	4	61	1	3	3
1988	5	2	21	3	62	1	3	3
1989	5	2	21	3	61	1	4	3
1990	5	1	19	3	64	1	5	3
1991	5	2	19	3	63	1	4	4
1992	4	2	19	3	64	1	3	3
Black Females								
1933	43	6	4	11	17	2	8	9
1934	42	7	3	13	22	3	7	3

1935	43	5	5	9	20	4	8	6
1936	41	5	5	9	26	0	8	6
1937	44	9	6	7	19	3	6	6
1938	40	6	8	13	15	3	7	8
1939-1978	no data							
1979	23	1	7	7	48	1	8	4
1980	22	2	11	6	43	2	11	4
1981	23	2	7	7	47	1	9	5
1982	23	4	9	6	41	1	12	4
1983	30	1	12	4	40	1	7	5
1984	21	3	10	7	47	1	9	2
1985	25	2	8	6	48	1	7	3
1986	23	2	10	5	46	1	6	6
1987	26	4	12	5	43	2	5	3
1988	26	4	8	5	45	1	5	6
1989	26	3	11	4	43	2	7	5
1990	26	2	12	4	43	1	6	5
1991	24	2	12	5	41	1	8	7
1992	27	2	9	6	40	1	6	9

	950	952	953	954	955	956	957	958
White Males								
1933	11	13	19	4	45	4	3	1
1934	11	11	20	4	45	5	3	1
1935	11	12	20	4	44	5	3	1
1936	11	12	21	4	43	5	3	1
1937	11	12	21	4	43	5	3	1
1938	10	15	20	4	43	5	3	1
1939-1978	no data							
1979	7	8	13	1	64	2	3	2
1980	7	9	14	1	63	1	3	2
1981	6	9	14	1	65	1	2	2
1982	6	8	15	1	65	1	2	2
1983	6	9	14	1	65	2	2	2
1984	6	9	15	1	65	1	2	2
1985	6	9	14	1	65	1	2	1
1986	6	9	15	1	65	1	2	1
1987	6	10	14	1	65	1	2	2
1988	6	9	14	1	66	2	2	1
1989	6	7	15	1	66	1	2	2
1990	6	7	14	1	67	1	2	2
1991	7	7	14	1	66	1	2	2
1992	7	7	15	1	65	1	2	2
White Females								
1933	32	18	14	8	17	3	6	2
1934	32	18	15	8	18	3	5	1
1935	30	18	15	7	17	3	6	4
1936	30	17	16	8	18	3	6	2
1937	30	18	17	8	16	3	7	1
1938	28	18	16	8	18	3	6	3
1939-1978	no data							

1979	29	12	11	3	38	1	4	2
1980	27	12	10	3	39	1	4	2
1981	27	11	10	3	41	1	4	2
1982	26	11	11	3	41	1	3	2
1983	26	12	10	4	41	1	3	2
1984	26	12	13	3	40	2	3	2
1985	26	12	11	3	41	1	3	2
1986	26	13	12	3	39	2	3	2
1987	26	13	11	3	40	1	3	2
1988	27	12	12	2	40	2	3	2
1989	28	9	12	2	41	1	3	2
1990	27	9	12	2	42	1	3	3
1991	29	9	13	2	40	1	3	2
1992	29	9	14	2	40	1	2	2

CHAPTER 6

BLACK SUICIDE IN THE STATES OF AMERICA[1]

S uicide and homicide rates show a wide variation over the American states, but there has been little attention given in by researchers to the similarities and differences in the social correlates of state rates of suicide for African Americans versus whites.

Durkheim's (1897) classic theory of suicide in societies was based on two dimensions. Suicide was predicted to be common in societies in which the degree of social integration (that is, the strength of the individual's social network) was very low (egoistic suicide) or very high (altruistic suicide). Suicide was also predicted to be common in societies in which the degree of social regulation (that is, the degree to which the individual's attitudes, desires and emotions were shaped and regulated by the society) was very low (anomic suicide) or very high (fatalistic suicide).

Durkheim's theory has been used to predict a variety of associations between suicide rates and social indicators. For example, societies with large numbers of migrants would appear to have lower levels of social integration than societies with more stable populations and, therefore, higher suicide rates. Similarly, societies with high rates of divorce would appear to have lower levels of social integration and regulation, and so higher suicide rates.

---

[1] This chapter is based in part on Lester (1990-1991, 1994, 1996).

In general, these predicted associations have been confirmed by research (Stack, 1980; Lester, 1994).

In the studies conducted by Lester, Stack and others, a large number of variables have been included in the correlational analyses. Whereas some researchers, such as Stack, prefer regression analyses which select the most powerful predictors of the suicide rate, Lester has preferred factor analysis which first clusters the social indicators and then examines the correlation of these clusters (technically known as factors) with the suicide rate. The present chapter reports such factor analyses.

The first study sought to examine the predictors of suicide rates for whites and African Americans in the United States using a data set for the 48 continental, contiguous states of America for 1980 prepared by Lester (1994). Thirty seven social indicators were obtained for each state and subjected to a factor analysis (a principal components analysis with a varimax rotation). Seven independent factors were identified, and their factor scores were correlated with the suicide rates of African Americans and whites over the 48 states.

Because the population of African Americans in the states can be quite small, suicide rates for African Americans were calculated for a four-year period, 1979-1982. The suicide rates for whites and African Americans are shown in Table 6.1, and the results of the factor analysis of the 37 social indicators in Table 6.2.

STUDY ONE

RESULTS

Black and white suicide rates were not associated over the 48 states, either overall, for males or for females (Pearson rs = 0.18, 0.18 and 0.18 respectively).

The correlations between the factor scores are shown in Table 6.3. For the total sample of 48 continental states, the suicide rates of whites and African Americans were both associated with Factor II (social disintegration) in the predicted direction. In addition, while white suicide rates were associated with Factor III (age), black suicide rates were associated with Factor IV (southern). Since the percentage of African Americans also loaded highly on Factor IV, this latter result is congruent with the results reported in Chapter 11 that black suicide rates are higher in states where there were fewer African Americans.

The associations by gender are quite different (see Table 6.3). For the all 48 states, black female suicide rates were associated with only scores on the urban/wealth factor, while black male suicide rates were associated with social disintegration scores (positively) and southernness scores (negatively). Interestingly, white female suicide rates were associated with urban/wealth scores as were black female suicide rates.

When only the nineteen states with black populations greater or equal to ten percent were studied, the pattern of correlations changed dramatically. While white suicide rates still correlated with scores on Factor II (social disintegration), black suicide rates now correlated with scores on Factors IV (southern), V (labor force participation), VI (unemployment) and VII (Roman Catholicism).

DISCUSSION

This study has shown that the social correlates of suicide over the states of the United States are sometimes similar and sometimes different for whites and for African Americans. For example, both black and white suicide rates are associated with indices of social disintegration, but black suicide rates are associated with southernness while white suicide rates are associated with the age structure of the states.

STUDY TWO

The first study used social indicators from the states based on the total population of the state. This second study took a smaller set of variables and located measures for both whites and African Americans individually. For example, while Study One examined the association between the total unemployment rate and white and black suicide rates, Study Two examines the impact of white unemployment rates and black unemployment rates separately.

DATA SOURCES

Data were obtained from the publications resulting from the 1980 Census, published by the Census Bureau, for African Americans and whites separately: the percentage of people over 25 years of age with four years of college completed, the male unemployment rate, the median family income, the fertility rate for women aged 35-44 ever married, the participation of women over 16 years of age in the labor force, the percentage of divorced and of separated men over 15 years of age, and the extent of inter-state migration from 1975 to 1980.

RESULTS

The results of the factor analysis, using SPSSX with a principal components extraction and a varimax rotation, are shown in Table 6.4. For the whites, four factors were identified: I education/wealth, II social disintegration, III fertility, and IV unemployment. For the African Americans, only three factors were identified: I education/wealth, II education/migration, and III unemployment/divorce. Factor I appears to be similar for both races, but the remaining factors differ considerably.

The correlations between factor scores and rates of suicide were also quite different. For example, suicide rates for whites were associated with social disintegration (Factor II), whereas suicide rates for African Americans were associated with education/wealth (Factor I).

Similarly, examination of the Pearson correlations between each social variable and suicide rates revealed differences for African Americans and whites (Table 6.5). Black suicide rates, but not white suicide rates, were associated with education, wealth and fertility.

DISCUSSION

The social correlates of black versus white suicide rates were different. The traditional associations for the total United States population described by Lester (1994, 1996) were found to be true only for whites.

The different patterns for African Americans may be a result of the characteristics of African Americans in states with high rates of black suicide, primarily states with small proportions of African Americans, as we will see in Chapter 11 where it is noted that African Americans in the states where African Americans are rare (such as Maine, Vermont and Montana) tend to be migrants and well-educated, and much more similar in general to the whites in those states than are the African Americans in states where African Americans are more numerous. It would appear that different sociological theories may be needed to account for the regional differences of black suicide rates as compared to white suicide rates.

STUDY THREE

The results reported so far have been for 1980. It is of interest to explore whether similar results would be found for more recent data. Accordingly, Study One was replicated for 1990 using a smaller set of variables than in Study One, but a set representing all of the factors identified for 1980.[2]

The simple correlations are reported in Table 6.6 and the results of the factor analysis in Table 6.7. In Table 6.6, it can be seen quite clearly that the general characteristics of the states were less often correlated with black suicide rates than with white suicide rates in both 1980 and 1990. However, the correlations for black suicide rates seem to be higher in 1990 as compared to 1980 -- six versus two significant correlations.

The results of the factor analysis (Table 6.7), indicate that white suicide rates in 1980 were associated with scores for Factors II (social disintegration) and IV (low birth rate), while black suicide rates were associated only with scores on Factor III (Southernness). For 1980, the five factors scores combined to give a multiple R of 0.84 for predicting the white suicide rate (with Factors II and IV contributing significantly). The same factor scores gave a multiple R of only 0.41 for predicting black suicide rates (with only Factor III contributing significantly).

In 1990, white suicide rates were associated with factor scores for Factor II (urban), Factor III (wealth), Factor V (social disintegration) and Factor VI (also social disintegration). Black suicide rates were not associated with any of the factor scores. The six factor scores combined to give a multiple R of

---

[2] Marriage rates were available for only 46 states in 1990, and this affects the data to some extent.

0.83 for predicting white suicide rates (with Factors II, III, V and VI contributing significantly); the same factor scores gave a multiple R of only 0.47 for predicting black suicide rates (with Factors I, III and VI contributing significantly).[3]

It is clear from the results of these studies that sociological theories of suicide need to be modified in order to account for the regional variation of black suicide rates in the states of America.

REFERENCES

Durkheim, E. *Le suicide*. Paris: Felix Alcan, 1897.

Lester, D. Mortality from suicide and homicide for African Americans in the USA. *Omega*, 1990-1991, 22, 219-226.

Lester, D. *Patterns of suicide and homicide in America*. Commack, NY: Nova Science, 1994.

Lester, D. Explaining the regional variation of suicide and homicide. *Archives of Suicide Research*, 1996, 1, 159-174.

Stack, S. The effects of marital dissolution on suicide. *Journal of Marriage & the Family*, 1980, 42, 83-91.

---

[3] An examination of the correlates of the ratio of the black/white suicide rates did not reveal any interesting correlates -- a negative association only with scores on Factor V (social disintegration).

Table 6.1
Rates of Suicide for Whites and African Americans
(per 100,000 per year)

	Whites (1980)			Blacks* (1979-1982)		
	total	males	female	total	male	female
AL	13.79	23.6	4.5	4.59	8.1	1.5
AZ	18.74	28.9	8.9	10.67	16.7	5.5
AR	12.96	20.5	5.9	5.15	9.2	1.6
CA	17.56	26.2	9.3	10.35	16.2	4.8
CO	17.89	27.9	8.1	10.08	17.7	2.0
CT	9.50	15.1	4.3	3.79	7.1	0.9
DE	13.53	20.3	7.2	6.00	10.0	2.5
FL	17.55	30.8	9.8	4.97	8.6	1.7
GA	8.84	24.2	7.3	5.41	9.1	2.1
ID	13.64	22.5	4.9	9.20	15.2	0.0
IL	10.61	17.0	4.6	5.74	9.9	2.1
IN	10.81	18.2	3.8	6.09	10.6	2.1
IA	11.17	19.3	3.5	9.59	18.0	1.2
KS	11.48	17.5	5.8	5.75	12.7	2.8
KY	13.32	21.6	5.4	5.88	11.5	2.4
LA	15.18	24.0	6.6	5.73	10.2	1.7
ME	12.43	20.1	5.3	15.98	26.2	0.0
MD	12.16	18.9	5.7	6.76	11.2	2.8
MA	8.52	13.3	4.2	5.31	9.3	1.7
MI	12.25	19.0	5.7	8.49	14.3	3.2
MN	10.82	17.0	4.9	9.84	14.7	4.8
MS	11.64	18.4	5.2	3.83	6.5	1.4
MO	12.73	20.2	5.8	6.13	11.3	1.5
MT	13.92	22.5	5.4	41.99	65.8	0.0
NE	10.53	17.9	3.5	10.33	14.9	6.0
NV	24.70	32.7	16.5	10.78	18.6	2.9
NH	11.21	17.6	4.9	6.27	11.0	0.0
NJ	8.18	13.8	3.0	4.35	7.9	1.3

NM	21.07	33.8	8.7	7.29	11.9	2.2
NY	10.70	16.1	5.8	5.54	9.3	2.3
NC	12.94	20.0	6.2	5.63	9.3	2.3
ND	10.39	17.2	3.5	0.00	0.0	0.0
OH	12.35	19.4	5.8	9.57	15.3	4.5
OK	14.05	21.5	7.4	7.21	11.3	3.3
OR	15.06	24.6	5.8	6.07	7.8	4.2
PA	11.60	18.8	5.0	8.26	14.5	2.9
RI	11.49	17.6	6.0	10.88	11.2	10.5
SC	11.55	18.2	5.1	4.19	7.4	1.3
SD	10.94	19.0	3.1	0.00	0.0	0.0
TN	13.51	20.8	6.6	5.85	9.6	2.6
TX	14.83	23.3	6.6	5.22	8.5	2.2
UT	13.67	20.0	7.4	2.71	4.6	0.0
VT	14.80	23.5	6.5	22.03	38.8	0.0
VA	15.23	24.4	6.3	7.29	12.6	2.3
WA	13.79	21.3	6.4	12.55	19.7	4.1
WV	12.70	20.9	5.0	6.53	12.3	1.4
WI	11.97	19.0	5.3	5.60	9.2	2.4
WY	16.13	24.5	7.3	0.00	0.0	0.0

* The estimates are based on the 1980 population

Table 6.2
Results of the Factor Analysis of Social Variables over the States of America
in 1980

	FACTOR						
	I	II	III	IV	V	VI	VII
median family income	74#	-04	-01	-14	58#	08	-11
% urban	92#	09	-08	13	-01	-05	06
per capita income	79#	08	21	-14	48#	-07	-16
population	62#	-19	14	25	-16	18	-40
population density	54#	-38	37	11	08	07	44#
personal income	80#	14	23	-13	47#	-07	-13
% in poverty	-50#	-06	-13	47#	-54#	02	01
gross state product	42#	26	-28	-09	33	-29	-33
% immigrants	86#	08	23	-03	-10	01	18
% Roman Catholic	60#	-08	32	-32	16	06	45#
% born in state	-40#	-81#	05	07	-12	19	-12
crime rate	72#	53#	-01	17	05	05	15
divorce rate	-02	88#	-16	02	-03	-01	-08
interstate migration	-04	83#	-27	-10	11	-32	13
church attendance	-10	-73#	-20	-20	-19	-33	21
% divorced	15	91#	-08	-07	06	13	-16
gun control strictness	27	-58#	18	13	13	20	-08
alcohol	31	53#	14	-16	39	-15	35

consumption							
females/males	10	-50#	55#	34	-31	21	26
longitude	10	50#	-54#	-28	-07	-09	-38
birth rate	-14	11	-92#	-14	-12	-18	-10
% voting for Reagan	05	23	-58#	-33	-08	-45#	-05
% over 65 years	-05	-22	69#	-29	-51#	-20	-02
death rate	-10	-32	79#	-05	-43#	-01	-04
% under 15 years	-32	-05	-91#	-01	-12	06	02
median age	31	03	92#	-02	-15	-01	01
southern index	-26	27	-12	73#	-30	11	-34
% separated	26	-04	18	84#	12	14	15
% black	-10	-16	04	92#	-10	13	-01
latitude	02	-13	08	-77#	43#	16	05
infant mortality rate	05	-25	17	82#	-17	15	01
females in labor force	12	10	-02	-15	81#	-32	14
males in labor force	19	03	-34	-26	80#	-29	-01
employment ratio	03	08	-15	-20	75#	-47#	02
unemployment rate	01	-05	03	07	-20	96#	-01
male unemployment	07	-07	06	-07	-17	93#	-08
female unemployment	-06	-01	-03	27	-21	88#	12
% of variance	26%	21%	13%	8%	7%	5%	3%

high loading (greater than 0.40)

Table 6.3
Correlations Between Factor Scores And Black And White Rates Of Suicide
In 1980

	FACTOR						
	I	II	III	IV	V	VI	VII
Correlations: All States							
white suicide rate	0.10	0.81*	-0.25*	0.08	-0.12	-0.04	-0.04
black suicide rate	-0.10	0.26*	0.13	-0.26*	0.06	0.14	0.09
white suicide rates							
male	0.01	0.79*	-0.23	0.15	-0.21	-0.05	-0.06
female	0.25*	0.79*	-0.13	0.21	-0.05	-0.07	0.03
black suicide rates							
male	-0.13	0.27*	0.15	-0.25*	0.07	0.15	0.07
female	0.35*	-0.01	0.17	0.04	-0.05	0.05	-0.02
States With % Black > 9.9%							
white suicide rate	-0.11	0.61*	0.14	0.07	-0.36	-0.36	-0.29
black suicide rate	0.19	-0.07	-0.01	-0.42*	0.40*	0.46*	-0.44*
white suicide rates							
male	-0.19	0.81*	0.17	0.22	-0.41*	-0.45*	0.22
female	-0.05	0.81*	0.32	0.10	-0.35	-0.39	-0.13

black suicide rates							
male	0.20	-0.07	0.02	-0.45*	0.38	0.46*	-0.45*
female	0.17	-0.07	-0.05	-0.32	0.37	0.42*	-0.37
labels: I	Urban/wealthy						
II	social disintegration						
III	age						
IV	southern						
V	labor force participation						
VI	unemployment						
VII	Roman Catholicism						

* statistically significantly at the 5% level or better

Table 6.4: Factor Analysis of Race-Specific Social Variables for African
Americans And For Whites In 1980

	Whites				Blacks		
	I	II	III	IV	I	II	III
college education	0.84#	0.07	0.13	-0.24	0.65#	0.65#	-0.06
male unemploy ment	-0.09	-0.01	-0.10	0.96#	-0.14	-0.57#	0.65#
med. fam. income	0.82#	-0.13	0.26	0.19	0.87#	0.09	0.31
fertility	-0.04	-0.09	-0.92#	0.08	-0.92	-0.11	0.05
females in labor force	0.77#	0.26	0.04	-0.09	0.72#	0.31	0.01
% divorced	0.06	0.91#	0.13	0.21	0.19	0.18	0.91#
% separated	0.31	-0.03	0.82# -	0.04	-0.04	-0.96#	-0.11
migration	0.10	0.90#	-0.06	-0.23	0.44#	0.83#	-0.03
Pearson r's							
suicide	0.01	0.80*	0.14	0.03	0.31*	0.20	0.15

high loading (> 0.40)
* significant at the 5% level or better

Table 6.5: Pearson Correlations between Race-Specific Social Variables and
Suicide In 1980

	Suicide	
	whites	blacks
college education	0.17	0.35*
unemployment	0.02	-0.09
med. fam. income	-0.05	0.32*
fertility	-0.10	-0.38*
females in labor force	0.07	0.16
% divorced	0.76*	0.25*
% separated	0.20	-0.25*
interstate migration	0.75*	0.26*

* significant at the 5% level or better

Table 6.6
Correlations between the Social Indicators and Suicide Rates in 1980 and
1990

	black suicide rates		white suicide rates	
	1980	1990	1980	1990
church	-0.28*	-0.25*	-0.49**	-0.39**
population density	-0.12	-0.21	-0.42**	-0.51**
female labor force	0.06	0.08	-0.02	-0.03
% black population	-0.28*	-0.36**	-0.12	-0.09
% Roman Catholic	0.20	0.14	-0.07	-0.26*
marriage rate	0.07	-0.15	0.56**	0.31**
alcohol consumption	0.19	0.32**	0.38**	0.32**
infant mortality	-0.20	-0.13	-0.18	0.03
% in poverty	-0.13	0.06	0.06	0.29**
birth rate	-0.09	-0.02	0.29**	0.39**
migration rate	0.09	0.31**	0.71**	0.69**
crime rate	0.10	-0.11	0.50**	0.35**
death rate	-0.01	-0.10	-0.44**	-0.40**
% urban population	-0.14	-0.05	0.20	0.06
population	-0.10	-0.22	-0.04	-0.15
unemployment rate	0.04	0.12	-0.04	0.05
divorce rate	0.11	0.15	0.74**	0.71**
males/females	0.14	0.34**	0.51**	0.59**
per capita income	-0.02	-0.16	0.01	-0.32**
homicide rate	-0.18	-0.24*	0.43**	0.18

*   two-tailed $p < .10$
** two-tailed $p < .05$ or better

Table 6.7: Factor Analysis of the Variables and Correlations with the Suicide
Rates in 1980 and 1990^

1980					
	I	II	III	IV	V
% urban population	91#	05	16	-05	04
per capita income	83#	13	-27	15	15
population	60#	-20	27	07	-44
crime rate	76#	46	12	-09	-06
pop. density	52#	-27	06	61#	17
% Roman Catholic	57#	01	-39	50#	07
% in poverty	-58#	-09	61#	-09	-20
church attendance	-17	-68#	01	01	42
marriage rate	06	82#	07	-04	19
alcohol consumption	35	65#	-28	17	31
migration rate	-04	74#	-17	-43	26
divorce rate	-02	88#	06	-30	-04
% black population	-05	-06	92#	13	-04
infant mortality	06	-15	83#	29	-09
homicide rate	15	31	82#	-09	-29
birth rate	-17	-05	-04	-91#	09
death rate	-24	-21	08	79#	-18
males/females	-06	42	-39	-70#	19
female labor force	32	17	-31	-07	67#
unemployment	02	-03	10	17	-80#
suicide rate:					
white	0.10	0.71*	0.06	-0.40*	-0.13
black	-0.05	0.21	-0.31*	0.09	-0.14

* two-tailed p < .05 or better

---

^ the decimal point has been omitted from the factor loadings.

\# loading > 0.50

Factor labels:

I	urban/wealth	IV	birth rate
II	social disintegration	V	unemployment
III	southern		

1990						
	I	II	III	IV	V	VI
% black population	96#	08	04	08	06	-11
infant mortality	82#	-02	-17	21	18	-10
males/females	-56#	47	-39	-35	10	25
homicide rate	79#	39	-05	39	01	-06
death rate	28	-68#	13	47	-10	-14
% urban population	-09	72#	59#	09	-07	-10
population	17	59#	14	34	-40	01
birth rate	14	91#	-10	-12	07	-08
crime rate	26	75#	28	17	16	21
populat. density	09	-02	89#	06	-25	-11
per capita income	-02	22	82#	-17	-28	28
% in poverty	36	02	-65#	49	13	-23
female labor force	-24	03	14	-87#	-08	17
unemployment	18	02	-01	81#	01	04
% Roman Catholic	-32	05	49	-05	-65#	25
marriage rate	21	03	-16	-05	73#	-03
divorce rate	-12	11	-28	38	78#	15
migration rate	-12	08	01	-31	56#	65#
alcohol consumption	04	04	23	-23	-35	77#
church adherents	25	-01	03	-12	-11	-82#
suicide rate:						
white	-0.05	0.38*	-0.48*	0.10	0.42*	0.35*
black	-0.27	-0.07	-0.24	0.06	-0.10	0.26

Factor labels:

I	southern	IV	unemployment
II	urban	V	social disintegration
III	wealth	VI	social disintegration

CHAPTER 7

SOCIAL CORRELATES OF LETHAL AGGRESSION

Whereas many researchers have explored the correlates of regional suicide rates or of regional homicide rates, Whitt (1969, 1985; Whitt, et al., 1972) suggested that suicide rates and homicide rates could be summed to give a measure of the lethal aggression rate of a society. Regardless of the direction in which aggression is expressed, inwardly as suicide or outwardly as homicide, some societies have high rates of lethal aggression whereas others have low rates. The direction in which the aggression is expressed is a separate variable and may have very different correlates from the lethal aggression rate. Whitt argued that the correlates of the lethal aggression rate might well be very different from those of the component parts of the rate (the homicide rate and the suicide rate).

Field (1963) proposed a similar idea. In discussing black suicide, Seiden (1974) noted that black homicide rates have also risen, alongside black youth suicide rates, and Seiden suggested, therefore, that scholars search for an explanation of *violent death* among black youth.

Whitt hypothesized that the lethal aggression rate of a society would vary directly with the proportion of frustrated individuals in the society. The ratio of the suicide rate in the society to the lethal aggression rate should vary with the extent to which individuals in the society perceive themselves to have control over the outcomes in the society or the reinforcements that they seek. In a study of census tracts in Atlanta, the lethal aggression rate was found to vary inversely with the median family income in line with his hypothesis.

The present analysis explored whether the lethal violence rates of African Americans and whites in the American states showed similar or different correlates with social characteristics of the states using the same factors identified in the previous chapter (Chapter 6).

Whitt's measure of the direction of aggression (the ratio of the suicide rate to the lethal violence rates) could not be used since it involved division by zero for some data points. As a result, the measure proposed by Field (of simply subtracting the rates) was used.

The results are shown in Table 7.1. It can be seen that the factor scores which are correlated with suicide and homicide rates considered separately are also those that are correlated with the composite measures. Thus, Whitt's assertion that the lethal aggression rate provides an important and different variable from the simple suicide and homicide rates was not confirmed. However, Whitt's suggestions are worth consideration in future research for they provide alternative conceptualizations of the variables which may, in different data sets, prove to be of interest.

REFERENCES

Field, F. B. Mortality rates and aggression management indices. *Journal of Health & Human Behavior*, 1963, 4, 70-78.

Seiden, R. H. Current developments in minority group suicidology. *Journal of Black Health Perspectives*, 1974, 1, 29-42.

Whitt, H. P. The lethal aggression ratio and the suicide-murder ratio. *Dissertation Abstracts*, 1969, 29B, 2624-2625.

Whitt, H. P. Comments on Stack's paper "Suicide: a decade review of the sociological literature." *Deviant Behavior*, 1985, 6, 229-231.

Whitt, H. P., Gordon, C. C., & Hofley, J. R. Religion, economic development and lethal aggression. *American Sociological Review*, 1972, 37, 193-201.

Table 7.1

Pearson Correlations between Factor Scores and Aggression Rates

	FACTOR						
	I	II	III	IV	V	VI	VII
suicide + homicide							
black	0.32*	0.29*	0.11	0.16	-0.19	0.31*	-0.28
white	0.20	0.69*	-0.22	0.31	-0.27	-0.01	-0.07
Suicide - homicide							
black	-0.42*	-0.08	-0.01	-0.38*	0.25	-0.21	0.37*
white	-0.20	0.29*	-0.07	-0.51*	0.34*	-0.06	0.07
suicide							
black	-0.10	0.26	0.13	-0.26	0.06	0.14	0.09
white	0.11	0.81*	-0.25	0.08	-0.12	-0.04	-0.04
homicide							
black	0.41*	0.21	0.07	0.29*	-0.24	0.29*	-0.36*
white	0.25	0.48*	-0.16	0.46*	-0.37*	0.02	-0.09

* two-tailed p < .05 or better

Factor Labels

I	urban/wealth	V	labor force participation
II	social disintegration	VI	unemployment
III	age	VII	Roman Catholicism
IV	southern		

CHAPTER 8

RESEARCH ON BLACK SUICIDE

There has not been very much research conducted on completed suicide in African Americans, but this chapter will review the research that has been published.

ARE PSYCHOLOGICAL MEASURES VALID FOR AFRICAN AMERICANS?

Some scholars have questioned whether the psychological tests devised for research into suicide in whites are valid for African Americans. Molock, et al. (1994) found a strong association between scores on a depression inventory and a measure of current suicidal ideation in African American college students. Those who had considered suicide in the past also differed in scores on these two scales. Finally, both scales proved to have good internal consistency. Thus, the scales appeared to be both valid and reliable for African Americans.

Blanton-Lacy, et al. (1995) administered standard scales for measuring suicidal ideation and depression (devised by Aaron Beck) to African American college students. Those who had attempted or thought about suicide were more depressed than the nonsuicidal students, and the suicidal ideation scale differentiated between the attempters and the ideators. Thus, the scales appeared to produce results similar to those obtained in white samples, suggesting that the scales could be used for African Americans.[1]

Molock, et al. (1996) examined the factor-analytic structure of several scales using African American and white college students. A suicidal ideation scale and a hopelessness scale gave similar factors for both groups. However, the factors identified for the Beck Depression Inventory did differ a little for the two groups of students. Despite this, the correlations between the factor scores were similar in both groups.

Thus, it appears that the standard psychological measures used in research on suicide are probably reliable and valid for use with African Americans.

RESEARCH FINDINGS

THE MODAL BLACK SUICIDE

Reingold (1975) found that the modal black suicide in San Francisco in 1970-1973 was male, over the age of 30, and used barbiturates or firearms. Davis (1976) found that the modal black suicide in New Orleans was a 39 year-old male laborer who was unmarried.

Peck (1983) studied a sample of 55 "nonwhite" suicides from a large Midwest city -- in the title and body of his article Peck talks of black suicides. The majority were male, less than 55 years of age, married or separated, Protestant, and employed full-time, although mainly as laborers. Thus, in this sample, coming from a lower social class and poverty seemed to characterize the suicides. Only nine (16%) left suicide notes, but 31 percent were judged to be depressed, 42 percent had been treated for physical ailments in the past, and 36 percent had expressed a wish to die. Twenty-five percent were heavy drinkers, 24 percent drug users, and 13 percent heavy users of medication. The most common method for suicide was a firearm, and many of the suicides had marital/romantic problems.

Christian (1974, 1977) studied black suicides in Los Angeles and found the median age to be 28 and modal age 21. Over half were under 30 years of age and only 21 percent over the age of 40. Fifty four percent were female, and the female suicides were younger than the male suicides (median ages

---

[1] The three groups of students did not differ on Beck's measure of hopelessness.

26.5 and 31 respectively). About half used an overdose (with barbiturates the most common choice), with firearms as the second most popular method. The largest occupational group was unskilled laborers, and the majority lived with others (42 percent with extended families and 35 percent with nuclear families). Romantic problems/loss of love was the most common precipitant, followed by poor health and financial problems. She suggested that loss of a love relationship for those who have no money or ego supports (such as position or prestige) may be especially difficult to survive. The majority had lived in California for eleven years or longer; only eight percent had arrived in the previous five years. A quarter had communicated their suicidal intent to others.

Christian described the typical female suicide as a young, low-income woman, married and living with her family. She had children under the age of thirteen and lived in California for a long time. The most common precipitant was an unhappy love relationship that seemed about to end. The typical male suicide was young, single, unskilled, and living with his family. His suicide too was precipitated by romantic problems with a loved one.

Mitchell (1985) found that half of black youth suicides in Washington, DC, involved drugs (with phencyclidine very common).

SUICIDAL BEHAVIOR IN AFRICAN-AMERICANS VERSUS OTHER ETHNIC GROUPS

Swanson and Breed (1976) compared black and white male suicides in New Orleans in 1954-1963 and found that the black suicides were younger, more often semi-skilled or unskilled workers, less educated, less often downwardly mobile, more often single or in common-law marriages, attended church more often, were more socially active, were more worried about debts, more often had alcohol problems and less often threatened suicide prior to their death.

Green (1977) compared black versus other suicides in Los Angeles and found few differences, though tests of statistical significance were not carried out on the data. The black suicides had a slightly higher proportion of men, used barbiturate overdoses less often, were more often unemployed or unskilled workers, less often retired, more often depressed, less often alcoholic, were less likely to have seen a private physician, had received psychiatric treatment more often, were more likely to be chronically unstable, were less often in poor health, less often left a suicide note, and were less likely to have been drinking prior to the suicide.

Marzuk, et al. (1992) examined completed suicides in New York City and found that the black (and Hispanic) suicides were more likely to have used cocaine prior to their death.

Studying female completed suicides in Alaska, Georgia, Nebraska and North Carolina, Alston (1986) found in general that suicide rates in women in highly-traditional occupations were lower than those of women in nontraditional occupations, which in turn were lower than those of women in moderately traditional occupations. The relationship was not, therefore, linear. As the occupation became less traditional, suicidal behavior first became more common and then less common.

Alston (1988) found that ethnicity played a role in this relationship. In North Carolina, African American women had higher suicide rates if they had clerical jobs and lower suicide rates if they had service jobs. European American women had higher suicide rates if they were in service jobs. In Georgia, however, the suicide rates of black women exceeded those of white women in all occupational categories.

THE ACCEPTABILITY OF SUICIDE

Stack (1998) examined responses to the General Social Surveys for black and white differences in the acceptability of suicide. Given four scenarios for suicide, African Americans rated suicide as a less acceptable option than did whites, significantly so for one scenario (a person with an incurable disease). Religiosity predicted the acceptability of suicide for both African Americans and whites, but much less strongly and consistently for African Americans. The strongest correlate of rating suicide as acceptable was living in the west for black men and educational level for black women. In contrast, religiosity was the most important predictor of viewing suicide as acceptable for both white men and white women. Thus, these results led Stack to question the role of the church in shaping black suicidal behavior. Jorgenson and Neubecker

(1980-1981) looked at national survey data and confirmed that blacks were less pro-euthanasia than were whites.

Lichtenstein, et al. (1997) surveyed residents in Detroit and found that African Americans were less in favor of physician-assisted suicide and active euthanasia, both in the abstract and for themselves. In a multiple regression, however, only feeling that religion was important predicted this attitude, suggesting that religiosity was the critical characteristic differentiating African Americans and whites (although Lichtenstein did not report on racial differences in the variables studied).

In South Africa, Forster and Keen (1988) surveyed Zulus in Durban and found that 80 percent considered suicide to be totally unacceptable -- both men and women and those of all religious affiliations.

MARITAL STATUS AND BLACK SUICIDE

Stack (1996a, 1996b) looked at African American suicides and natural deaths from urinary cancer in 1989 in the United States. He found that divorce and widowhood increased the risk of suicide over natural deaths, while age decreased the risk. For whites, divorce, widowhood and being single increased the risk of suicide over natural deaths, and age decreased the risk. The regression coefficients were larger for whites than for African Americans, suggesting to Stack that marriage is a much greater protector against suicide for whites than for African Americans, perhaps because extended family ties are larger and stronger for African Americans than for whites, though Stack provided no research data relevant to this suggestion.

EXPERIENCING A FRIEND'S SUICIDE

Williams, et al. (1996) presented vignettes to African American college students in which the protagonist had a friend commit suicide in either a non-sensationalized or a sensationalized way or who had not experienced a friend commit suicide. Regardless of whether the friend's suicide was sensationalized or not, the respondents predicted a suicidal outcome more often if the protagonist had a friend commit suicide.

MULTIVARIATE STUDIES

Davis and Short (1977) studied black mortality in New Orleans from 1954 to 1973, including all suicides, homicides, and accidental deaths and a 25 percent sample of natural deaths. The percentage of deaths due to suicide rose over the period, from 0.31% in 1954 to 0.91% in 1973. The report is not clear, but it appears that the correlations between the predictor variables and the occurrence of suicide was carried out over the 779 deaths in the sample.

Males were more likely to commit suicide than females, but in the multiple regression the association was reversed (that is, females were more likely to die from suicide when all other variables were controlled for). Age was associated with a lower risk of suicide, as was marriage. Occupational status was positively associated with the risk of suicide, while community integration (measured by the use of crime rates[2]) decreased the likelihood of suicide. Slight differences in these results were found between the first ten year period and the second ten year period. Davis and Short felt that their study was a test of Henry and Short's (1954) theory of suicide, but it seems more relevant to testing Durkheim's (1897) theory.

Davis (1980) looked at correlates of the nonwhite suicide in 1970 and 1975 in the 17 states with large black populations. In both years, the nonwhite suicide rate was positively correlated with the percentage of black migrants, the percentage of African Americans living alone, the percentage of African Americans aged 20-34 and the percentage of African Americans with low education. In a multiple regression analysis, only migration and low education contributed significantly to the prediction of the black suicide rate. Black suicide rates were higher when African Americans had more education and were more often migrants to the states. The youth cohort size and living alone were only weak predictors of black suicide rates. Thus, these results support the "middle-class acculturation" theory of black suicide, that is, as African

---

[2] They switched to an ecological analysis for this analysis.

Americans become more educated and more geographically mobile, their suicide rates rise.

TIME SERIES STUDIES

Martin (1984) found that measures of church attendance were inversely associated with suicide rates for all gender-by-race groups in the United States from 1972 to 1978.

Hamermesh (1974) analyzed the variation in black suicide rates from 1947-1967 over five age groups (giving him 189 observations). The results showed that the effect of individual income on black suicide rates was positive. This was opposite to what Hamermesh expected and opposite also to the result for whites. Second, the effect of unemployment on black suicide rates was positive and increased with age. This finding paralleled that for whites. Third, the white suicide rate also predicted the black suicide rate.

Using cross-sectional data for both 1950 and 1960 from 20 states with large black populations, a positive association between income and black suicide rates was observed. The association between suicide rates and unemployment was now negative.

Assuming that the suicide rates are accurate, Hamermesh suggested that black suicide rates may be higher when income is higher because African Americans have become more aware of the economic conditions of whites. Blacks whose incomes are higher are more likely to come into contact with whites and so be more aware of their relative economic status.

Stewart (1980) replicated Hamermesh's study, but introduced social variables (demonstrations and riots by African Americans and the black illegitimacy rate). He found that the addition of these variables improved the predictive power of Hamermesh's regression equations by up to seven percent.

South (1984) studied age-standardized suicide rates for whites and nonwhites for 1949 to 1979 and found that the as nonwhite incomes rose relative to white incomes, the nonwhite suicide rate rose relative to the white suicide rate also. Unemployment had a positive effect also on nonwhite and white suicide rates on the nonwhite/white suicide rate ratio, but only for males.

Lester (1993) explored the association between economic indices and suicidal behavior for African Americans in the United States from 1967-1986. Indices of dissimilarity in income and unemployment for African Americans versus whites were correlated with white and nonwhite suicide rates for both genders, but no associations were found for the absolute suicide rates or for the ratio of the nonwhite/white suicide rates. Lester (1996) correlated a measure of general income inequality in the United States from 1947 to 1972 with nonwhite and white suicide rates. Income inequality was associated with lower nonwhite suicide rates, but was not associated with white suicide rates. Lester (1997) found that the number of riots by African Americans in America from 1960 to 1992 was associated with lower black suicide rates, but the association did not reach statistical significance.

Yang (1992; Yang and Lester, 1994) applied her real-income hypothesis of suicide to a study of suicide rates in the United States from 1940 to 1984. She examined the role played by the gross national product per capita (both without a lag and with a one year lag), the unemployment rate, female participation in the labor force, the divorce rate, the percentage of Roman Catholics, and the Second World War in accounting for the suicide rate.

For the overall suicide rate, a multiple regression analysis indicated that the gross national product per capita (both without a lag and with a one year lag), the unemployment rate and female participation in the labor force all played a significant role in predicting the suicide rate. The effects of unemployment and the unlagged gross national product per capita were positive, while the effects of the lagged gross national product per capita and female participation in the labor force were positive.

Yang looked at the ability of these socioeconomic variables to predict the suicide rates of white males, white females, nonwhite males and nonwhite females separately (see Table 8.1). The lagged gross national product per capita had a negative influence for all four groups. Unemployment rates had a statistically significant influence only for white males. The unlagged gross national product per capita had a statistically significant influence only for white females and nonwhite females. Female participation in the labor force had a negative influence for females, a positive influence for nonwhite males and no influence for white males. Thus, it is clear that the relationship of these economic variables to the suicide rate differs for the different groups.

Yang concluded that the beneficial impact of economic growth was present only for males. For females economic growth had a negative impact.

With other variables held constant, both female participation in the labor force and unemployment rates had a rather modest impact on the suicide rate.

Lester (1995) studied the period of 1933 to 1985 and took eighteen social indicators for the United States and factor analyzed them. He identified five independent factors which he labeled (based on the social indicators loading most strongly on the factors) year, military involvement, marriage, social and political threat, and business failures.

Whereas the suicide rates of white males and female were not associated with "year," nonwhite male and female were positively associated with "year," increasing over time. All four suicide rates were negatively associated with military involvement, lower when the military was proportionately greater. The suicide rates of only the white males was positively associated with marriage and social threat, while the suicide rates of white and nonwhite males were negatively associated with business failures. Again, therefore, Lester found differences in the time-series predictors of white and nonwhite suicide rates, as did Yang.

Some of these studies utilized nonwhite suicide rates rather than black suicide rates because the *Vital Statistics of the United States*, which is published annually, did not provide suicide rates for African Americans by age and gender until 1979. It is hoped that the inclusion of black suicide rates by age and gender back to 1933 in the present book will stimulate time-series research on black suicide.

DISCUSSION

It is clear from this review that research into black suicide is rare. Although there have been a few comparisons of the superficial characteristics of black and white suicides, there have been no sound psychological autopsy studies, no multivariate studies, and no studies of suicide notes in which black and white suicides are compared.

In particular, there are important ways in which black and white suicides might differ. For example, one of the strongest correlates of suicidal behavior is psychiatric illness (Lester, 1992). Earls and Jemison (1986) pointed out that African Americans and whites differ in their experience of psychiatric illness - - they differ in symptoms, diagnosis, frequency of misdiagnoses, severity of dysfunction, age at onset, etc. Thus, it would seem crucial to explore whether the differences in the clinical picture of African Americans and whites could account for, in part, the differences in suicidal behavior. Studies of young adults and the elderly with this is mind might clarify the relatively high suicide rates of young black adults and the relatively low suicide rates of black elderly. This kind of research is needed if we are going to shed light on black suicide and how its causes and motivations might differ from those of white suicide.

REFERENCES

Alston, M. H. Occupation and suicide among women. *Issues in Mental Health Nursing*, 1986, 8, 109-119.

Alston, M. H. Occupational correlates of suicide in black and other nonwhite women. In D. Lester (Ed.) *Suicide '88*, p. 206. Denver, CO: American Association of Suicidology, 1988.

Blanton-Lacy, M., Molock, S. D., Kimbrough, R., Williams, S., Nicholson, M., & Hamilton, D. Validity of the use of suicide scales with African Americans. In D. Lester (Ed.) *Suicide '95*, p. 117. Washington, DC: American Association of Suicidology, 1995.

Christian, E. R. An exploratory study into suicides among urban blacks. In J. A. Bush (Ed.) *Suicide and blacks*, unpaged. Los Angeles: Charles R. Drew Postgraduate Medical School, 1974.

Christian, E. R. Black suicide. In C. L. Hatton, S. M. Valente & A. Rink (Eds.) *Suicide*, pp. 143-159. New York: Appleton-Century-Crofts, 1977.

Davis, R. A statistical analysis of the current reported increase in the black suicide rate. *Dissertation Abstracts International*, 1976, 36A, 5573.

Davis, R. Black suicide and the relational system. *Research in Race & Ethnic Relations*, 1980, 2, 43-71.

Davis, R., & Short, J. F. Dimensions of black suicide. *Suicide & Life-Threatening Behavior*, 1978, 8, 161-173.

Durkheim, E. *Le suicide*. Paris: Felix Alcan, 1897.

Earls, F., & Jemison, A. Suicidal behavior in American blacks. In G. Klerman (Ed.) *Suicide and depression among adolescents and young adults*, pp. 133-145. Washington, DC: American Psychiatric Press, 1986.

Forster, H. W., & Keen, A. W. Black attitude in suicide. In L. Schlebusch (Ed.) *Suicidal behaviour*, pp. 98-109. Durban: University of Natal, 1988.

Green, J. Ethnic aspects of suicide statistics. In C. L. Hatton, S. M. Valente & A. Rink (Eds.) *Suicide*, pp. 139-143. New York: Appleton-Century-Crofts, 1977.

Hamermesh, D. The economics of black suicide. *Southern Economic Journal*, 1974, 41, 188-199.

Henry, A. F., & Short, J. F. *Suicide and homicide*. New York: Free Press, 1954.

Jorgenson, D. E., & Neubecker, R. C. Euthanasia. *Omega*, 1980-1981, 11, 281-291.

Lester, D. *Why people kill themselves*. Springfield, IL: Charles Thomas, 1992.

Lester, D. Economic status of African-Americans and suicide rates. *Perceptual & Motor Skills*, 1993, 77, 1150.

Lester, D. Combining opposing methodologies in studies of suicide and homicide. *Quality & Quantity*, 1995, 29, 67-72.

Lester, D. Inequality of income and rates of violence in Caucasian and black groups. *Psychological Reports*, 1996, 79, 978.

Lester, D. Black riots and black suicide rates. *Psychological Reports*, 1997, 81, 1134.

Lichtenstein, R. L., Alcser, K. H., Corning, A. D., Bachman, J. G., & Doukas, D. J. Black/white differences in attitudes toward physician-assisted suicide. *Journal of the National Medical Association*, 1997, 89, 125-133.

Martin, W. T. Religiosity and United States suicide rates. *Journal of Clinical Psychology*, 1984, 40, 1166-1169.

Marzuk, P. M., Tardiff, K., Leon, A. C., Stajic, M., Morgan, E. B., & Mann, J. J. Prevalence of cocaine use among residents of New York City who committed suicide during a one-year period. *American Journal of Psychiatry*, 1992, 149, 371-375.

Mitchell, L. E. The effect of drug abuse on suicide rates among black youth in the District of Columbia. In *Youth Suicide*, pp. 63-66. Washington, DC: Youth Suicide National Center, 1985.

Molock, S. D., Kimbrough, R., Lacy, M. B., McClure, K. P., & Williams, S. Suicidal behavior among African American college students. *Journal of Black Psychology*, 1994, 20, 234-251.

Molock, S. D., Williams, S., & Kimbrough, R. Measuring suicidality in African American college students. In J. L. McIntosh (Ed.) *Suicide '96*, pp. 127-128. Washington, DC: American Association of Suicidology, 1996.

Peck, D. L. "Official documentation" of the black suicide experience. *Omega*, 1983, 14, 21-31.

Reingold, E. Black suicide in San Francisco. In Anon, *Miniconsultations on the mental and physical health problems of black women*, pp. 111-120. Washington, DC: Black Women's Community Development Foundation, 1975.

South, S. J. Racial differences in suicide. *Social Science Quarterly*, 1984, 65, 172-180.

Stack, S. The effect of marital integration on African American suicide. *Suicide & Life-Threatening Behavior*, 1996a, 26, 405-414.

Stack, S. The effect of marital integration on African American Suicide. In J. L. McIntosh (Ed.) *Suicide '96*, pp. 125-126. Washington, DC: American Association of Suicidology, 1996b.

Stack, S. The relationship between culture and suicide. *Transcultural Psychiatry*, 1998, in press.

Stewart, J. B. The political economy of black male suicides. *Journal of Black Studies*, 1980, 11, 249-261.

Swanson, W. C., & Breed, W. Black suicide in New Orleans. In E. S. Shneidman (Ed.) *Suicidology*, pp. 99-128. New York: Grune & Stratton, 1976.

Williams, S., Molock, S. D., & Kimbrough, R. Glamorized suicides and their contagious effects. In. J. L. McIntosh (Ed.) *Suicide '96*, pp. 129-130. Washington, DC: American Association of Suicidology, 1996.

Yang, B. The economy and suicide. *American Journal of Economics & Sociology*, 1992, 51, 87-99.

Yang, B., & Lester, D. Crime and unemployment. *Journal of Socio-Economics*, 1994, 23, 215-222.

Table 8.1
Time-Series Correlates Of The Suicide Rate In The United States, 1940-1984
(from Yang, 1992)

	GNP	GNP^{-1}	UN	WAR	FLFP	DIV	CATH
white male	0.19	-0.36*	0.02*	-0.10*	0.00	0.21*	-0.01
white female	1.35*	-0.99*	0.01	0.12*	-0.05*	0.73*	0.06*
nonwhite male	0.08	-0.76*	0.01	-0.24*	0.02*	0.45*	0.04*
nonwhite female	1.80*	-1.33*	0.02	-0.09	-0.04*	0.89*	0.11*

GNP	gross national product per capita
GNP^{-1}	GNP lagged by one year
UN	unemployment rate
WAR	dummy variable for 1942-1945
FLFP	female labor force participation
DIV	divorce rate
CATH	percentage of population Roman Catholic

CHAPTER 9

THEORIES OF BLACK SUICIDE

One of the first commentators this century on black suicide was Prudhomme (1938). Prudhomme was aware that scholarly thinking on this issue was dominated by white Eurocentric scholarship and, therefore, might not be relevant to understanding black suicide. Despite this, Prudhomme attempted to account for low suicide rates in African Americans using then current theories of suicide.

Prudhomme noted that suicide rates seem to increase with civilization, by which he meant an increase in the well-being of people, and which today we would prefer to call "modernization." Things which were once luxuries become necessities, and people seem to develop passions which the modern society cannot always satisfy. Modernization also seems to result in a weakening of traditional religion, which not only weakens inhibitions against suicide, but also weakens social integration and social regulation.

Prudhomme observed that African Americans were economically far worse off than whites, and in the Depression lost little since they had so little to start with. African Americans were also far less educated than whites. Therefore, modernization had, to a large extent, passed African Americans by. Furthermore, African Americans were more likely to live in rural areas at the time that Prudhomme was writing and in warmer climates (where suicide was less common). (Prudhomme thought that suicide rates tended to be higher in the more northern states.) Prudhomme suggested that African Americans have more close interpersonal ties and are able to express their concerns and misery more easily. They are also more committed to their religion than are whites. Thus, Prudhomme focused on the social differences between African Americans and whites in order to account for the differences in suicide rates.

Although nominally free, Prudhomme noted that African Americans were not free in reality, and so their desires have to be channeled into vicarious activities. He noted that African Americans aspire to live like whites, but find it difficult to do so. As a result, Prudhomme thought, African Americans tend to form a negative image of themselves and to value "light-skin" and other "white" physical characteristics (such as straight hair).[1]

Prudhomme saw the heightened emotionality and possible impulsiveness of African Americans as a result of their continual humiliation, inferiority and insecurity in the society. Since African Americans have obvious enemies in the dominant whites, there is less need to suppress and repress their anger and turn it inward onto themselves and more reason to discharge their anger outwardly, leading to a higher homicide rate. Since inhibitions against expressing anger result from education and culture, according to Prudhomme, African Americans have less inhibition against expressing their anger. Thus, by white standards, African Americans may appear to be more "neurotic."

Prudhomme gave examples of both completed suicide and attempted suicide in African Americans. Prudhomme saw completed suicide as more likely in psychotic individuals, while attempted suicide, a hysterical act, was more common in neurotic individuals. However, after presenting some cases, Prudhomme concluded that the causes of suicide were the same in African Americans as in whites, and that racial prejudice (in the society or introjected as self-hatred) played only a secondary role. For example, one completed suicide, a forty-one year-old dentist, was light-skinned but had married a dark-skinned woman. He never referred to himself as a "negro," and he refused to have children with his wife because he did not want dark-skinned children; he also wanted to move away from Texas, where he worked, to Chicago or Detroit. He accused his wife of infidelity and began divorce proceedings. This cost him income because of the scandal, and he lost more money in foolish investment schemes and from gambling. He remarried a light-skinned woman and, although poorer than before, lived reasonably well. He was now determined to have children, but his wife did not become pregnant. He began to suspect his wife of infidelity (in the case of his second wife, with white co-workers), as he did his first wife, and one Sunday morning he skipped mass (his wife was a Catholic) and shot himself. He had recently changed his will to

---

[1] Prudhomme stated, without evidence, that suicide was less common in the "more typical black Negro" than in lighter-skinned blacks.

disinherit his wife, leaving his estate to his sister living in the north. Prudhomme suggested that the man's suspicions of infidelity in his wives suggested paranoia, and that he may have had psychosexual difficulties. On the other hand, the racial factors seem quite important here, in that the skin color of his wives was very important to him and affected his desire to have children. If this case is typical of those that Prudhomme encountered, it would seem that Prudhomme underestimated the role of racial factors in this case -- rather than playing only a secondary role, they seem to have played a major role.

WOODFORD: MIDDLE-CLASS BLACK SUICIDE

The next major commentator was Woodford (1965). Writing in *Ebony*, Woodford noted that the suicide rate of black men had doubled since 1946 and that the majority of the suicides occurred in those who were financially secure or wealthy, that is to say, in the black middle class, especially those whose family roots were in the South but who had migrated to Northern cities (see also Seiden [1970]). Woodford saw suicide as a result of luxury. The American myth which promises happiness along with success is a myth -- when people find that success does not bring happiness, they become suicidal. When people have to deal with everyday hassles, they are less suicidal -- for example, the black suicide rate dropped by 20 percent during the Second World War. Although Woodford does not cite Henry and Short's (1954) theory of suicide, it is clear that Woodford's ideas are similar to those proposed by Henry and Short (see Chapter 10).

Woodford also noted some interesting epidemiological facts. Black suicides are younger than white suicides -- 30 versus 39 years of age for men and 28 versus 34 years of age for women. More African Americans cite romantic problems as a motive for suicide in their suicide notes. The marital status of black and white suicides, however, is similar. Black women tend to use dramatic, violent and disfiguring methods for suicide more often than white women, perhaps motivated by revenge. Among African Americans in Northern states, jumping is relatively more common than in whites. In attempts at suicide, more often found in black women than in black men (as is the case for white women and men), black women tend to use slow-acting poisons more often than white women.

Woodford gave many examples of prominent African Americans who committed suicide. For example, Jack Claybourne, a black wrestler, shot himself in 1960 at the age of 49, as his career declined. Buford Conley, an official in Cincinnati's NAACP, killed himself with car exhaust on the eve of an election in which he was running for city office.

Consistent with Woodford's views, Holmes (1977), after conducting psychological autopsies on six black suicides from Los Angeles, concluded that their suicides were caused by problems arising from the transition to the middle-class.

HENDIN: BLACK RAGE

Hendin (1969, 1978) focused on attempted suicide, but generalized his results to completed suicide, perhaps not a wise decision. He first noted the high suicide rate among urban, young black males aged 20 to 35. He argued that suicide in these men was the result of their conscious rage and murderous impulses.[2] Coming from violent homes, where mothers and fathers were typically violent and abusive, and living in violent neighborhoods, they grew up to be violent adolescents. Hendin gave an example of black male who did complete suicide who, as a child, had been trapped in a room while his father, a wife abuser, was shot by the police after a gun battle. This boy grew up to admire Hitler, was in frequent fights (for which he had been arrested), and contemplated killing his brother and mother before attempting suicide himself.

Hendin argued that cultural stress increased this rage. The national rejection of African Americans through discrimination and racism reinforces both their anger and their feelings of worthlessness. They grow up feeling trapped -- by their lack of education and job opportunities, by aspirations that they can never realize, by their families, by the ghetto, and by their own personalities.

Such individuals may become homicidal, may try to calm their rage with alcohol or drugs, or may turn the rage inward on themselves. Thus, Hendin

---

[2] Hendin felt that his characterization of suicidal black men applied also to black women.

argued that the Freudian hypothesis that suicide results from anger turned inward upon the self did not apply to black suicide. While Freud's hypothesis requires that the anger felt toward others be unconscious, the anger and rage in African Americans is conscious. Thus, for African Americans, suicidal and homicidal behavior are positively associated rather than inversely associated. Furthermore, the African Americans whom Hendin interviewed alternated between overt violent and suicidal behavior, rather than being simply self-destructive as the Freudian hypothesis demands.

For African Americans, the feelings of hopelessness and despair occur early in life, and so their suicide rates peak early in life, much earlier than in whites. Whereas black suicide rates peak in young adults, white suicide rates do not peak until middle age and after.

Unfortunately, Hendin based his conclusions on interviews with twenty-five black attempted suicides, and most scholars argue that attempted and completed suicides have very different psychodynamics. Second, he failed to interview nonsuicidal African Americans or white attempted suicides so that we cannot be sure that the dynamics Hendin described are true for *suicidal* African Americans rather than being true for African Americans in general or attempted suicides in general.

Hendin reported objective psychological test data for his sample of attempted suicides. Over half had intelligence test scores of 80 or below versus only one above 110. On measures of hostility, the group scored higher than the mean scores of several comparison groups. The patients' anger appeared to be precipitated most often by the anger of others directed toward them. Their depression, on the other hand, appeared to result from their own failures and inadequacies. The group showed little achievement motivation and had low aspirations, and the men did not view father-son relationships in a positive manner.

Slater (1973), who thought that the suicide rate of black women was rising dramatically (as we have seen in Chapter 5, it was not), felt that Hendin's ideas were relevant to black women. Slater argued that suicide in black women was a result of the oppression and racism, as well as violence experienced at the hands of black men. Slater also saw the decline in the strength and relevance of black community organizations, such as the church, as a factor, and in addition rising social and economic expectations which the society fails to meet.

Bagley and Greer (1972) presented data on twenty-five black suicidal individuals (23 attempters and two completers) which seemed to contradict Hendin's thesis. However, not only were Bagley and Greer's attempters in England rather than New York City, they were *not* black. Rather they were from the Caribbean, India, Pakistan, Africa and Cyprus, a fact which those who have cited the study seem to have missed. As compared to English attempted suicides, the immigrant attempters were more often judged to have acute situational stress and less often an antisocial personality disorder, psychosis or brain-damage. They were younger and more often discharged without psychiatric treatment. They were recent immigrants suffering from external stress, primarily from interpersonal conflicts.

BREED AND FATALISTIC SUICIDE

Breed (1970) carried out a psychological autopsy study on African Americans who completed suicide in New Orleans from 1954 to 1963, that is, he interviewed friends and relatives in order ascertain the behavior and emotional state of people prior to their suicides. The black suicides tended to be younger, with lower status jobs, more frequently living alone and less likely to be married than the average black in New Orleans.

The black suicides had fewer occupational problems and showed less downward mobility than the whites, though this latter difference was confounded of course by their lower occupational status -- they were less able to move downward since they were already at the bottom (almost one third were laborers). The black and white suicides were similar in size of household, whether living with a mate and number of children. More African Americans were living with their mate but unmarried, than were the whites. The black suicides had more extended kin living in the area, they were more sociable with friends and neighbors, and they attended church more than the white suicides.

The black and white suicides did not differ much in mental disorder, physical health, drug and alcohol abuse or gambling. The black suicides had been injured more at work, perhaps a function of their low status jobs.

The younger black suicides were more often lower class than the older black suicides, had lower incomes, were more often single, attended church less often, abused alcohol more and had more problems with the police. They had better health and less downward mobility.

However, Breed focused his report on the one single area which differentiated the black and white suicides most -- difficulties with the police and other authorities. As compared to only 10 percent of the white suicides, 71 percent of the black suicides had such problems. Twenty-one of the 42 black suicides had problems with the police -- in fact four of the suicides occurred in jail and a fifth in a hospital to which the police had taken him. Four others committed suicide while being chased or sought by the police. Several of the suicides had stated that they would kill themselves rather than go to jail, and African Americans in the community who were interviewed also expressed a fear of the police. Breed gave many other examples of problems with authorities, such as wages being garnished to pay for a son's car, being served with an eviction notice, being guilty of income tax fraud, and awaiting trial for rape.

Breed noted that the black men seemed to have little information about the community resources at their disposal. For example, those facing criminal proceedings did not know about Legal Aid, and those needing support did not know about the range of agencies which could help them. Even if they did know about them, they seemed reluctant to use them, perhaps because they had already had bad experiences with these agencies or because they feared difficulties and rejection of their requests.

Breed noted that Durkheim (1897) had defined fatalistic suicide as that resulting from too much social regulation and had given suicides among slaves as an example of fatalistic suicide. Breed felt that today, long after slavery has been abolished, African Americans are still subjected to excessive regulation, inflexible rules, and moral despotism. They have not obtained freedom from unjust and arbitrary authorities, and so their suicides are fatalistic in nature. While noting that anomic and egoistic suicide can also be found in African Americans, these types of suicide are not as common. They may, however, be a little more common in older African Americans, who have experienced fatalistic pressures early in life but moved to an anomic and egoistic position later in their suicidal career.

On the other hand, Breed noted that black suicide rates were lower than white suicide rates, and he warned that the black suicide rate might rise as their social situation improved and become more similar to that of whites.

Swanson and Breed (1976) noted that five themes are commonly found in suicides: (1) rigidity, an inability to be flexible and to shift roles, (2) commitment to high aspirations, (3) failure when role performance falls short of these aspirations, (4) shame when this failure is a publicly recognizable event, and (5) social isolation in response to the failure and shame. Swanson and Breed formulated these themes based on white suicides, and they noted that they failed to find it in their study of black suicides in New Orleans. They noted particularly the low aspirations of the African Americans in their sample, partly resulting from the oppression and racism in the society, but partly also from their nonutilitarian world view which perhaps results from their history as slaves in the United States. Their religion did not encourage a "Protestant ethic" but rather helped African Americans survive in their hostile world. Religion made life safer and more tolerable.

In New Orleans, Swanson and Breed speculated that African Americans are less suicidal because of three forces acting against self-destruction: (1) greater sociability in black neighborhoods, (2) segregation and competition between the sexes, a rivalry which seems to increase morale and cohesion, and (3) the varied ethnic identity in New Orleans (with American Indians and Creoles in addition to African Americans) which reduces the emotional affronts from racism felt by the African Americans.

DAVIS: YOUTH SUICIDE

Davis (1980, 1981), noting that recent years had seen a rise in youth suicide rates in the United States, particularly among young black males, noted that many suggestions had been made as to the causes of this increase, including, the stresses associated with urbanization (such as migration, unemployment and frustration),[3] movement into the American mainstream and conflictful male/female relationships.

Urbanization seems to be associated with poverty and unemployment, resulting in inadequate education, poor housing, poor parenting and socialization into a violent way of life. This model sees black suicide as

---

[3] Kirk (1977) proposed that general stress from social, physical, political, economic and psychological forces played a role in black suicide.

fatalistic in nature. Wyche and Rotheram-Borus (1990) also suggested urban stress as a possible contributing factor in black youth suicide, and Gibbs (1990) has noted the high frequency of all kinds of behavioral and psychological problems in black youth, including delinquency, substance abuse, teenage pregnancy and homicide, which may be a result of this urban stress.

The "culture shock" hypothesis argues that, as African Americans move into the middle classes, they encounter the different stressors common in this social class, stressors which appear to increase the risk of suicide, as witnessed by the fact that white suicide rates are higher than black suicide rates. The economic advances of young educated African Americans, in addition to the Black Liberation Movement, may have increased the rate of egoistic and anomic suicide among this group because, as this group moves into the middle class, their situation is more stressful than that for comparable whites. African Americans are subjected to greater adjustment and assimilation problems because of the racism endemic in the society, and this may increase their alienation.

Davis noted that other explanations proposed have included the "weakness" of the black family, a history of authority problems with the police, retroflected anger and distorted psychosocial patterns. Davis (1981) called these explanations patronizing, which I think is an unfair judgment. If differences in these variables can be documented for African Americans and whites, then they are possible explanations for the differences in black and white suicide rates and for the differences in the personal and social meanings for suicides in African Americans and whites.

In order to account for the suicide rate of black females (which Davis [1980] claimed was higher than for white females, a claim which appears to be false [see Chapter 5]), Davis noted that black females experience more domestic and work stress than white females. The deficit of black men as suitable mates, in addition to the frequent desertion of black men from their mates and children increases the stress on black women even more. The shortage and absence of black males means that black youths often lack a good role model with which to identify, leading to psychological problems in adolescence. Davis (1978) termed these factors a "black family deficit theory."

Davis noted also that, while the black community has functioned in the past to provide support, cooperative effort and a sense of belonging, this role has weakened in recent year, particularly for black youths.

In a later article, Davis (1981) noted similar factors. For example he argued that the factors which promoted group solidarity, such as the stress of discrimination and racism, have weakened, especially for black youth, as they perceive greater opportunities in American society. This perception has increased their individualism and weakened the effect of communal and family ties (see also Seiden [1972]).

ROBINS: ELDERLY SUICIDE

Robins, et al. (1977) examined the usefulness of ten theories of suicide in order to explain why elderly white men had higher suicide rates than elderly black men:

1) differences in social integration, that is, the strength of social networks and relationships, in particular marital status and contacts with children and friends,
2) differences in the tendencies to express anger and violence outwardly,
3) differences in their acquaintanceship with others who had attempted or completed suicide,
4) differences in the importance of occupational roles so that retirement is less threatening to some,
5) differences in attitudes toward the elderly and old-age,
6) differences in feelings of lack of control in their own lives,
7) differences in self-blame over the failure to achieve and the perception of external obstacles to their achievement,
8) differences in religiosity,
9) differences in the use and abuse of alcohol, and
10) differences in depression.

To test these hypotheses, Robins interviewed samples of psychiatric patients and community residents, all men between the ages of 45 and 65. Among the psychiatric patients, similar proportions of African Americans and whites had thought about suicide, but more white men had attempted suicide.

Comparing the suicidal and nonsuicidal men, explanations 1 (integration), 3 (differential association), 5 (no role for the aged), 8 (secular norms), 9 (heavy drinking) and 10 (depression) received support. The suicidal patients were more socially isolated, knew more others who had been suicidal, felt no pride in aging and expected poor treatment from relatives as they grew older, approved more of suicide and were less likely to believe in an after-life, had less heavy alcohol use (the opposite of what was expected), and had been depressed or had a family history of depression.

These same six explanations worked equally well for suicidal versus nonsuicidal whites and suicidal versus nonsuicidal African Americans, except that the differential association explanation (number 3) did not apply to the African Americans in the sample.

Robins then turned to the community sample to see whether these six factors occurred more in elderly white men than in elderly black men. First, he showed that the patients of both ethnic groups were more socially isolated, and more depressed than the community sample. White patients also had more suicidal relatives than did the white community sample. Second he showed that white men in the community were slightly less socially integrated than the black men in the community (explanation 1), had more suicidal relatives (explanation 3), had more negative expectations about aging (explanation 5), had more secular attitudes (explanation 8), had less heavy drinking (explanation 9), and were more depressed (explanation 10).

Thus, six of the explanations proposed by Robins showed promise in explaining black and white differences in elderly male suicide.

OTHER THEORIES

Howze (1977) reviewed many theories of suicide in African Americans. She noted that many African Americans are moving into the middle class and have had their hopes and aspirations raised since the 1960s. Along with this, they are internalizing more responsibility for their failures, and so they are beginning to resemble the white majority more, a majority which has a higher suicide rate. On the other hand, studies in urban areas show that African American female suicides are typically unmarried, cut off from the church, and feeling lonely and isolated.

Poussaint (1975, 1977) pointed to several factors which might be relevant to black suicide: (1) the disruption of social relations, especially the absence of one or both parents, (2) assimilation into the white life style which is clearly more suicidogenic, (3) feelings of oppression from living in a society that does not permit African Americans, especially black youth, to realize their aspirations,[4] (4) a greater tolerance for deviant behavior among the black community which reduces the guilt and stigma for those who have behaved deviantly, and (5) a lower incidence of depression (especially severe depression) among African Americans.

Seiden (1974) attributed the greater increase in black youth suicide as compared to white youth suicide to the cultural conflict which black youths have to face. He attributed the increasing equality of black and white suicide rates in general to the acculturation of African Americans and their improved social, economic and educational status. He noted also that there had been a large migration this century of African Americans from the rural south to the urban centers of the north, that is, from regions with a low suicide rate to regions with a high suicide rate. Finally, Seiden attributed the peak in suicide rates among the youth in African Americans (as in Chicanos and Native Americans) to the history of racism common to all three ethnic groups.

Frederick (1984) noted several possible reasons for the relatively low black suicide rates: more tightly knit and supportive family groupings and community (the latter perhaps a result of the racism and discrimination to which they have been subjected), acceptance of lower socioeconomic status and therefore less frustration at this status, and inaccurate counting of black suicides. The increase in suicide rates among young black males in the 1970s, therefore, could be attributed to the breakdown of the black family, but this does not explain why the increase in suicide rates was not as great in young black females. The increase in the suicide rate of young black males may also have resulted from increased aspirations and expectations in those who do not yet have the skills to achieve in the mainstream society.

Frederick also noted the high rates of many forms of deviance among young black males, including addiction, criminal behavior, and violent death as well as suicidal behavior. Thus, the increasing rates of suicide among young black males may be part of a broader change, which would, therefore, require perhaps a different kind of explanation.

The role of alcohol and drug abuse is unclear. Some commentators see such substance abuse as increasing the risk of suicide since suicidal behavior

---

[4] Black youth have one of the highest unemployment rates in America.

is frequent in substance abusers. Others, however, see substance abuse and suicidal behavior as sharing a common set of causes and precipitating factors.

Spaights and Simpson (1986) noted that anger, low self-esteem, depression, an inability to express emotions, and difficulties in family structure were probably common to both black and white suicides. However, black suicides may be more likely to experience upward mobility in modern times. In addition, the cultural expectations for black males may differ from those for white males. For example, black males may be expected to suppress emotions more and to display stricter obedience to parents and elders than are white males.

Bush (1976, 1978) proposed three factors which might account for black suicidal behavior: extragroup pressures (primarily racism), intragroup pressures (including role expectations, language, and child rearing practices common in the black community), and values (a black perspective or "an interactive set of norms or...shared cultural standards," p. 219). Bush saw as suicidogenic those cases in which the black person's value orientation conflicted with that of his or her intragroup.

Smith and Carter (1986) reviewed the major theories of black suicide: culture-shock as African Americans move into the middle class, the family-deficit theory which focuses on problems in the typical African American family[5], and revolutionary suicide to bring about changes in the society (which Smith and Carter felt was rare among African Americans). They felt, however, that a broad sociocultural theory made sense, especially as an explanation of black youth suicide -- they noted the stress from minority status, economic deprivation and situational stressors. They suggested also that social progress, such as school desegregation, subjected black youth to more stress as they had to confront the stress of white classmates and white teachers.

Early (1992) focused on the role of the church in the low black suicide rate. He argued that the church constructed and reinforced a social meaning for suicide that acted as a counter to suicide, and that the black community, which is strongly involved in the church, shares this meaning. He went on to argue that the church view promulgated by the pastors is that suicide is sinful, opposes God's authority, and is unacceptable whatever the motive or stress. Suicide is a denial of black identity and culture -- indeed, it is a "white thing."

---

[5] including female-headed households, physical abuse of children, poverty and alienation, few black role models, erosion of respect for black institu tions such as the church, physical illnesses, absentee parents, psychiatric illness and the presence of firearms in the household.

There is some evidence for Early's hypothesis. First, a recent study by Taylor, et al. (1996) found that African Americans are more religious than whites -- they are more likely to attend church services, to pray and to say that religion is more important in their lives, even after controls for income, religious affiliation, and geographical distribution.

Second, Early himself surveyed African American church members and found that the majority agreed on the central role of the church for the black community and also that suicide was against God's will and a sin to be punished by being condemned to Hell. Early's conclusions would have been more forceful if he had conducted a similar survey of white church members.

Reviewing the factors in African Americans which increase the risk of suicide, Gibbs (1997) noted some factors which increase the risk of suicide in all ethnic groups: being male, age, substance abuse, depression, family dysfunction and conflict, interpersonal and marital conflict, acting-out and delinquency, psychiatric disorders, homosexuality and AIDS. Some of these factors may play more of a role in black suicide because they are more common in the black population, such as substance abuse and delinquency.

Gibbs also noted protective factors for suicide, such as religiosity, living in the South, and social support, factors which may be more common or stronger for African Americans. The majority of African Americans are affiliated with Protestant religions, such as the Baptists and the Methodists, and there is a history of moral condemnation of suicide in these churches. The churches also provide social support and social cohesion, and the involvement of black religious leaders in the civil rights movement has helped inspire African Americans with hope.

Gibbs noted that black women have a history of providing strong support to their children, their families and their community, and these experiences may have helped them develop effective strategies for warding off depression and suicidal ideation. The extended families and kin networks of African Americans appear to be stronger than those for whites, and this may offer protection against the risk of suicide. The ethnic neighborhoods, though often quite poor, are more cohesive than the neighborhoods of whites, and this may increase the level of social integration and social support for African Americans.

African American elderly appear to play a more important role in the community than elderly whites. They are less likely to be in nursing homes and more likely to be living independently in the community or with their families. Gibbs attributed the rising suicide rate among black male youth to despair and hopelessness over the dwindling opportunities, especially resulting from the high levels of unemployment, and to their increasing involvement in gangs, drugs and violence.

Allen (1973) noted that many African Americans have migrated in recent years, especially from the South to other states. Consequently, we would expect suicide rates to be higher than expected since research seems to indicate that migrants have higher suicide rates than native-born.

Earls, et al. (1990) suggested that segregation may play a role in black suicide, especially since reports indicate that suicide may be especially common in urban areas of the Midwest and Northeast. Lester (1971) presented some results relevant to this possibility by examining the association between residential segregation and white and nonwhite suicide rates in cities in the United States in 1960. Within each of the nine major regions of the United States, he found a tendency for nonwhite suicide rates to be higher where residential segregation was less and for white suicide rates to be higher where residential segregation was greater.

THE GENDER DIFFERENCE

Gibbs and Hines (1989) attributed the rising black youth suicide rate to the breakdown in traditional family structure, the decreasing influence of the church and religion, the declining impact of middle-class African Americans as they move to the suburbs, the deterioration of inner city schools, and the weakening of social support systems provided by employment. However, Gibbs and Hines argued that these social changes would have a greater impact on black males than on black females.

They noted that research suggests that it is harder for black males to develop a positive self-concept and a healthy psychosocial identity, probably because black males experience more stress, have more negative experiences and receive less positive feedback from the environment. As for the family, Gibbs and Hines argued that the absence of fathers has a more detrimental impact on black males than on black females. Black parents also tend to provide more nurturance and emotional support for female children than for male children, to use physical punishment more for boys, and to abuse male children more than female children.

Black males also fare worse on measures of performance in the educational system. Black males also have higher rates of delinquency, substance use, AIDS and accidents, and more often experience criminal victimization. Black males seem to use community resources, such as health care, less often than black females, and employers are much less willing to hire black males than black females. Black females have better work skills and habits and are viewed more favorably by employers.

The result is that black males are disadvantaged, not only as compared to white males, but also as compared to black females.

THE AGE DISTRIBUTION OF BLACK SUICIDE

Seiden (1981), noting the decrease in suicide rates with age in African Americans (and also Native Americans), proposed several possible explanations for the low suicide rate in the black elderly.

(1) *Differential Life Expectancy*: Seiden noted that African Americans have lower life expectancies than whites; perhaps only the strongest survive into old age and so they are less likely to be suicidal. This particular explanation was supported by Markides and Machalek (1984) who noted that, after the age of 75, African Americans have a longer life expectancy than whites -- that is, they appear to be more physically healthy and, therefore, possibly "stronger" in a broader sense.

(2) *Deviant Burnout*: Studies on some forms of deviance, such as drug and alcohol abuse and criminal behavior, indicate that the behavior decreases in frequency with age. Seiden suggested that suicidal behavior precipitated by aggression turned inward upon the self might also become less common with age. For this to apply to black suicide, then the causes of black suicide would have to be quite different from those for white suicides for, if not, then both ethnic groups would have the same age distribution for suicide rates.

(3) *Screening Out The Violence Prone*: Seiden noted that, at the time of writing, both suicide and homicide rates were very high for young African Americans. Therefore, these causes of death might remove African Americans from the population who might, in old age, commit suicide.

(4) *Role And Status Of The Elderly*: Seiden suggested that some ethnic cultures may hold their elderly in higher status and assign them important roles in the community. Some ethnic groups may be more disposed to keep the elderly living at home in multi-generational families. This may be more true for the African American culture than for the white culture.

(5) *Traditional Values*: Related to this, Seiden suggested that some cultures place more value on age and the elderly, especially cultures that are less urbanized and less industrialized. This would mean that the age distribution of black suicide rates would be clearer in rural areas than in urban areas in America. Seiden also suggested that black cultural attitudes are quite negative toward suicide -- indeed, the black community shows pride in overcoming adversities.

(6) *Age-Specific Motives*: Since the motives for suicide change with age, it may be that the motives for elderly suicide are less common in the black community than in the white community. For example, elderly African Americans are less likely to show downward social mobility in old age since they are less likely to be members of the higher social classes. Perhaps also, the stress from racial discrimination is less for elderly African Americans than for younger black adults.

These suggestions made by Seiden are useful and could have stimulated much research. Unfortunately, it is impossible to locate research which has sought to test the validity of any of his hypotheses.

THEORETICAL PROBLEMS

There are grave theoretical problems in trying to account for black suicide. An attempt by Gibbs (1988) to account for black youth suicide rates illustrates these problems. Gibbs described three approaches to explaining black suicide: sociological, psychological and ecological. In the sociological approach, Gibbs used Durkheim's (1897) theory of suicide and cast black suicide as partly egoistic in nature[6] (as a result of decreased social integration) and partly fatalistic (as a result of overly strong social regulation). Gibbs felt

---

[6] Actually Gibbs used the term "anomic" but defined it as involving decreased social integration. Decreased social integration leads to egoistic suicide, not anomic suicide.

that this conceptualization would predict high suicides rates for elderly African Americans, especially those who have migrated from the South to the northern states. Yet this is not the case. Black suicide rates are lower than white suicides in general, and black male youth suicide rates are higher than those of other black groups; the concepts of social integration and social regulation seem inadequate to explain all of these phenomena.

Psychological theories of suicide derive primarily from the psychoanalytic notion that suicide is a result of repressed anger turned inward onto the self, anger that is felt toward a lost love object (Litman, 1967). Yet African Americans, especially young black males, seem to have less of a problem in expressing anger outwardly than whites, older black males and black females.

Gibbs noted that the ecological approach, exemplified by Holinger's (1987) research on the effect of cohort size on opportunities and frustrated behavior (see Chapter 11), would seem to apply better to black youth than to white youth, but Holinger found that his results were clearer for white youth than for nonwhite youth.[7] The ecological approach also focuses on such factors as urban stress, including high rates of unemployment, dysfunctional families, police brutality, racism and chaotic environments (see also Seiden [1970]). Gibbs noted that these conditions are similar for black females as well as black males and, furthermore, black youth suicide rates peaked in 1967, two years after the passage of major civil rights legislation and the occurrence of urban riots. Gibbs suggested that "relative deprivation" might be a more important explanatory factor than absolute deprivation, that is, the discrepancy between rising aspirations and economic opportunities, but this factor is rather subjective and much harder to operationalize for the purposes of research.

To explain the rising suicide rate in African Americans in recent years, Gibbs noted the breakdown of traditional support networks, including the family, the church, fraternal and social organizations, community schools, extended kin and social support networks. Urbanization, racial integration, and social and economic changes have weakened all of these support networks after African Americans began to migrate in large numbers from the South in the 1930s and 1940s. Black families are increasingly headed by females, the church has less influence especially with young black males, fraternal organizations have declined as middle-class African Americans migrated from

---

[7] Holinger studied nonwhite youth in general and did not isolate the effects for black youth.

the cities to the suburbs, inner-city schools have deteriorated, and unemployment and welfare have weakened social support systems by decreasing the dignity, initiative and aspirations of urban African Americans. Again, Gibbs suggested that the discrepancy between aspirations and opportunities may account for the recent increases in black suicide rates.

Gibbs felt the explanatory value of this factor was weakened by the fact that black female suicide rates, though rising, have not risen as fast as those of black males. She noted that black males are more often involved in deviant and self-destructive behavior than are black females, such as school problems, criminal behavior, murder and accidental deaths, and drug use. Black males have higher rates of employment than black females, and black males may also be treated more harshly by their parents than are black females. As a result they may mature with lower self-esteem and self-confidence than their sisters.

However, perhaps the gender difference in black suicide rates should be treated simply as the same phenomenon that is found in white suicide rates, and thus a result of more general physiological, sociocultural and psychological factors which differentiate women and men (Canetto and Lester, 1995).

Thus, Gibbs highlights the problem -- how can one theory explain low black suicide rates relative to white suicide rates, rising black suicide rates in recent years, high black male suicide rates relative to black female suicide rates, and high black male youth suicide rates relative to older black male suicide rates. No single theory may be able to explain all of these phenomena.

PRISON SUICIDE

It has been generally agreed upon that black suicidal behavior, both fatal and nonfatal, is less common in prison as compared to white and Hispanic suicidal behavior (Anson, and Cole, 1984; Haycock, 1989; Johnson, 1976; Lester and Danto, 1993), similar to the differentials found in the general community. Toch (1975) saw self-injurious behavior as a response to the stress of being in prison, but it a response that is not goal-oriented. It is deviant from inmate norms and a sign of crisis. Toch implied, therefore, that prison is less stressful for African Americans than for whites and Hispanics.

Johnson (1976) suggested that this might be so because prison life has norms similar to the survival norms of the black ghetto.

Haycock (1989) argued that the conclusions of both Toch and Johnson were wrong. First, he suggested that self-injury may be a purposeful and goal-oriented act. For example, self-injury is a form of communication with institutional and governmental authority -- a means of protest, grievance or appeal, much as hunger strikes are. Haycock supported this suggestion by documenting how inmates educate one another on methods for self-mutilation, such as how to cut wrists with pieces of plastic or paint chips.

Haycock noted also that there may be many ways of responding to crises, and the relative frequency of one single mode of response may not be valid as a measure of the level of stress. Furthermore, since African Americans have lower suicide rates in general, the lower rate of suicidal behavior in prisons may simply be a reflection of this ethnic difference. Haycock also suggested that the overwhelming preponderance of white correctional officers may lead to under-reporting of black suicidal behavior.

The importance of this debate between Haycock on the one hand and Toch and Johnson on the other is that they have proposed different intervention and prevention approaches for black and white inmates. Johnson has suggested that the use of black peers may be more beneficial for helping black inmates in crisis, and that peer support may be less useful for white inmates. Correctional staff may be better able to provide intervention for white inmates in crisis. Johnson also suggested that white inmates may benefit more from counseling, especially counseling that fosters self-insight, and from educational programs about the ways of prison life. Haycock views these recommendations as misguided and urges the hiring of more black correctional staff and a more sympathetic and understanding approach to the relief of stress among black inmates.

CONCLUSIONS

There are many difficulties in efforts to explain black suicide rates. First, it is difficult to explain both the low rate of black suicide *and* the rising suicide of African Americans in the 1970s. The low rate of black suicide means that we must find explanatory variables which put African Americans at an *advantage* over whites. However, times of rising black suicide rates, especially when these increases are greater than for whites, means that we have to find explanatory variables which place African Americans at a *disadvantage* over whites. It is difficult to accomplish both tasks with the same theory.

Second, even if some variable which differentiates African Americans from whites is proposed, not only do we have to document that it truly differs in the black and white communities, we also have to show that the difference is associated with the difference in suicidal behavior.

Gibbs (1988) also pointed out the diversity of suicidal behavior which any theory, or set of theories, has to explain. She presented two cases.

(1) Karen had graduated from an Ivy League school and could not decide whether to go to graduate school or look for a job. She broke up with her boyfriend, withdrew from her friends and quarreled with her parents. Along with her self-doubts, she had ambivalent attitudes toward whites. After an argument with her father, she died in a single car-crash when she hit a bridge abutment.

(2) Robert had been abused and abandoned by his alcoholic mother at the age of three. Reared in foster homes, he became involved in delinquent acts, was failing in school and was a loner. At age 16, his foster parents could no longer tolerate his aggressive behavior, and he was moved to a group home. After attacking one of the counselors, he was sent to the juvenile hall where he hung himself in his room.

The fact that both of these individuals are African Americans may lead us to group them together in order to explain their deaths, but to do so is perhaps foolish. Karen and Robert are as different as any two American individuals, and their common ethnic identity is perhaps only of minor relevance to their self-destructive acts.

REFERENCES

Allen, N. H. *Suicide in California 1960-1970.* Sacramento, CA: Department of Public Health, 1973.

Anson, R. H., & Cole, J. N. Inmate suicide. *Justice Quarterly,* 1984, 1, 563-567.

Bagley, C., & Greer, S. Black suicide. *Journal of Social Psychology,* 1972, 86, 175-179.

Breed, W. The Negro and fatalistic suicide. *Pacific Sociological Review,* 1970, 13, 156-162.

Bush, J. A. Suicide and blacks. *Suicide & Life-Threatening Behavior,* 1976, 6, 216-222.

Bush, J. A. Similarities and differences in precipitating events between black and Anglo suicide attempts. *Suicide & Life-Threatening Behavior,* 1978, 8, 243-249.

Canetto, S. S., & Lester, D. The epidemiology of women's suicidal behavior. In S. S. Canetto & D. Lester (Eds.) *Women and suicidal behavior,* pp. 35-57. New York: Springer, 1995.

Davis, R. *Black suicide in the seventies.* Institute for Research on Poverty, University of Wisconsin, Madison, WI, 1978.

Davis, R. Suicide among young blacks. *Phylon,* 1980, 41, 223-229.

Davis, R. Black suicide and support systems. *Western Journal of Black Studies,* 1981, 5, 219-223.

Durkheim, E. *Le suicide.* Paris: Felix Alcan, 1897.

Earls, F., Escobar, J., & Manson, S. M. Suicide in minority groups. In S. J. Blumenthal & D. J. Kupfer (Eds.) *Suicide over the life cycle,* pp. 571-598. Washington, DC: American Psychiatric Press, 1990.

Early, K. E. *Religion and suicide in the African-American community.* Westport, CT: Greenwood, 1992.

Frederick, C. J. Suicide in young minority group persons. In H. S. Sudak, A. B. Ford & N. B. Rushforth (Eds.) *Suicide in the young,* pp. 31-44. Littleton, MA: PSG, 1984.

Gibbs, J. T. Conceptual, methodological, and sociocultural issues in black youth suicide. *Suicide & Life-Threatening Behavior,* 1988, 18, 73-89.

Gibbs, J. T. Mental health issues of black adolescents. In A. R. Stiffman & L. E. Davis (Eds.) *Ethnic issues in adolescent mental health*, pp. 21-52. Newbury Park, CA: Sage, 1990.

Gibbs, T. J. African-American suicide. *Suicide & Life-Threatening Behavior*, 1997, 27, 68-79.

Gibbs, J. T., & Hines, A. M. Factors related to sex differences in suicidal behavior among black youth. *Journal of Adolescent Research*, 1989, 4, 152-172.

Haycock, J. Race and suicide in jails and prisons. *Journal of the National Medical Association*, 1989, 81, 405-411.

Hendin, H. *Black suicide*. New York: Basic Books, 1969.

Hendin, H. Suicide. *Suicide & Life-Threatening Behavior*, 1978, 8, 99-117.

Holinger, P. C. *Violent deaths in the United States*. New York: Guilford, 1987.

Holmes, C. E. An ethnographic look at black upward mobility as it relates to internalization versus externalization factors in the increase in black suicide. *Dissertation Abstracts International*, 1977, 38B, 902.

Howze, B. Suicide. *Journal of Non-White Concerns*, 1977, 5, 65-72.

Johnson, R. *Culture and crisis in confinement*. Lexington, MA: D. C. Heath, 1976.

Kirk, A. R. A stress component in black males. *Urban Health*, 1977, 6, 38-40.

Lester, D. Residential segregation and completed suicide. *Crisis Intervention*, 1971, 3, 7-9.

Lester, D., & Danto, B. L. *Suicide behind bars*. Philadelphia: Charles Press, 1993.

Litman, R. E. Sigmund Freud on suicide. In E. S. Shneidman (Ed.) *Essays in self-destruction*, pp. 324-344. New York: Science House, 1967.

Markides, K. S., & Machalek, R. Selective survival, aging and society. *Archives of Gerontology & Geriatrics*, 1984, 3, 207-222.

Poussaint, A. Black suicide. In R. A. Williams (Ed.) *Textbook of black-related diseases*, pp. 707-714. New York: McGraw-Hill, 1975.

Poussaint, A. Rising suicide rates among blacks. *Urban League Review*, 1977, 3(1), 22-30.

Prudhomme, C. The problem of suicide in the American negro. *Psychoanalytic Review*, 1938, 25, 187-204, 372-391.

Robins, L. N., West, P. A., & Murphy, G. E. The high rate of suicide in older white men. *Social Psychiatry*, 1977, 12, 1-20.

Seiden, R. H. We're driving young blacks to suicide. *Psychology Today*, 1970, 4(3), 24-28.

Seiden, R. H. Why are suicides of young blacks increasing? *HSMHA Health Reports*, 1972, 87, 3-8.

Seiden, R. H. Current developments in minority group suicidology. *Journal of Black Health Perspectives*, 1974, 1, 29-42.

Seiden, R. H. Mellowing with age. *International Journal of Aging & Human Development*, 1981, 13, 265-284.

Slater, J. Suicide. *Ebony*, 1973, 28(11), 152-160.

Smith, J. A., & Carter, J. H. Suicide and black adolescents. *Journal of the National Medical Association*, 1986, 78, 1061-1064.

Spaights, E., & Simpson, G. Some unique causes of black suicide. *Psychology*, 1986, 23(1), 1-5.

Swanson, W. C., & Breed, W. Black suicide in New Orleans. In E. S. Shneidman (Ed.) *Suicidology*, pp. 99-128. New York: Grune & Stratton, 1976.

Taylor, R. J., Chatters, L. M., Jayakody, R., & Levin, J. S. Black and white differences in religious participation. *Journal for the Scientific Study of Religion*, 1996, 35, 403-410.

Toch, H. *Men in crisis*. Chicago: Aldine, 1975.

Woodford, J. N. Why Negro suicides are increasing. *Ebony*, 1965, 20(9), 89-100.

Wyche, K. F., & Rotheram-Borus, M. J. Suicidal behavior among minority youth in the United States. In A. R. Stiffman & L. E. Davis (Eds.) *Ethnic issues in adolescent mental health*, pp. 323-338. Newbury Park, CA: Sage, 1990.

CHAPTER 10

FRUSTRATION, AGGRESSION AND THE OPPRESSED

Henry and Short (1954) presented a theory of suicide that was based the frustration-aggression hypothesis developed by Dollard et al. (1939). They began by examining the relationships between the business cycle and suicide and homicide rates.

In order to explain the relationship between the business cycle and suicide and homicide rates, they made two predictions: (a) Suicide rates will rise during times of business depression and fall during times of business prosperity, while crimes of violence against people will rise during business prosperity and fall during business depression; and (b) the correlation between suicide rates and the business cycle will be higher for high status groups than for low status groups, while the correlation between homicide rates and the business cycle will be higher for low status groups than for high status groups. Henry and Short considered that their predictions had been confirmed by the data.

The data presented, however, did not in fact support their predictions. The only status category with data available for both suicide and homicide rates was that of race (white versus black). The correlations between suicide and homicide rates and the business cycle in the United States for whites were -0.81 and -0.51 respectively, and for African Americans -0.38 and +0.49 respectively (Henry and Short, 1954, pp. 29, 49).

The second prediction (point b above) was confirmed. The negative correlation between suicide rates and the business cycle was greater for the high status group (whites) than it was for the low status group (African Americans), whereas the positive correlation between homicide rates and the business cycle was higher for the low status group than for the high status group. However, the first prediction (point a above) was not confirmed. The prediction of a positive correlation between homicide rates and the business cycle was not found for whites.

Henry and Short attempted to interpret their results in terms of the frustration-aggression hypothesis. Their assumptions were (a) aggression is often a consequence of frustration, (b) business cycles produce variations in the hierarchical rankings of persons by status, and (c) frustrations are generated by a failure to maintain a constant or rising position in the status hierarchy relative to the status position of other groups.

The interpretation of their results required two additional assumptions: (a) high status persons lose status relative to low status persons during business contraction while low status persons lose status relative to high status persons during business expansion, and (b) suicide occurs mainly in high status persons while homicide occurs mainly in low status persons. Thus, during business contractions in the United States, whites should lose status relative to African Americans, and so their suicide rate should increase. During business expansions, African Americans lose status relative to whites, and so their homicide rate should increase.[1]

Consider those who lose income during business contraction. The higher status person has more income to lose and his fall is greater than that of the low status person. The high status person loses status relative to the low status person. The low status person may actually experience a gain in status relative to the high status person. Thus in times of business contraction, high status people lose status relative to low status people and this generates frustration. The aggression consequent to this frustration in high status people is predominantly self-directed aggression, and so suicide rates rise in times of business contraction in high status people. This analysis explains why suicide

---

[1] The statistics presented by Henry and Short in the first part of their book were based on the suicide and homicide rates of societal subgroups, such as white versus black. However, Henry and Short extended their thesis by considering high and low class whites and high and low class African Americans. In so extending their analysis, they went beyond the bounds of their data. Thus their arguments become speculative and not grounded in empirical facts.

rates and the business cycle are negatively correlated in whites, a high status group.

If suicide occurs mainly in whites and in particular in high status whites, then why should the correlation between the business cycle and suicide rates be larger in whites than in African Americans? Henry and Short predicted this difference since whites are of higher status than African Americans and high class whites are of higher status than low class whites.

When all of their explanations are considered together, it becomes clear that Henry and Short assume that whites assess their relative status by comparing themselves to African Americans and vice versa; that high class whites assess their status relative to low class whites and vice versa; and that high class African Americans assess their status relative to low class African Americans and vice versa. The first of these assumptions is incompatible with the latter two. Do high class African Americans assess their status relative to low or high class whites or African Americans? Henry and Short assume, for example, that when a black is considered as a black, he assesses his status relative to whites, but that when he is considered as a high class black he assesses his status relative to low class African Americans. This makes less than good sense. A person's assessment of himself is independent of how we may choose to label him.

In conclusion, Henry and Short have to resort to changing the reference groups for particular groups of individuals in order to account for the particular associations that arise. There is no general rule possible to decide which reference group a particular societal subgroup will choose, whether it will be within racial groups or across racial groups for example. The system becomes, therefore, post hoc. The reference groups are deduced after the correlations between the suicide and homicide rates and the business cycle have been determined.

SOCIOLOGICAL AND PSYCHOLOGICAL DETERMINANTS OF THE CHOICE BETWEEN SUICIDE AND HOMICIDE

Henry and Short assumed that the basic and primary target of aggression is another person rather than the self. They then attempted to identify the sociological and psychological bases of the legitimization of other-oriented aggression. What enables the child to develop so that his primary response to frustration, that of other-oriented aggression, is seen as legitimate, while other children develop in such a way that this primary response is inhibited and self-directed aggression becomes legitimate?

Sociologically, the strength of external restraint was seen as the primary basis for the legitimization of other-oriented aggression. When behavior is required to conform rigidly to the demands and expectations of others, the share of others in the responsibility for the consequence of the behavior increases, thereby legitimizing other-oriented aggression. When external restraints are weak, the self must bear the responsibility for the frustration generated, and other-oriented aggression fails to be legitimized.

Henry and Short found two psychological correlates of other-oriented aggression in people, low superego strength which results in low guilt, and a specific type of cardiovascular reaction during stress similar to the effects of norepinephrine. They presented evidence to indicate that in the male child, these two factors are associated with the use of physical punishment as opposed to love-oriented punishment and punishment by the father rather than punishment by the mother.

Henry and Short then sought to show how experience of love-oriented punishment dealt out by the parent who is the source of nurturance and love leads to the development of tendencies to inhibit the primary other-oriented expression of aggression. The argument centers around the idea that when the source of nurturance and love also administers, the punishment, then the primary other-oriented expression of aggression threatens to end the flow of love and nurturance. If the child retaliates, he will receive no nurturance. Therefore, the child develops habits of inhibiting this primary other-oriented aggression.

Gold (1958) felt that Henry and Short's theory was useful for explaining differences in suicide rates between subgroups of the population. He used a ratio measure (the suicide rate divided by the suicide plus homicide rates) and found that females, military officers, whites and urban dwellers were relatively more suicidal than males, enlisted men, African Americans and rural dwellers respectively.

Explaining Black Suicide Rates
The Presence of External Restraint

It can be predicted from Henry and Short's theory that groups exposed to more external restraint would be more homicidal and less suicidal than groups exposed to less external restraint. Lester (1989a) showed that the suicide and homicide rates of whites and blacks in both the United States and South Africa fitted this prediction, since the blacks in both nations were oppressed and the whites the oppressors. The whites had higher suicide rates and the blacks higher homicide rates.

The Quality of Life and Personal Violence

Common sense suggests that, as we improve conditions in the world, people should be much happier. If we can eliminate poverty and oppression (such as sexism and racism), if we clean up the environment, and if we improve the educational and cultural offerings for our citizens, then we should be much happier. In contrast, as the quality of life declines, life should be less worth living.

In contrast, using Henry and Short's theory, it can be argued that when external conditions are bad, we have a clear source to blame for our own misery, and this makes us outwardly angry rather than inwardly angry or depressed. When times are good, there is no clear external source of blame for our misery, and so we are more likely to become inwardly angry or depressed and less likely to be outwardly angry. Henry and Short would argue that a higher quality of life would lead to higher rates of suicide and lower rates of homicide, whereas a lower quality of life would lead to lower rates of suicide and higher rates of homicide.

These contrasting ideas lead to opposite predictions, and Lester (1989b) has conducted a series of studies which support the prediction from Henry and Short's theory. In regions where the quality of life is higher, suicide rates are higher and homicide rates are lower. If the hypothesis holds in other

situations, then in a society in which there are two social groups differing in
the quality of life, as in whites and African Americans in the United States,
then the suicide rate should be higher in whites and the homicide rate higher
in African Americans. The suicide and homicide rates in the United States of
African Americans and whites clearly fit this prediction. African Americans
have a lower quality of life, lower suicide rates and higher homicide rates than
whites.

OTHER COMMENTATORS

Powell (1970) had views similar to those of Henry and Short. He
attributed the low suicide rate in African Americans to the fact that they live
with "clear and present complications.....(T)herefore the guilt of his hostility
can be externalized. The enemy is outside the ego....."(p. 46). In contrast,
whites are pursuing happiness which is never attained, making the present
existence painful, and have only themselves to blame for their failures. Powell
noted too that, as African American move into the middle classes, the pattern
of their suicidal behavior may come to resemble that of whites.

Maris (1969) felt that the high degree of external constraints on African
Americans was responsible for their low suicide rate, but he suggested that
their stronger involvement in social relationships also protected them from
suicide. Looking at the causes of individual suicides among African
Americans, Maris noted that psychiatric problems played a major role, while
physical illness played almost no role. Rather than the suicidal individuals
being social isolated, their suicides seemed to be precipitated by disruptions in
social relationships ("transient domestic crises" p. 107) and to be more
impulsive. However, Maris did not present numerical data on the black versus
white differences in motives for suicide.

Lalli and Turner (1968) used the categories of open and closed societies to
explain the ethnic differences in suicide rates. An open society is one where
the status is achieved rather than ascribed and where personal freedom is
emphasized. A closed society is a tribal or caste society, where ascriptive
status spells out people's rights and duties. Although American society may be
viewed as open, African Americans have been excluded from it, and instead
have constituted a closed society within the larger, open society.

Lalli and Turner suggested that suicide would be rare in closed societies and, when it does occur, be altruistic in nature. Suicides in open societies will be more frequent and egoistic in nature. Although homicide was expected to be rare also in closed societies, in those cases where the whole society is not closed, but rather a smaller subculture within the larger society, then Lalli and Turner predicted that homicide would be more common.

The only data presented by Lalli and Turner to support their theory were suicide rates by occupational status for whites and nonwhite males aged 20-64 in 1950. According to Lalli and Turner, whereas the suicide rates for whites varied greatly by occupational level -- from 21.5 in the highest level (I) to 35.5 in the lowest level (VI) -- the variation for nonwhites was much smaller -- from 8.9 in level IV to 14.1 in level VI. They claimed the social conditions leading to suicide did not differ much among the social strata for nonwhite males. However, I calculate the variation by occupational level to be larger in the nonwhites than in the whites, and I think that these data are, at the best, only tangentially related to Lalli and Turner's theory.

COMMENT

Black suicide rates are lower in the United States than white suicide rates, while black homicide rates are higher than white homicide rates. It is clear that Henry and Short's theory explains this difference, both using their concept of the strength of external restraints and using the prediction based on their theory relating the quality of life to rates of suicide and homicide.

There are two other phenomena for which Henry and Short's theory provides an explanation. First, the rising black suicide rates in recent years may be associated with an increasing standard of living, consistent with the prediction from Henry and Short's theory that suicide becomes more common when the quality of life improves. Second, the higher black suicide rates in states with a smaller proportion of African Americans may be a result of the higher standard of living of African Americans in those states (see Chapter 11).

These three phenomena, which are consistent with Henry and Short's theory, have not been explicitly tested with empirical data, and such tests are important before we place confidence in the explanations. It is particularly important in this regard to examine the relationship between the rate of suicide and social class (and the movement of individuals between social classes) in African Americans.

However, the phenomena of black suicide are more extensive than this simple overall ethnic difference. Henry and Short's theory may have limited applicability to explaining the age variation in black suicide rates or changing black suicide rates over time, and may need to be supplemented by other theories.

REFERENCES

Dollard, J., Doob, L., Miller, N., Mowrer, O., & Sears, R. *Frustration and aggression*. New Haven: Yale University Press, 1939.

Gold, M. Suicide, homicide, and the socialization of aggression. *American Journal of Sociology*, 1958, 36, 651-661.

Henry, A. F., & Short, J. F. *Suicide and homicide*. New York: Free Press, 1954.

Lalli, M., & Turner, S. H. Suicide and homicide. *Journal of Criminal Law, Criminology & Police Science*, 1968, 59, 191-200.

Lester, D. Personal violence (suicide and homicide) in South Africa. *Acta Psychiatrica Scandinavica*, 1989a, 79, 235-237.

Lester, D. *Suicide from a sociological perspective*. Springfield, IL: Charles Thomas, 1989b

Maris, R. W. *Social forces in urban suicide*. Homewood, IL: Dorsey, 1969.

Powell, E. H. *The design of discord*. New York: Oxford University Press, 1970.

CHAPTER 11

SOCIAL DEVIANCY AND AFRICAN AMERICAN SUICIDE

Wechsler and Pugh (1967) argued that the ready availability of a peer group facilitates the formation of interpersonal relationships. If an individual does not have a peer group, then he or she may experience a greater degree of stress and social isolation, a situation which may be more conducive to the development of psychiatric illness.

Pursuing this idea, they argued that people with particular personal characteristics who live in communities where that characteristic is less common should have higher rates of psychiatric illness and higher rates of psychiatric hospitalization.

They confirmed this hypothesis for various age groups, marital statuses, places of birth (in-state versus out-of-state) and occupational statuses. Thus, for example, old people living in communities with a high proportion of old people had lower rates of psychiatric hospitalization than old people living in communities where there were fewer older people.

This suggests a hypothesis which might account for the variation by state of black suicide rates. Black suicide rates might be higher in those states with a smaller proportion of black residents. Why might a deviant status increase the risk of suicide? The mediating variables may include lack of social contact with others in the community, a feeling of alienation and insecurity because one is surrounded by people from other ethnic or cultural groups, and frustrations generated by dealing with a possibly prejudiced and hostile majority group. Lester (1980, 1987) found that states with fewer nonwhites had higher suicide rates for nonwhites. Lester did not study black suicide rates in these two studies.

In order to explore this further, the association was explored for black suicide rates and the proportion of African Americans in the states. The National Center for Vital Statistics publishes an annual volume, *Vital Statistics of the United States*, which is the primary source of mortality statistics. Unfortunately, prior to 1979, this volume reported data by state only for nonwhites as a whole, and so data for African American suicides by state are not available prior to 1979. Lester (1994; see Chapter 6) calculated black suicide rates by state for the period 1979-1982, using four years of data in order to make the estimated rates more reliable. For the 48 contiguous continental states, the Pearson correlation between the black suicide rate in the states and the percentage of the population which was black was negative as predicted ($r = -0.28$, one-tailed $p = .026$). Thus, the greater the proportion of African Americans living in a state, the lower the black suicide rate.

This result was replicated in Chapter 6 of the present book for 1990, where we reported a correlation of -0.36 (two-tailed $p < .05$) between the black suicide rate and the proportion of African Americans in the states.

For the present book, the black suicide rates were calculated for black males and females separately for the period 1979 to 1982. The correlation with the proportion of African Americans in the state populations was negative for black male suicide rates ($r = -0.27$, $p < .05$) but not for black female suicide rates ($r = -0.02$). This may reflect a difference in the phenomenon for men and women or simply that the black female suicide rates were less reliable since they were based on so few suicides.

Lester (1988) looked at the personal characteristics of African Americans in states where there were few African Americans as compared to states where there were many African Americans. For example, the African Americans in Maine and Idaho were more educated, earned higher incomes and had more stable families and so were more similar to whites in these states than were the African Americans in Mississippi and South Carolina. Thus, the higher suicide rates of minorities in states where minorities are few may be a result of these social characteristics rather than their low representation in the states, in this case consistent with Henry and Short's theory (see Chapter 10).

THE RELATIVE COHORT SIZE HYPOTHESIS

The social deviancy theory is similar to the relative cohort size hypothesis. Easterlin (1980) studied the baby boomers, the generation of Americans born after the Second World War, and argued that their large cohort size would result in economic, social, educational and political changes. Larger birth cohorts, Easterlin argued, would create increased competition for existing limited resources and, as a result, the cohort would be and feel relatively deprived. Holinger (1987) hypothesized from this idea that, in years when the size of the cohort of Americans aged 15-24 was relatively larger, the cohort would have relatively higher rates of psychopathology, in particular suicidal behavior.

In a time series study of the United States from 1933 to 1975, Holinger and Offer (1982) found that the suicide rate of those aged 15 to 19 was positively correlated with the percentage of adolescents in the population. For those aged 65 to 69, the suicide rate of the group was negatively correlated with the percentage of older adults. Holinger, et al. (1987) found the positive correlation for 15 to 24 year-olds, a negative correlation for 35 to 44 year-olds and for 55 to 64 year-olds, and no significant correlation for 25 to 34 year-olds and 35 to 44 year-olds.

Thus, for adolescents, the larger the size of the age group in the society, the higher the suicide rate. The question here is whether this hypothesis applies to the suicide rates of black youth.

There are several ways of calculating the proportion of a cohort in the population (Leenaars and Lester, 1996): for example, the proportion of 15-24 year-olds relative to the total population or relative to the population aged 25-64. For the present analysis, several options are possible for the base population: the percentage of all 15-24 year-olds relative to the total population, the percentage of black 15-24 year-olds relative to the total black population, or the proportion of black male 15-24 year-olds relative to the total black male population. I chose the latter, that is, the proportion of black male 15-24 year olds relative to the total black male population. The results were calculated for the modern period, 1960-1991, for which government estimates of the black population are available (see Chapter 5) and for the total period for which data are available, 1933-1991.

The results are shown in Table 11.1. It can be seen that for black 15-24 year-olds of both genders and for both time periods the association of cohort size and suicide rate was positive. Thus, for this group, Holinger's hypothesis was confirmed.

Interestingly, positive associations were found for other age groups for some time periods -- for example, black males aged 75-84 and 85+ for 1960-1991. These results were not found by Holinger for whites, for whom these associations were negative. This difference is noteworthy and merits further study to see whether a large cohort in old age is not as advantageous for African Americans as it is for whites.

If some cohorts of black youth have high suicide rates as compared to others, it will be of interest to follow these cohorts over time to see whether their suicide rates remain high or whether they follow the trend in cross-sectional studies of black suicide rates to show a decrease with age. If the rates remain high, this may reflect some factor such as changed socialization experiences in the black family or changed social conditions for the black community (Earls, et al., 1990).

REFERENCES

Earls, F., Escobar, J., & Manson, S. M. Suicide in minority groups. In S. J. Blumenthal & D. J. Kupfer (Eds.) *Suicide over the life cycle*, pp. 571-598. Washington, DC: American Psychiatric Press, 1990.

Easterlin, R. A. *Birth and fortune*. New York: Basic Books, 1980.

Holinger, P. C. *Violent deaths in the United States*. New York: Guilford, 1987.

Holinger, P. C., & Offer, D. Prediction of adolescent suicide. *American Journal of Psychiatry*, 1982, 139, 302-307.

Holinger, P. C., Offer, D., & Ostrov, E. Suicide and homicide in the US. *American Journal of Psychiatry*, 1987, 144, 215-219.

Leenaars, A. A., & Lester, D. Testing the cohort size hypothesis of suicide and homicide rates in Canada and the United States. *Archives of Suicide Research*, 1996, 2, 43-54.

Lester, D. Regional suicide rates and the hazards of minority status. *American Journal of Psychiatry*, 1980, 137, 1469-1470.

Lester, D. Social deviancy and suicidal behavior. *Journal of Social Psychology*, 1987, 127, 339-340.

Lester, D. Demographic attributions related to black suicide. *Journal of Social Psychology*, 1988, 128, 407-409.

Wechsler, H., & Pugh, T. F. Fit of individual and community characteristics and rates of psychiatric hospitalization. *American Journal of Sociology*, 1967, 73, 331-338.

Table 11.1
Correlations between Cohort Size and Black Suicide Rates #

	1960-1991	1933-1991
males		
15-24	0.655***	0.671***
25-34	0.618***	0.112
35-44	0.105	-0.581***
45-54	-0.217	-0.609***
55-64	0.110	0.051
65-74	-0.040	0.444***
75-84	0.559***	0.553***
85+	0.555***	0.532***
females		
15-24	0.460**	0.584***
25-34	-0.469**	-0.346*
35-44	-0.592***	-0.759***
45-54	0.144	-0.343*
55-64	0.087	0.393**
65-74	0.267	0.409**
75-84	0.271	-0.140
85+	-0.170	-0.126

*   two-tailed $p < .05$
** two-tailed $p < .01$
*** two-tailed $p < .001$

For 1940, the census did not count African Americans by age for the age groups 75-84 and 85+. As a consequence, the estimates of the proportion of African Americans aged 75-84 and 85+ for men and women from 1930 to 1950 are less accurate than the estimates for younger age groups.

CHAPTER 12

NONFATAL SUICIDAL BEHAVIOR

The epidemiology of nonfatal suicidal behavior is less well documented than that of fatal suicidal behavior, and this is true for black suicidal behavior. As far as we can tell, the greater frequency of nonfatal suicidal behavior in women than in men, found in the United States in general, is found also for African Americans too (Alston and Anderson, 1995).

EPIDEMIOLOGICAL SURVEYS
YOUTH

Garrison, et al. (1993a, 1993b) surveyed high school students in South Carolina in 1990. The incidences of suicidal ideation and attempted suicide in the prior year were:

	ideation	attempts
white males	7.4%	4.6%
white females	14.6%	8.5%
black males	8.4%	2.3%
black females	12.1%	6.4%

The attempts of the black students were less serious than those of the white students, even after controls for other variables (such as aggressive behavior, drug use and sexual behavior).

In New York City junior high school students, Walter, et al. (1995) found that 12.0 percent of the black students had attempted suicide during their lifetime as compared to 14.0 percent of the Hispanic students.

Earls (1989) surveyed youths attending health clinics in ten cities in America. The incidence of suicidal ideation in the prior 12 months was higher in white females than in black females and in those aged 13-16 than in those aged 17-18. Too few males were in the sample and too few youths with a history of attempted suicide for those data to be reliable. However, Earls attributed the higher incidence in white females in part to the possibility that white adolescents in urban clinics may have been more likely to have left their families and so be at higher risk for psychological problems.

Reynolds (1992) surveyed high school students in the Midwest and found that black students had higher scores on a scale of suicidal ideation than did white students.

Rotheram-Borus (1993) found that 37 percent of a sample of runaway youths (primarily African and Hispanic Americans) had previously attempted suicide, with the incidence higher in females than in males. This percentage is much higher than in the general population.

In a sample of minority adolescents presenting at an emergency room after a suicide attempt, Summerville, et al. (1992) found only 21 percent to be not depressed: 38 percent were mildly depressed, 17 percent moderately depressed and 24 percent severely depressed.

Farrow and Schwartz (1992) noted that white suburban adolescents reported more suicidal ideation in association with drug and alcohol use than did black urban adolescents.

COLLEGE STUDENTS

In a survey of African American college at a predominantly black university, Molock, et al. (1994) found that 49 percent had thought about suicide during their lifetime, and eleven percent had attempted suicide.

ADULTS

Moscicki, et al. (1989) examined data from the five-site catchment area study and found a lifetime incidence of suicidal ideation of 11.3 percent in whites and 6.8 percent in African Americans and a lifetime incidence of attempted suicide of 3.0 percent in whites and 2.3 percent in African Americans.[1]

Swanson and Breed (1976) surveyed African Americans and whites in New Orleans and found that only 8 percent of the African Americans as compared to 23 percent of the whites had a history of suicidal ideation or attempts. African Americans were much less likely to view suicide as justifiable under any circumstances (24% versus 41%). Incidentally, the African Americans were more likely than whites to view religion as truth rather than myth, to participate in church activities, to pray often and to believe that everything has a divine purpose. Unfortunately, in their brief report of this study, Swanson and Breed did not report on the associations of the religious variables with the suicide variables for the two ethnic groups.

Wenz (1978-1979) compared African Americans and whites in four census tracts in Flint, Michigan, who were given a survey which included questions on whether they had thought about, threatened or attempted suicide in the past. Approximately similar percentages of African Americans and whites had thought about suicide (52% and 55% respectively) and threatened suicide (49% and 53% respectively). However, more of the African Americans had attempted suicide (44% versus 20%), a difference which is statistically significant, although Wenz did not carry out a statistical test himself. He found that these three items formed a reasonable Guttman scale for both African Americans and whites. Calculating a total suicidality score for each subject based on these three responses, Wenz found that the African Americans and whites did not differ overall in suicidality, but that those of both ethnic groups in the poorer census tracts had greater suicidality than those in the wealthier census tracts.

In a study of inner-city women in West Philadelphia, Grisso, et al. (1991) found that the rate of attempted suicide was highest in those aged 15 to 24

---

[1] These percentages were weighted to correct for differences between the samples.

(660 per 100,000 per year as compared to a rate of 50 for those 65 years of age and older).

MEDICAL AND PSYCHIATRIC PATIENTS

Cochran and Mays (1994) found that black homosexual men (but not black homosexual women) had more suicidal ideation if they were diagnosed as HIV positive than if they were HIV negative.

Frederick, et al. (1973) found that black hard-core heroin addicts in a methadone treatment program had made no more prior suicide attempts than black non-addicted men.

Raskin, et al. (1975) found that, among depressed psychiatric inpatients, black males had more often threatened and attempted suicide than white males, while the females showed little difference by ethnic group.

Horwath, et al. (1993) found no differences in prior suicide attempts between African Americans and whites who suffered from panic disorder. Browning, et al. (1970) found no differences in suicidal ideation or suicide attempts by black and white psychiatric emergency patients.

Collins, et al. (1992) found that white patients referred for psychiatric consultation were more often suicidal than black patients. However, Frierson and Lippman (1990b) found no differences between African Americans and whites with suicidally self-inflicted gunshot wounds in the proportion referred for psychiatric consultation.

STUDIES OF ATTEMPTED SUICIDES

Pedersen, et al. (1973) calculated attempted suicide rates for Rochester (NY) for 1964-1967. The crude rates were

white males	29.9
white female	74.3
nonwhite males	48.8
nonwhite females	266.1

The peak ages for all four race-by-gender groups was 15-24, and all groups had a greater proportion of people from the lower social classes than the general population. The nonwhite attempters were younger than the white attempters, had a greater proportion of females, had more separated, divorced and widowed females and more single males, were less often judged to have a psychiatric disorder and received less psychiatric care prior to and after the attempt.

Alston and Anderson (1995) noted also that African American women may also have a high incidence of covert nonfatal self-destructive behavior, such as contracting HIV infections, partly because of the disapproval of overt suicidal behavior in the African American community, and in particular the church. Alston and Anderson felt that nonfatal suicidal behavior was especially common in black women because they are particularly disadvantaged in the occupational field as regards earnings, occupational status and job mobility, and in addition have to face racism. African American women remain concentrated in low-paying and low-status jobs, and they are eight times more likely to live in poverty than women from other ethnic groups. African American women are also more likely to be unemployed, particularly for long periods of time, the so-called "discouraged" workers.

Alston and Anderson suggested that inadequate support systems may contribute to the suicidality of African American women. Primary support systems, that is, family friends and religious institutions, may be failing African American women, and the African American church may have been especially inadequate in providing support. Alston and Anderson also noted that the welfare system for African American women is inadequate and perpetuates feelings of powerlessness and hopelessness.

Alston and Anderson presented the case of a 42 year-old African American women who was raised by her mother in a major city. She never knew her father but was attached to her mother's boyfriend. Her mother worked but also obtained support from AFDC. She learned early to fear the "welfare lady" who could stop the support if the family violated the rules, and she also learned to fear the police, all white males, and anyone who asked questions about the family. Her childhood was happy, but in high school she dated a man who drank heavily and introduced her to alcohol.

She first attempted suicide by overdosing when her mother was about to move to another state. Her mother allowed her to remain behind with friends, but she got pregnant as a junior in high school and dropped out. The baby was born dead and the father abandoned her, whereupon she cut her wrists. She moved in with an older man and began to use drugs. She attempted suicide for the third time (with drugs and alcohol) three years later when she was told by a physician that she was unable to have children. After this attempt, she was given inpatient psychiatric care for drug abuse and depression.

She continued to use drugs, but in sufficient moderation that she held a steady job. By age 40, she was again involved with a drug addict who physically abused her. After two years of abuse, she again attempted suicide with drugs and alcohol and was admitted for psychiatric care.

This women was limited educationally and occupationally, and she seems to have learned to use suicidal behavior as a means of communicating distress to others. With little expectation of changing her life situation, she used drugs and alcohol to cope. She had few support systems other than her current male friend, but these partners tended to come from the same social situation and, in particular, to also use drugs and alcohol.

Howze (1977) described the characteristics of thirteen black women who had attempted suicide, ranging in age from 18 to 34. There was no typical family background for the group, some growing up with parents and others in foster homes. However, all experienced frustration in childhood and adolescence. Their needs to be loved and cared for were not met; instead they were thwarted and rejected. None could recall close trusting relationships with others in childhood. Thus, they developed an inability to form these kinds of relationships themselves, and they developed feelings of low self-worth.

The women felt rage and hostility, probably directed toward their caretakers in childhood, but later displaced onto others and toward the world in general. They perceived the world as untrustworthy and ungiving, and they ended up isolated and estranged from their family members and friends. In additional to the emotional neglect of childhood, the women were also physically abused, reinforcing their feelings of worthlessness and leading to feelings of guilt. They often felt rage toward their own children and relatives, and they responded to these feelings with further guilt and a need to punish themselves, until death seemed to be the only way out.

The women had strong dependency needs, coupled with an intense fear of abandonment, a history of angry acting-out, and conflicts about developing close relationships. If their relationships were disrupted or were threatened with disruption (by, for example, a hint of unfaithfulness or loss of a job), they reacted strongly, often with suicidal behavior.

Christian (1977) speculated that black attempted suicides typically act impulsively in crisis situations. They are less likely to be chronically suicidal and may merely want to alert others to their distress. However, she did not present data to support this speculation.

Summerville, et al. (1994) studied a sample of adolescent black suicide attempters and found that two-thirds rated their families as moderately or severely dysfunctional, especially as regards to family cohesion. However, apart from finding that the highly depressed attempters differed from the non-depressed attempters, this study provided little useful information.

Molock, et al. (1994) found that college students who reported having attempted suicide at some point in their lives typically spent less than three hours considering their plan before attempting. The majority did not tell anyone about their attempt. The major reasons for suicidal ideation or attempts were school problems, family problems and relationship problems.

Baker (1984, 1988) examined black suicide attempters from New Haven (CT) and found that the modal attempter was aged 16-29, single, with a prior psychiatric history, and used a drug overdose. Forty-eight percent had made a prior attempt.

HENDIN'S WORK

Hendin's (1969a, 1969b) study of 25 black attempted suicides deserve mention (see Chapter 9). His conclusions are based on clinical judgment about the attempters, but he did not study a comparable group of nonsuicidal African Americans. Thus, his conclusions are unjustified, even though they are provocative.

Based on his cases, Hendin concluded that the attempters, both male and female, were typically assaultive and homicidal as well as suicidal. This combination of anger and suicide did not fit well with standard psychoanalytic assumptions about suicide which propose that suicide (and depression) result from suppressed and repressed anger.

Hendin also noted extreme neglect and abuse in the childhoods of these attempters, primarily from the mothers since the fathers had abandoned the families early on. The rage felt toward the mothers generalized later in life to substitute figures. Their childhood experiences destroyed their capacity for love and friendship as adults. Hendin also noted extreme self-hatred in these attempters which generalized to a hatred of African Americans in general. The homosexuals in his sample, for example, typically sought white male sexual partners.

In contrast, the few older African Americans in his sample had been obedient and submissive members of the society and became suicidal when their adaptation failed, typically through their own misbehavior. (One man attempted suicide after sexually molesting a nine-year-old girl whose mother he had once dated.)

Goldberg and Hodes (1992) proposed some psychoanalytic speculations that are congruent with Hendin's ideas. In looking at cases of nonfatal suicidal behavior in adolescents in Great Britain among immigrants (not all of whom were of African descent), they noted that the individual, the family and the social group are isomorphic and can stand for one another. Minorities are "denigrated and dehumanized by racism" (Goldberg and Hodes, 1992, p. 61), and this often leads to depression, low self-esteem and feelings of worthlessness. If the dominant social group labels a minority group as vile or non-human, then members of the minority group may act out this view by poisoning themselves in a nonfatal suicidal act. This seems to stem from an identification of the minority members with the aggressors. Suicidal acts can also be viewed as attempts to take control in situations where control and power are lacking.

MALE SUICIDE ATTEMPTERS

Kirk and Zucker (1979) compared a sample of black men who had attempted suicide in Detroit with a control group of black men from the same neighborhoods. The two groups were similar in age, marital status, occupational status, religious background and level of education.

The attempters had lower scores on a test of black consciousness, higher anomie scores (but no different alienation scores), higher depression scores on the MMPI, but no difference in scores for depression and hostility on the Multiple Affect Adjective Check List or in group cohesiveness. Thus, the attempters were more anomic and lacked a positive black identity.

Salter (1978) compared eight black attempted suicides with nonsuicidal controls (matched for age, education, marital status and psychiatric diagnosis). The attempters were less self-confident, had worse personal adjustment and felt less autonomy. They did not differ in self-control, affiliation, intropunitiveness or impunitiveness. Salter judged that the attempters had greater difficulty coping with life's everyday hassles and had an inadequate coping style.

MALE VERSUS FEMALE BLACK ATTEMPTERS

Frierson and Lippman (1990a) compared large samples of black men and women who had attempted suicide in Louisville. The two groups did not differ in age or marital status. Both chose solid and liquid substances most often for suicide (88% of the women and 57% of the men), followed by firearms (primarily by a shot to the abdomen). Men chose stabbing and carbon monoxide more often, while women chose jumping and burning more often. The men were more often diagnosed with schizophrenia and alcohol abuse while the women were more often diagnosed with a major depression. The groups did not differ in prior attempts or past psychiatric history. Both groups were most often motivated by difficulties with a relationship or marriage, whereas white attempters in the community were more often motivated by job and money problems. The numbers of black attempters appeared to have increased in recent years.

Molock, et al. (1994), in a study of college students who reported having considered or attempted suicide during their lives, found a higher incidence of both ideation and attempts in women, and the women used less lethal methods for the attempt.

Baker (1984) found that black female attempters were younger than the male attempters, less often diagnosed as schizophrenic and more often diagnosed as having an affective disorder or adjustment reaction. The genders did not differ in prior psychiatric history, prior suicide attempts, use of alcohol before the attempt, family history of psychiatric illness or the method used. The females were accompanied more often by family members to the emergency room.

Baker summarized the profiles as follows. The female attempters were single, stressed after an argument with a significant other, impulsive, and with a history of family discord and difficulty in relationships. The men were single, in on-going psychiatric treatment, and attempted suicide during an episode of psychotic decompensation (schizophrenic or manic).

BLACK VERSUS WHITE ATTEMPTED SUICIDES

Tuckman and Youngman (1963) looked at attempted suicides in Philadelphia from 1959-1961 and noted that women, nonwhites and the young were over-represented as compared to the general population of Philadelphia (30 percent of the suicide attempters were nonwhite versus only 24 percent in the general population).

Lester and Beck (1975) compared the African Americans and whites who had attempted suicide in their sample and found some differences. Out of 54 characteristics, black and white male attempters differed on only five: the black males were more likely to be Protestant, less likely to be living with others, had more often been separated from their fathers, obtained lower scores on a vocabulary test, and if schizophrenic were more likely to be diagnosed as paranoid.

The black and white female attempters differed on twelve characteristics: the black females had not completed as much education, had more unofficial marital arrangements (such as cohabitation and separation), had worse physical health, used alcohol more, had made fewer previous suicide attempts, were more often Protestant, lived more often in low rent districts, had experienced more separation from their fathers, and if separated from their mother had experienced this at an earlier age. They had poorer vocabulary scores and lower suicidal intent scores. If diagnosed as schizophrenic, they were more likely to be paranoid.

The black male and female attempters differed on five characteristics: the black females were more often living with others, more often unemployed, more likely to attempt suicide at home, more likely to attempt suicide later in the year, and less psychiatrically disturbed.

Lester and Beck noted that some of black versus white differences seemed to reflect general differences in the life situation of black and whites in general, such as the differences in religious affiliation and absent fathers. The precipitants and circumstances of the suicidal acts were similar in both ethnic groups. In particular the groups did not differ in self-reported depression scores (including the item on self-hate), hopelessness, post-attempt suicidal ideation, or the medical lethality of the attempt.

Bush (1978) compared black and white suicidal patients whom he saw in psychotherapy. He noted that, for most of the African Americans, recent or threatened loss of a spouse or lover was the most common precipitant of the suicidal behavior, whereas this was rare in the whites. For the whites, there was more often a chronic history of poor interpersonal and work functioning and daily problem-solving. The majority of the African Americans were closely involved with their families, whereas this was rare in the whites. Thus, the contexts in which African Americans and whites turned to thoughts of suicide and attempted suicide were very different.

In a hospital in the Bronx, Berne (1983) found that female attempters outnumbered males by a factor of 2.62 for African Americans but only 1.02 for whites. There were more attempters under the age of 21 among the black attempters than among the white attempters (26% versus 3%). However, Berne did not give details of the composition of the population served by the hospital so that we can determine whether these figures deviate from the population percentages.

Hickman (1984) compared black and white suicide attempters seen at a psychiatric emergency service. The African Americans had a higher proportion of women (75% versus 67%). The modal age was 16-20 for black females, white males, and white females, but the modal age for black males was 21-25. The black attempters were more often single or separated and less often married or divorced. The black attempters used drug overdoses more and cutting less; they also attempted suicide more often in response to girl/boyfriend problems and less often as a result of marital problems and with manipulative intent. The two groups did not differ in psychiatric diagnosis (with a depressive reaction most common in both groups), time of day, or disposition. However, the whites appear to have visited the service more under their own initiative, which is in line with the common assertion that African Americans are more often suspicious of community services.

Alessi, et al. (1984) found that white incarcerated juvenile delinquents had attempted suicide more often in the prior year than black delinquents. Kempton and Forehand (1992) found that same difference for lifetime suicide attempts. Furthermore, whereas the number of depressive symptoms predicted a history of attempted suicide for the white delinquents, it did not for the black delinquents.

Kiev and Anumonye (1976) compared black suicide attempters in Newark (NJ) with white middle class attempters in New York City. They claimed that the black attempters were more often male, were more disoriented, had abused drugs and alcohol more often, showed more distrust of the hospital personnel, and were more ignorant of the medical care system. The black attempters more often denied that they had problems and gave situational explanations for the self-destructive acts. The two groups were similar in their psychiatric symptoms, impulsivity, and the circumstances of the suicidal act. However, this report is very poor -- it fails to describe the samples, provides no tables of data and reports no statistical tests of significance on the data.

Steele (1977) compared black and white attempters in New Haven. On 42 variables, the two groups were similar on 32, and so Steele concluded that similarities outweighed the differences. In particular, the groups did not differ in suicidal intent, the risk to life from the attempt, or the presence of a thought disorder or delusions. The black attempters had less specific plans for their suicidal act, had less manipulative intent, and showed less depression, guilt or self-punishment, hopelessness and anxiety.

Stein, et al. (1974) found that black and white men and women who had attempted suicide had all experienced more separations between birth and age seven than nonsuicidal psychiatric controls. The same was true for separations between birth and age seventeen, except for black males. All groups had experienced more separations prior to the suicide attempt, except for black females. However, for none of the four gender-by-racial groups was there an association between early and later separations.

Key (1986) compared black and white suicide attempters in Los Angeles County on eleven variables. The two groups were similar in age, gender, marital status, employment status, referral source, psychiatric diagnosis, previous hospitalizations, presenting problems, suicidal intent, or disposition. The groups differed in method, with the whites using cutting, jumping, firearms and gas more and African Americans using poisoning and walking in front of moving vehicles more.

Molock, et al. (1994) compared their data on college students who had considered or attempted suicide with data from other researchers on white students and concluded that the similarities outweighed the differences. They mentioned only two differences: (1) the incidence of suicidal ideation seemed to be lower in the black sample and (2) the black students seemed to be less likely to use alcohol or drugs prior to and during the suicide attempt.

Tardiff, et al. (1981) studied psychiatric inpatients and found that 23.0% of the white females had suicidal problems, 12.1% of the black females, 13.3% of the white males and 7.8% of the black males. Using more detailed comparisons, however, some deviations from this trend were found. For example, more black males aged 16-18 had suicidal problems than white males of the same age; more black separated and divorced women had suicidal problems than white separated and divorced women; and more black male Catholics (a double minority) had suicidal problems than white male Catholics. From a clinical standpoint (diagnosis, symptoms and source of referral), the black and white suicidal patients were similar

Nisbet (1996) compared black and white female suicide attempters from a large catchment area study conducted by NIMH in 1980-1985. He found that emotional and psychological support from family and friends protected against nonfatal suicidal behavior for all race-by-gender groups. The strength of the different factors in the multiple regression analysis, however, did differ. For example, marriage was a stronger protective factor for white females than for black females. The major difference was that household income was positively associated with nonfatal suicide in black women but negatively in white women. Nisbet concluded that he had failed to find unique protective factors for nonfatal suicidal behavior in black women.

SUICIDAL IDEATION

Goldberg (1981) surveyed the 18-24 year olds in the general population in Kansas City, Missouri, and found that more whites had thought about suicide in the past month than African Americans (11.6% versus 7.7%), even after controls for age, education, marital status and occupation. However, the sample size was so small that this difference was not statistically significant.

In an academically select public high school in New York City, Friedman, et al. (1987) found no differences in the frequency of suicidal ideation (or attempted suicide) between the black and white students.

Lester and Anderson (1992) gave urban high school students a self-report depression inventory and a measure of hopelessness. The black students obtained lower depression scores and lower suicidal ideation scores than the Hispanic students. The two groups of students did not differ in hopelessness. The two groups of students were similar in gender, age, and self use and parental use of alcohol and drugs. The black students were, however, less likely to be living with both parents.

Lester and DeSimone (1995) compared black and white high school and college students on a self-report depression inventory and found no differences by race (or gender) in depression scores or current suicidal ideation. High school students of both ethnic groups were more depressed than the college students.

Kimbrough, et al. (1996) found that suicidal ideation was predicted by perception of the amount of family support, but not support from the college community. Furthermore, these results were found for black college students attending a predominantly black and a predominantly white college, and these two groups of black students did not differ in their mean scores on any of the psychological measures.

PREDICTING SUICIDALITY IN AFRICAN AMERICANS

Lewis, et al. (1995) studied suicidal ideation in a sample of black undergraduates. They found that, while perception of poor family support and cohesion predicted suicidal ideation in the students, a measure of "communalism" did not.

Vega, et al. (1993a) studied sixth and seventh grade male children in Dade County (Florida), and found that suicidal ideation was most common in the African-Americans, followed in order by the Haitians, whites, other Hispanics, Cuban Americans, Nicaraguans and Caribbean African Americans. Attempted suicide was most common in the Haitians, followed in order by the other Hispanics, Cuban Americans, Nicaraguans, African Americans, whites and Caribbean African Americans.

In predicting suicide attempts during the next year, the variable of history of a suicide attempt at the beginning of the study was significant for all ethnic groups. For African Americans, a history of suicidal ideation and psychoactive drug use also predicted a suicide attempt in the following year, but cocaine/crack use, alcohol use and cigarette use did not contribute significantly to the prediction, results similar to those found for whites.

Vega, et al. (1993b) also explored whether other risk factors predicted a history of attempted suicide. They found that the different groups of adolescents differed in the frequency of risk factors. For example, black youth more often had low self-esteem, perceived poor life chances, teacher derogation (negative attitudes on the part of teachers), parent derogation and delinquent behavior than white youth, but less often had high alcohol use and perceived peer substance use. However, psychosocial, deviance and family risk factors all contributed significantly to the multiple regressions predicting a history of suicide attempts.

Using data from the five-site Epidemiological Catchment Area study, Earls, et al. (1990) reported that the predictors of past suicidality (ideation and attempts combined) for African Americans included psychiatric symptoms. Depressive symptoms, daily drug use, multiple childhood conduct problems and multiple somatic symptoms were stronger predictors for African Americans than unstable marriage, unemployment, low wages or low education. Violent behaviors (including fist fighting, using a weapon in fights, child abuse and being victimized by violence) also predicted suicidality.

Garrison, et al. (1991b) studied a large of sample of 12-14 year olds and reported that race did not contribute to the prediction of suicidal ideation or suicide attempts. In another paper (Garrison, et al., 1991a) in which they followed up the sample for three years, they reported that suicidal ideation was more common in African Americans than in whites (and in females more than in males), but again race did not contribute to the prediction of suicidal ideation -- depression and experience of stressors were the significant predictors of suicidal ideation.

Bettes and Walker (1986) studied suicidal and nonsuicidal black adolescents aged 11 to 18 in outpatient and inpatient psychiatric units from 1968-1976 in New York City and Buffalo. Adolescents with prior suicidal ideation were more depressed and more anxious than the nonsuicidal adolescents, but less angry. The suicidal adolescents had more internalization, somatic and psychiatric symptoms (such as depression and hallucinations) but fewer externalization symptoms (such as antisocial behavior).[2] The adolescents who had attempted suicide were more depressed than the nonsuicidal children but differed less in the other variables. The girls and the older adolescents more often had suicidal symptoms than the boys and younger adolescents.

ATTITUDES TOWARD SUICIDE

Marks (1988-1989) surveyed 491 residents of Arkansas by telephone in 1984 and asked them about their attitudes toward suicide and compared the responses of whites and nonwhites (most of whom were black in Arkansas). Nonwhites were more likely than whites to view suicide as immoral (71% versus 51%) and to think that normal people do not think of committing suicide (70% versus 48%), but did not differ in whether they saw suicides as mentally ill.

In contrast, Parker, et al. (1997) surveyed elderly inner city residents and found no differences between African Americans and whites in their sympathy and agreement with suicides presented to them in vignettes.

DISCUSSION

Although a number of studies have been reviewed in this chapter, a valid conclusion is that not much has been learned about nonfatal suicidal behavior in African Americans. The reason for this is that the studies have been conducted on samples that happened to be available, with some data in their files, with almost no regard for psychological theory. Thus the results, limited as they are, have few implications either for theory or prevention. Future research should begin with theory, and design research studies to test predictions made from the theory. Then the results would be more useful.

---

[2] A slight gender difference appeared in that boys with a history of suicide attempts as well as suicidal ideation resembled the boys with only suicidal ideation more, but the girls with a history of both suicide attempts and suicidal ideation resembled the nonsuicidal adolescents more.

REFERENCES

Alessi, N. E., McManus, M., Brickman, A., & Grapentine, L. Suicidal behavior among serious juvenile offenders. *American Journal of Psychiatry*, 1984, 141, 286-287.

Alston, M. H. Occupation and suicide among women. *Issues in Mental Health Nursing*, 1986, 8, 109-119.

Alston, M. H. Occupational correlates of suicide in black and other nonwhite women. In D. Lester (Ed.) *Suicide '88*, p. 206. Denver, CO: American Association of Suicidology, 1988.

Alston, M. H., & Anderson, S. E. Suicidal behavior in African-American women. In S. S. Canetto & D. Lester (Eds.) *Women and suicidal behavior*, pp. 133-143. New York: Springer, 1995.

Baker, F. M. Black suicide attempters in 1980. *General Hospital Psychiatry*, 1984, 6, 131-137.

Baker, F. M. Suicide attempters in New Haven. *Journal of the National Medical Association*, 1988, 80, 889-895.

Berne, J. E. The management of patients post-suicide attempt in an urban municipal hospital. *Psychiatria Fennica*, 1983, supplement, 45-54.

Bettes, B., & Walker, E. Symptoms associated with suicidal behavior in childhood and adolescence. *Journal of Abnormal Child Psychology*, 1986, 14, 591-604.

Browning, C. H., Tyson, R. L., & Miller, S. I. A study of psychiatric emergencies. *Psychiatry in Medicine*, 1970, 1, 359-366.

Bush, J. A. Similarities and differences in precipitating events between black and Anglo suicide attempts. *Suicide & Life-Threatening Behavior*, 1978, 8, 243-249.

Christian, E. R. Black suicide. In C. L. Hatton, S. M. Valente & A. Rink (Eds.) *Suicide*, pp. 143-159. New York: Appleton-Century-Crofts, 1977.

Cochran, S. D., & Mays, V. M. Depressive distress among homosexually active African American men and women. *American Journal of Psychiatry*, 1994, 151, 524-529.

Collins, D., Dimsdale, J. E., & Wilkins, D. Consultation/liaison psychiatry utilization patterns in different cultural groups. *Psychosomatic Medicine*, 1992, 54, 240-245.

Earls, F. Studying adolescent suicidal ideation and behavior in primary care settings. *Suicide & Life-Threatening Behavior*, 1989, 19, 99-107.

Earls, F., Escobar, J., & Manson, S. M. Suicide in minority groups. In S. J. Blumenthal & D. J. Kupfer (Eds.) *Suicide over the life cycle*, pp. 571-598. Washington, DC: American Psychiatric Press, 1990.

Farrow, J. A., & Schwartz, R. H. Adolescent drug and alcohol usage. *Journal of the National Medical Association*, 1992, 84, 409-413.

Frederick, C. J., Resnik, H. L. P., & Wittlin, B. J. Self-destructive aspects of hard core addiction. *Archives of General Psychiatry*, 1973, 28, 579-585.

Friedman, J. M. H., Asnis, G. M., Boeck, M., & DiFiore, J. Prevalence of specific suicidal behaviors in a high school sample. *American Journal of Psychiatry*, 1987, 144, 1203-1206.

Frierson, R. L., & Lippman, S. B. Attempted suicide by black men and women. *Journal of the Kentucky Medical Association*, 1990a, 88, 287-292.

Frierson, R. L., & Lippman, S. B. Psychiatric consultation for patients with self-inflicted gunshot wounds. *Psychosomatics*, 1990b, 31, 67-74.

Garrison, C. Z., Abby, C. L., Jackson, K. L., McKeown, R. E., & Waller, J. L. A longitudinal study of suicidal ideation in young adolescents. *Journal of the American Academy of Child & Adolescent Psychiatry*, 1991a, 30, 597-603.

Garrison, C. Z., Jackson, K. L., Abby, C. L., McKeown, R. E., & Waller, J. L. Suicidal behaviors in young adolescents. *American Journal of Epidemiology*, 1991b, 133, 1005-1014.

Garrison, C. Z., McKeown, R. E., Valois, R. F., & Vincent, M. L. Aggression, substance use, and suicidal behaviors in high school students. *American Journal of Public Health*, 1993, 83, 179-184.

Goldberg, D., & Hodes, M. The poison of racism and the self-poisoning of adolescents. *Journal of Family Therapy*, 1992, 14, 51-67.

Goldberg, E. L. Depression and suicide ideation in the young adult. *American Journal of Psychiatry*, 1981, 138, 35-40.

Grisso, J. A., Wishner, A. R., Schwarz, D. F., Weene, B. A., Holmes, J. H., & Sutton, R. L. A population-based study of injuries in inner-city women. *American Journal of Epidemiology*, 1991, 134, 59-68.

Hendin, H. Black suicide. *Archives of General Psychiatry*, 1969a, 21, 407-422.

Hendin, H. Black suicide. *Columbia Forum*, 1969b, Fall, 13-17.

Hickman, L. C. Descriptive differences between black and white suicide attempters. *Issues in Mental Health Nursing*, 1984, 6, 293-310.

Horwath, E., Johnson, J., & Hornig, C. D. Epidemiology of panic disorder in African-Americans. *American Journal of Psychiatry*, 1993, 150, 465-469.

Howze, B. Suicide. *Journal of Non-White Concerns*, 1977, 5, 65-72.

Kempton, T., & Forehand, R. L. Suicide attempts among juvenile delinquents. *Behavior Research & Therapy*, 1992, 30, 537-541.

Key, L. J. Clinical comparison of black and white suicide attempters. In R. Cohen-Sandler (Ed.) *Proceedings of the 19th Annual Meeting*, pp. 78-80. Denver, CO: American Association of Suicidology, 1986.

Kiev, A., & Anumonye, A. Suicidal behavior in a black ghetto. *International Journal of Mental Health*, 1976, 5(2), 50-59.

Kimbrough, R., Molock, S. D., Williams, S., & Blanton-Lacy, M. Perception of social support (family and college community), acculturation and their relationship to depression and suicidal ideation. In J. L. McIntosh (Ed.) *Suicide '96*, pp. 164-165. Washington, DC: American Association of Suicidology, 1996.

Kirk, A. R., & Zucker, R. A. Some sociopsychological factors in attempted suicide among urban black males. *Suicide & Life-Threatening Behavior*, 1979, 9, 76-86.

Lester, D., & Anderson, D. Depression and suicidal ideation in African-American and Hispanic American high school students. *Psychological Reports*, 1992, 71, 618.

Lester, D., & Beck, A. T. Racial background and suicidal behavior. *Psychology*, 1975, 12(2), 3-5.

Lester, D., & DeSimone, A. Depression and suicidal ideation in African American and Caucasian students. *Psychological Reports*, 1995, 77, 18.

Lewis, T. T., Molock, S. D., Williams, S., Kimbrough, R., Blanton-Lacy, M., Hamilton, D., & Nicholson, M. Suicide ideation among African American college students. In D. Lester (ed.) *Suicide '95*, p. 112. Washington, DC: American Association of Suicidology, 1995.

Marks, A. Structural parameters of sex, race, age, and education and their influence on attitudes toward suicide. *Omega*, 1988-1989, 19, 327-336.

Molock, S. D., Kimbrough, R., Lacy, M. B., McClure, K. P., & Williams, S. Suicidal behavior among African American college students. *Journal of Black Psychology*, 1994, 20, 234-251.

Moscicki, E. K. O'Carroll, P. W., Rae, D. S., Roy, A. G., Locke, B. Z., & Regier, D. A. Suicidal ideation and attempts. In M. L. Rosenberg & K. Baer (Eds.) *Report of Secretary's Task Force on Youth Suicide, Volume 4*, pp. 115-128. Washington, DC: United States Government Printing Office, 1989.

Nisbet, P. A. Protective factors for suicidal black females. *Suicide & Life-Threatening Behavior*, 1996, 26, 325-341.

Parker, L. D., Cantrell, C., & Demi, A. S. Older adults' attitudes toward suicide. *Death Studies*, 1997, 21, 289-298.

Pedersen, A. M., Awad, G. A., & Kindler, A. R. Epidemiological differences between white and nonwhite suicide attempters. *American Journal of Psychiatry*, 1973, 130, 1071-1076.

Raskin, A., Crook, T. H., & Herman, K. D. Psychiatric history and symptom differences in black and white depressed inpatients. *Journal of Consulting & Clinical Psychology*, 1975, ,43, 73-80.

Reynolds, W. M. Measurement of suicidal ideation in adolescents. In D. Lester (Ed.) *Suicide '92*, pp. 230-232. Denver, CO: American Association of Suicidology, 1992.

Rotheram-Borus, M. J. Suicidal behavior and risk factors among runaway youth. *American Journal of Psychiatry*, 1993, 150, 103-107.

Salter, D. S. Personality differences between suicidal and non-suicidal blacks. *Dissertation Abstracts International*, 1978, 38B, 3473.

Steele, R. Clinical comparison of black and white suicide attempters. *Journal of Consulting & Clinical Psychology*, 1977, 45, 982-986.

Stein, M., Levy, M. T., & Glasberg, H. M. Separations in black and white suicide attempters. *Archives of General Psychiatry*, 1974, 31, 815-821.

Summerville, M. B., Abbate, M. F., Siegel, A. M., Serravezza, J., & Kaslow, N. J. Psychopathology in urban female minority adolescents with suicide attempts. *Journal of the American Academy of Child & Adolescent Psychiatry*, 1992, 31, 663-668.

Summerville, M. B., Kaslow, N. J., Abbate, M. F., & Cronan, S. Psychopathology, family functioning, and cognitive style in urban adolescents with suicide attempts. *Journal of Abnormal Child Psychology*, 1994, 22, 221-235.

Swanson, W. C., & Breed, W. Black suicide in New Orleans. In E. S. Shneidman (Ed.) *Suicidology*, pp. 99-128. New York: Grune & Stratton, 1976.

Tardiff, K., Sweillam, A., & Jacque, C. Suicide and race. *Journal of Psychiatric Treatment & Evaluation*, 1981, 3, 275-278.

Tuckman, J., & Youngman, W. F. Identifying suicide risk groups among attempted suicides. *Public Health Reports*, 1963, 78, 763-766.

Vega, W. A., Gil, A., Warheit, G., Apospori, E., & Zimmerman, R. The relationship of drug use to suicide ideation and attempts among African American, Hispanic, and white non-Hispanic male adolescents. *Suicide & Life-Threatening Behavior*, 1993a, 23, 110-119.

Vega, W. A., Gil, A. G., Zimmerman, R. S., & Warheit, G. J. Risk factors for suicidal behavior among Hispanic, African-American, and non-Hispanic white boys in early adolescence. *Ethnicity & Disease*, 1993b, 3, 229-241.

Walter, H. J., Vaughan, R. D., Armstrong, B., Krakoff, R. Y., Maldonado, L. M., Tuzzi, L., & McCarthy, J. F. Sexual, assaultive, and suicidal behaviors among urban minority junior high school students. *Journal of the American Academy of Child & Adolescent Psychiatry*, 1995, 34, 73-80.

Wenz, F. V. Suicide-related experiences among blacks. *Omega*, 1978-1979, 9, 183-191.

CHAPTER 13

AN INTERNATIONAL PERSPECTIVE

It is of interest for the present book to look at data and research on suicidal behavior in African nations in order to see what are the similarities to and differences from black suicide in the United States. Lester (1997) collected 1990 suicide rates for as many nations as possible (see Table 13.1). It can be seen that the only African nation for which suicide rates were available was Zimbabwe, although three Caribbean nations also reported suicide rates. These four suicide rates were quite low in comparison to suicide rates in the rest of the world.

More nations had data available for 1969-1971 and for 1979-1981, collected by Lester (1996), and these rates are shown for nations with a significant black population in Table 13.2. It can be seen that the suicide rates in the African nations of Angola, Kenya, Mozambique and Zimbabwe were relatively low. Similarly, the suicide rates of most of the Caribbean Islands were also relatively low.

DETAILED STUDIES

More detailed studies of suicide have appeared for some African and Caribbean nations. In general, it has been suggested by scholars that suicidal behavior is rare in Africa (Binitie, 1981), but that somatic complaints of psychological origin are more common (Ebigbo, et al., 1987).

BENIN

Bertschy, et al. (1992) found that 35 percent of depressed outpatients at a clinic in Benin had suicidal ideation, a percentage that they considered low in comparison with data from Europe.

THE CARIBBEAN

Caribbean islands differ in the proportion of those of African descent (for example, 41% in Trinidad and Tobago, 92% in Barbados and 90% in St. Lucia) and in religion (for example, 33% Roman Catholic in Trinidad and Tobago, 4% in Barbados and 90% in St. Lucia).

Mahy (1993) reported that official completed suicide rates (as reported to WHO) were 2.3 for Barbados for 1968-1971, 1.4 for Jamaica and 2.8 for the Bahamas during the same period, 7 for Trinidad in 1974, and about 4 for St. Lucia in 1991. Mahy reported a rate of attempted suicide rate of 98 in Bermuda.

(1) *The Bahamas*

Spencer (1972) reported a Bahamian suicide rate for 1959-1969 of 2.8 as compared to 8.8 for non-Bahamians. The Bahamian suicide rate was higher in the urban New Providence than in the outer islands. The men used shooting and hanging most often while the women used poisons.

(2) *Barbados*

In Barbados in 1984, the completed suicide rate was 4.0 (Mahy, 1987b). The rate was similar in men and women, and the modal suicide was aged 20 to 35 and used a solid or liquid substance. However, there were only ten suicides in that year, and so conclusions are unreliable.

Mahy (1980) found that the modal attempted suicide in Barbados in 1974-1975 was female, making a first attempt, younger then 21 if female and 22-26 if male, using Valium if female and poison if male, and attempting suicide after a dispute with a spouse or lover.

Mahy (1987a) reported on attempted suicide in Barbados in 1984. There were 28 men and 56 women in his sample. The most common age for the attempts was 25-29 for women. The men showed a more even distribution of numbers over the age range 15 to 34. Mahy did not attempt to calculate rates per 100,000, however. The most common method for attempting suicide was medication, in particular benzodiazepines. The most common precipitant of the attempts in women was an argument with a lover, and for the men an argument with a lover and depression. For the adolescents, disputes with their mother was the most common precipitant.

Mahy (1993) reported rates of attempted suicide in Barbados ranging from 45 to 74 per 100,000 per year. For 1985 to 1989, Mahy presents data suggesting an attempted suicide rate of 33 and a completed suicide rate of 0.4, but both of these rates increased from 1985 to 1989. For the period 1974-1978, there were twenty completed suicides and 250 first-time attempted suicides. The modal suicide was male and under the age of 45; the modal attempted suicide was under the age of 25, female, suffering from a transient situation disturbance who used most often a medication for the suicide attempt (Diazepam, barbiturates or other minor tranquilizers).

(3) *Jamaica*

Burke (1985, 1990) reported a suicide rate of 1.4 in Jamaica for 1975-1976, with the male suicide rate 2.3 and the female suicide rate 0.6. The suicide rate was higher in urban regions, in single men and widowed/divorced/separated women, and in professionals and managerial workers. The most common method was hanging in men and drowning/poisoning in women.

(4) *Trinidad and Tobago*

Mahy (1993) reported that the proportion of Africans among the completed suicides in Trinidad matched their proportion in the population. The most popular method for suicide was the herbicide Paraquat. The African suicides on the island tended more often to have a past history of psychiatric illness and were less often precipitated by disputes with family members or loved ones (Hutchinson, et al., 1991). The Indians on the island had higher rates of attempted suicide than those of African descent, but another study found no differences by ethnicity. Hutchinson, et al. (1991) confirmed the common use of paraquat for completed suicide in Trinidad, with the use of this poison more common in men than in women and in those aged 11 to 34.

Burke (1974a, 1974b) reported on attempted suicide among women in Trinidad and Tobago. The modal attempter was aged 15-24, used tablets, was provoked by a dispute with a lover and suffering from an affective disorder. Compared to other psychiatric patients, the suicide attempters were younger, more often had an affective disorder or no diagnosis and less often were schizophrenic or neurotic.

(5) *Other Caribbean Nations*

In the mid-1980s, there was a report of an increase in the use of paraquat for suicide in Dominica and agricultural poisons in general in Surinam as they became increasingly used by farmers (Anon, 1986). In Surinam, from 1976 to 1983, paraquat gradually replaced other agricultural poisons as the preferred agent for suicide. The use of agricultural poisons appears to have been common in many Caribbean countries during this period (Rahaman and Poon-King, 1983; Singh and West, 1985).

GHANA

Sefa-Dedeh and Canetto (1992) presented two cases of attempted suicide by women in Ghana who were both perceived by their families as having deviated from the culturally expected submissive role.

NIGERIA

Asuni (1962) reported a very low suicide rate (only 0.4 per 100,000 per year) in Western Nigeria in 1957-1960. The rate was lower in the Yoruba than in non-Yoruba and lower in Muslims than in Christians. The suicide rate seemed higher in administrative and professional workers and in rural areas. The most common method for both men and women was hanging and the most common precipitant mental illness. There did not appear to be a significant variation by age.

Later, Asuni (1967) described the characteristics of a small sample of attempted suicides from the same region. The modal attempter was male, used slashing/stabbing, and was psychiatrically disturbed (with a diagnosis of schizophrenia or depression equally likely). The attempters were equally likely to be under or over the age of 50.

Salako (1970) found that the majority of the suicide attempters by self-poisoning in Ibadan (in Western Nigeria) in the 1960s were male, with a mean age of 31. Forty eight percent used barbiturates (especially those in the higher social classes), bought from a drug store without a prescription, and 39 percent used poisons. The most common psychiatric diagnosis was depression, but in the non-depressed patients the suicidal action seemed to be impulsive. The most common precipitant in women was marital discord and in men failure or unhappiness at work or in studies.

Eferakeya (1984) reported an attempted suicide rate of 7.0 for Benin City and a male:female ratio of 1.2:1. The modal attempter was aged 15-19, a student, of low social class, using solids or liquids, and precipitated by mental illness. Odejide, et al. (1986) found that the modal attempter in Ibadan was under the age of thirty, a Christian, a student, single, a first-born, using solid or liquids, and responding to an acute stress, usually interpersonal problems with a significant other. Ebigbo, et al. (1987) reported that battery acid was becoming a common method for attempting suicide in Nigeria, and they reported four cases.

SOUTH AFRICA

Lester (1989) examined suicide in South Africa for the years 1978 to 1984, prior to end of the white-controlled government. In 1984, for example, the suicide rates were 18.4 for whites, 4.6 for coloreds, 9.9 for Asians, and 3.0 for blacks. The lower suicide rate for blacks matches that found in Zimbabwe and in the United States. The suicide rates were much lower in females than in males, but followed the same rank order. However, in Pretoria in 1968-1973, Van Zyl (1988) found similar suicide rate for whites and blacks: for men, 20.4 for whites and 22.2 for blacks, for women 5.4 for whites and 4.0 for blacks.

Flisher, et al. (1997) found that South African suicides peaked in January and were at a low in June for the 1980s, and this pattern was clearer in blacks and coloreds than in whites.

Lester (1989) found that blacks preferred hanging for suicide (both males and females) whereas whites preferred firearms (both males and females). Asians preferred hanging, as did colored males, while colored females preferred poison. Car exhaust was primarily used by white males.

Similar results were reported for 1980 by Wyndham (1986a, 1986b) -- the age-adjusted suicide rates were 13.0 for whites, 4.8 for coloreds, 8.7 for Asians and 3.4 for blacks. The peak for white suicide rates was 45-54 years of age as compared to 25-34 years of age for blacks.

Breetzke (1988) looked at suicide in Cape Town, where in 1983-1984 the suicide rates were 14 for whites, 3 for coloreds, and 0.7 for blacks. There were too few black suicides for analysis, but Breetzke found that colored female suicides were younger than white female suicides, that male single colored suicides were under-represented, and that whites used firearms more while colored males used hanging more and colored females used drugs more.

As for motives, the majority of the white females were depressed whereas interpersonal problems motivated the colored females' suicides. In line with this finding, the white female suicides were the group most often judged to be mentally ill, and more of this group had seen a psychiatrist or physician within two weeks of committing suicide. For white male suicides, depression and interpersonal problems were equally common, while colored male suicides had no clearly dominant precipitant.

Breetzke suggested that white-colored-black differences could result from differences in choice of method for suicide (with more colored and black suicidal people surviving their attempts to kill themselves), differences in the incidence of depression, a greater resilience to the harsh realities of life among blacks and coloreds, different strategies for handling aggression (inward versus outward), differences in the tendency to express conflicts somatically rather than psychologically or behaviorally, the lower life expectancy of coloreds and blacks, differences in social class, and a lesser tendency for coloreds and blacks to visit physicians and psychiatrists when in distress.

Thomson (1980) reported a low completed suicide rate for one community of Xhosa in 1957-1965 of 3.1 (whereas the homicide rate was 8.2).

Walton (1950) found very few black attempted suicides as compared to whites and coloreds at one hospital in Cape Town in the late 1940s. The whites and coloreds used different methods for attempting suicide (for example, the coloreds used poisons more often and medications less often). The colored attempters were younger, made less lethal attempts and their attempt was more often a gesture of anger or resentment directed toward another.

Naidoo and Pillay (1993) reported that the modal attempted suicide seen at their general hospital was female, making a first attempt, single and living with their family of origin, used self-poisoning, with a mean age of 23, and commonly having experienced loss of parent during childhood or adolescence and reacting to conflict with parents or partners.

Wilson and Wormald (1994) reported on 25 black South Africans over a three-year period who had attempted suicide with battery acid. The modal attempter was male, unemployed, unskilled or laborer, with limited schooling and without an Axis I psychiatric disorder. The most common precipitant was a domestic argument with a spouse or family member.

Flisher, et al. (1993) surveyed high school students and reported on the incidence of suicidal behavior in the previous year by language spoken at home. Serious thoughts about suicide were most common in those speaking English, next in Afrikaans and least in Xhosa. The ordering of the groups for attempts at suicide was Afrikaans, Xhosa and English.

A survey of early suicide prevention efforts in South Africa was provided by Bloomberg (1972), director of a telephone crisis intervention service in Johannesburg.

UGANDA

Ovuga, et al. (1995, 1996) surveyed students at Makerere University in Uganda and found that 8.4 percent had a personal history of suicide (though they did not define this), and 8.8 percent had a family history of suicide (again not defined). There was no gender difference in these incidences.

ZAMBIA

Rwegellera (1978) found suicide rates for Lusaka for 1967-1971 as follows:

black males	11.2
black females	2.2
European males	20.7
European females	21.0

The African male suicide rate peaked for those aged 35-54 and the African female suicide rate peaked for those aged 55-74, a pattern quite different from African Americans in the United States. The suicides showed no seasonal distribution. The Africans used hanging more than the Europeans.

ZIMBABWE

Lester and Wilson (1988) studied suicide in Zimbabwe, after the nation had won independence from the British, and compared their results with an earlier study by Rittey and Castle (1972) when Zimbabwe was still a British Colony. For 1981-1982, the suicide rate in Zimbabwe was 6.8 per 100,000 per year. The rate for men was 10.5 and for women 3.3. Data by ethnic group for the two periods are shown in Table 13.3. It can be seen the rates for Africans and Europeans have remained rather constant over the years. (The rise in the Asian/colored suicide rate is based on very small numbers of suicide and so is unreliable.) The suicide rate of African females has risen proportionately more between the two time periods, reducing the male/female suicide rate from 4:1 to 3:1.

Lester and Wilson reported on the African suicide by age (see Table 13.4). The suicide rates appear to rise with age in both genders, a pattern different from that observed for African Americans.

The methods used for suicide changed over the period (see Table 13.5). In 1970, Africans used primarily hanging, but by the 1980s they had begun to use poisons more, with women using fire on occasion. (Nhachi [1988] identified 133 cases of organophosphate poisoning presenting at one hospital in Harare over a five and one half year period, of which 73 percent were attempted suicides.) Europeans were much more likely to use firearms and car exhaust for suicide than were Africans.

Rittey and Castle (1972) reported mean ages for suicides in 1970 of 40 for African suicides and 46 for European suicides; For 1983-1986, the means ages were 37.4 (SD = 16.9) and 47.3 (SD = 16.9) respectively.

Gelfand (1976) confirmed the lower suicide rate in Africans as compared to whites for 1972-1974 (5.4 versus 17.1) and that Africans used hanging for suicide while whites used guns and poisoning (solids and gases). His data suggested that the African suicide rate was higher in rural areas than in urban areas.

Clarke and Lester (1989) have noted that the availability of methods for suicide affects their use. In this regard, it is interesting to note that, whereas only 3.1% of Africans used firearms for suicide during 1983-1986, 56.5% of the police officers committing suicide and 63.5% of the soldiers committing suicide used firearms. The availability of firearms for these men clearly affected their choice of method.

Lester and Wilson (1990) examined changes in the suicide rate in Zimbabwe by age during the 1970s. They found that, while the male teenage suicide rate stayed roughly the same, the female teenage suicide rate doubled. In contrast the suicide rate for elderly females in Zimbabwe dropped dramatically. Male suicide rates peaked in old age both in 1969-1970 and 1983-1986, whereas females suicide rates peaked for those aged 70+ in 1969-1970 (at 28.8 per 100,000 per year) but for those aged 60-69 in 1983-1986 (at

10.2). The methods used by teenage and adult males were quite similar, but whereas adult females preferred hanging (62% of all adult female suicides used hanging), teenage females preferred poison (58% used poisons). Lester and Wilson noted that suicide by self-immolation grew in frequency from 1983 to 1986 (from 5.6% to 12.1%) and almost all these suicides were teenage females residing in the capital of Zimbabwe, Harare.

RESEARCH ON CARIBBEAN NATIONS

Yang and Lester (1994) calculated suicide rates for fourteen Caribbean nations for 1970 to 1979: Antigua and Barbuda, the Bahamas, Barbados, Cuba, Dominica, the Dominican Republic, Grenada, Guadeloupe, Martinique, Puerto Rico, St. Kitts and Nevis, St. Lucia, St. Vincent, and Trinidad and Tobago. Suicide rates were higher in those nations with larger populations, less female participation in the labor force, and higher divorce and marriage rates.

The percentage of the population of these islands which was of African descent was obtained from the Central Intelligence Agency (1990).[1] The correlation between the suicide rates and the percentage of the population of African descent was -0.73 (two-tailed p = .003); thus, islands with more of the population of African descent had lower suicide rates.

A multiple regression was carried out to see if the proportion of the population of African descent added power to the prediction of the suicide rates. In the backward multiple regression, the percentage of the population of African descent, the gross national product per capita, male and female participation in the labor force, and the divorce rate all contributed significantly, giving a multiple R of 0.98.

---

[1] Islands whose populations were described as mainly, mostly or almost entirely of African descent were assigned 99%.

STUDIES BY ANTHROPOLOGISTS

Anthropologists have typically studied historical societies or societies which have been relatively less influenced by modernization -- often called preliterate or primitive societies. Bohannan (1967) edited a book on suicide in Africa in which the contributors looked at suicidal behavior in several tribes from Uganda and Kenya.

Bohannan noted first that earlier investigators had differed greatly in whether they thought that suicide in primitive societies was rare (Cavan, 1928) or common (Steinmetz, 1894). It is more reasonable to conclude that the range for the incidence of suicide in primitive societies may be as great as in modern societies (Westermarck, 1908). Not only may the rate of suicide vary from one primitive society to another, but these differences may be stable even after emigration, free or forced as a result of slavery. For example, Bastide (1952) noted that Mina, Dahomeans and Yoruba slaves in Brazil tended more often to assault and kill their slave owners, whereas Fulani slaves and those from Gabon and Mozambique tended more often to kill themselves.

As an anthropologist, Bohannan was not so much interested in the individual motives that people had for killing themselves in a society (he viewed what was in the mind of the suicide as unknowable), but rather he was interested in the causes ascribed to the suicide by members of the society. These popular ideas about suicide tell us something about the culture.

Fallers and Fallers (1967) described suicide among the Busoga of southeastern Uganda. The Busoga view suicide as an irresponsible and foolish act, probably impulsive. Thus, suicide, like homicide, is an act which must be punished. The body of a suicide is burnt, along with the tree or hut from which the person hung himself, and buried in waste land or at a crossroads. For the period from 1952 to 1954, the suicide rate for the society was 7.0 per 100,000 per year, which the Fallers thought was a slight underestimate.

Taking one hundred cases of suicide, the Fallers found that 86 percent hung themselves, in most cases impulsively. Sixty-nine percent were men. The most common motive was disease (31%) followed by quarrels with spouse, lover or kinsman (23%). Quarrels with a spouse was present in 48 percent of the homicides and 21 percent of the suicides, suggesting that marriage was full of conflict. The patrilineal nature of the society means that spouses have divided loyalties. The wife, in particular, feels drawn back to her family, and wives who feel oppressed by their husbands (which is not uncommon) often flee back to their father. The Fallers noted that the breaking down of the cultural traditions in recent times had decreased the incidence of suicide and homicide, probably as a result of the weakening of intergenerational family ties, which in turn has reduced marital conflicts.

La Fontaine (1967) described suicide among the Gisu, who live on the eastern border of Uganda. The Gisu view suicide as a choice made between life and death when life is too much trouble. The mentally disturbed cannot make this decision and so do not kill themselves. The suicide suffers from *litima*, a syndrome with fits of anger, jealousy and spite, thought to be inherited. Suicide is considered to be evil and also contagious. Physical contact with a suicide or his surroundings may cause you to commit suicide, and so unrelated people are paid to remove the body, and the suicide's hut may be destroyed or ritually cleaned. If the suicide hung himself from a tree, the tree will be cut down and burnt. The suicide is buried without ceremony, and the suicide's name is never mentioned. The memory of the person who brought this evil into the community is quickly blotted out.

The majority (94%) of the suicides use hanging. The Gisu maintain that three motives are found in suicides: failure to have children, quarrels with close relatives or spouse, and the death of several children or siblings, although La Fontaine found that physical illness was quite common as a motive in the suicides that he studied. La Fontaine also felt that the men responded more to economic conditions than did women, with a higher incidence of suicide in the years *after* famines or rises in prosperity. La Fontaine noted that the numbers of suicide peak in men aged 26 to 35, but he did not calculate suicide rates by age.

Beattie (1967) reported a similar pattern for the Bunyoro in the west of Uganda. The Bunyoro disapprove strongly of suicide and carry out a destruction of the suicide's property, including the tree used for hanging or the house in which he hung himself. The method used most commonly for suicide is hanging and the most common motive is disease, followed by quarrels with spouses.

The data from societies in Kenya were much less detailed, but the Joluo perform cleansing rituals after a suicide to prevent bad supernatural consequences (Wilson, 1967). Wilson felt that men commit suicide mostly as a result of loss of status, while women kill themselves as a result of domestic quarrels and fear of violence from their husbands.

In commenting on these reports, Bohannan (1967) noted that domestic institutions are responsible for the greatest number of the suicides. Women committed suicide as wives; they were unable to play the role of wife or mother because of husbands or fathers, co-wives or fate. Men, to a lesser extent, committed suicide as husbands, but impotence and loss of status played roles too. Suicide is consistently viewed as irresponsible and evil, and rituals involve destruction of the suicide's possessions and ritual cleaning. Bohannan felt that the suicide rates were moderate to low, though accurate estimates were absent except for the Busoga.

Brown (1981) reported on suicide among the Sara Nar, a tribe living in the south-central part of Chad. The Nar do not approve of suicide, but they find it understandable that people do occasionally engage in suicidal behavior. The rate was estimated at about 20 per 100,000 per year, although this estimate was based on small numbers. Women were more likely than men to both complete and attempt suicide. Of the eleven completed suicides and six attempted suicides that Brown studied, ten used poison and five hanging. Attempted suicides are not believed by the Nar to have intended to fail.

The Nar believe that suicide is precipitated by anger over painful words or shocking statements (often made when people are drinking) and loss of a loved one, especially among widowers. However, Brown found no cases precipitated by the latter, perhaps because the Nar watch widows and widowers carefully until their grief subsides. Suicides are not considered to be mentally unbalanced, except for teenagers, whose suicides do not make sense to the Nar. Suicidal preoccupation is an acute rather than a chronic condition.

In contrast to the beliefs about suicide held by the Nar, Brown considered falling short of ideals to be the most common motive for suicide. Feeding kin, gaining popularity, and retaining status in the community are important goals for the Nar, and failure in these areas can precipitate suicide. Several of the suicides were losing control over their wives, others had lost children and were believed to be witches. Nine of the seventeen cases involved people who had fallen short of one of the societal goals.

Role conflict also played a part. Women who feed their kin anger their husbands, and six of the cases involved such role conflicts. In contrast, people who were neglected by the community or isolated (and thus poorly integrated, that is egoistic[2]) did not however typically become suicidal.

---

[2] Brown mistakenly calls them anomic.

Brown felt that all of the suicides involved the suicidal person blackmailing the community and seeking vengeance or were the result of the community pressuring the suicide. Thus, issues of social control were behind many of the suicides.

Suicides are buried like those dying from other causes, and the suicide's soul is believed to behave as do other souls. Suicides need not fear the afterlife; those living need not fear the suicide's soul.

Jeffreys (1952) felt that Durkheim's (1897) categories of suicide, based on the concepts of social integration and social regulation, were not sufficient to explain cases of suicide he found in African tribes. He found suicide committed in order to revenge oneself on those one is angry at -- a type of suicide he called "Samsonic suicide" after the story of Samson in *The Bible*.

Revenge can be obtained in two ways. In some societies, the belief is that one's ghost can return and harm those at whom one is angry, as among the Herero of South West Africa (Vedder, 1928). Alternatively, the societal laws demand that those who provoked a suicide must pay some penalty, usually a fine, but in some societies death. The payment of a heavy fine by the person who provoked a suicide is customary, for example, among the Bavenda (Stayt, 1931) and the Kassena (Cardinall, 1920).

DISCUSSION

Two conclusions stand out from this research. First, many of the reports indicate that Africans view suicide as a bad act which merits sanctions and requires rituals to remove the harm that it may cause. Thus, the relatively negative view of modern African Americans toward suicide (as compared to the views held by whites) may be part of this long tradition.

Second, the low suicide rate of African Americans as compared to whites is found in multiracial African nations such as South Africa and Zimbabwe. The generality of this phenomenon and its stability suggests that the explanation based upon Henry and Short's theory (see Chapter 10) may not be valid. In Zimbabwe, black suicide rates continue to be low, even though the blacks there are no longer oppressed. However, many African nations are composed of more than one tribe, not all of whom share power equally, and it would be interesting to compare suicide rates in these different tribes within a nation.

REFERENCES

Anon. Paraquat poisoning in two Caribbean countries. *CAREC Surveillance Report*, 1986, 12(1/2), 1-9.

Asuni, T. Suicide in Western Nigeria. *British Medical Journal*, 1962, (2), 1091-1096.

Asuni, T. Attempted suicide in Western Nigeria. *West African Medical Journal*, 1967, 16(2), 51-54.

Bastide, R. Le suicide du nègre brésilien. *Cahiers Internationaux de Sociologie*, 1952, 7(12), 79-90.

Beattie, J. H. M. Homicide and suicide in Bunyoro. In P. Bohannan (Ed.) *African homicide and suicide*, pp. 130-153. New York: Atheneum, 1967.

Bertschy, G., Viel, J. F., & Ahyi, R. G. Depression in Benin. *Journal of Affective Disorders*, 1992, 25, 173-180.

Binitie, A. The clinical manifestation of depression in Africans. *Psychopathologie Africaine*, 1981, 17(1-3), 36-40.

Bloomberg, S. G. The present state of suicide prevention. *International Journal of Social Psychiatry*, 1972, 18, 104-108.

Bohannan, P. (Ed.) *African homicide and suicide*. New York: Atheneum, 1967.

Breetzke, K. A. Suicide in Cape Town. *South African Medical Journal*, 1988, 73, 19-23.

Brown, E. P. The ultimate withdrawal. *European Journal of Sociology*, 1981, 22, 199-228.

Burke, A. W. Clinical aspects of attempted suicide among women in Trinidad and Tobago. *British Journal of Psychiatry*, 1974a, 125, 175-176.

Burke, A. W. Attempted suicide in Trinidad and Tobago. *West Indian Medical Journal*, 1974b, 23, 250-255.

Burke, A. W. Suicide in Jamaica. *West Indian Medical Journal*, 1985, 34, 48-53.

Burke, A. W. Suicide in Jamaica. In J. P. Soubrier and J. Vedrinne (Eds.) *Depression and suicide*, pp. 99-103. Paris: Pergamon, 1981.

Cardinall, A. W. *Natives of the northern Territories of the Gold Coast*. London: G. Routledge & Sons, 1920.

Cavan, R. S. *Suicide*. Chicago: University of Chicago, 1928.

Central Intelligence Agency. *World Factbook*. Washington, DC: Central Intelligence Agency, 1990.

Clarke, R. V., & Lester, D. *Suicide: Closing the exits*. New York: Springer-Verlag, 1989.

Ebigbo, P. O., Aghaji, M. A. C., & Obiako, M. N. Battery acid intake as a method of suicide attempt in Nigeria. *International Journal of Family Psychiatry* 1987, 8, 375-385.

Eferakeya, A. E. Drugs and suicide attempts in Benin City, Nigeria. *British Journal of Psychiatry*, 1984, 145, 70-73.

Fallers, L. A., & Fallers, M. C. Homicide and suicide in Busoga. In P. Bohannan (Ed.) *African homicide and suicide*, pp. 65-93. New York: Atheneum, 1967.

Flisher, A. J., Parry, C. D. H., Bradshaw, D., & Juritz, J. M. Seasonal variation of suicide in South Africa. *Psychiatry Research*, 1997, 66, 13-22.

Flisher, A. J., Ziervogel, C. F., Chalton, D. O., Leger, P. H., & Robertson, B. A. Risk-taking behaviour of Cape Peninsula high-school students. *South African Medical Journal*, 1993, 83, 474-476.

Gelfand, M. Suicide and attempted suicide in the urban and rural African in Rhodesia. *Central African Journal of Medicine*, 1976, 22(10), 203-205.

Hutchinson, G., Daisley, H., Simmonds, V., & Gordon, A. Suicide by poisoning. *West Indian Medical Journal*, 1991, 40, supplement 1, 56-57.

Jeffreys, M. D. W. Samsonic suicide or suicide of revenge among Africans. *African Studies*, 1952, 11(3), 118-122.

La Fontaine, J. Homicide and suicide among the Gisu. In P. Bohannan (Ed.) *African homicide and suicide*, pp. 94-129. New York: Atheneum, 1967.

Lester, D. Personal violence (suicide and homicide) in South Africa. *Acta Psychiatrica Scandinavica*, 1989, 79, 235-237.

Lester, D. *Patterns of suicide and homicide around the world*. Commack, NY: Nova Science, 1996.

Lester, D. Suicide in an international perspective. *Suicide & Life-Threatening Behavior*, 1997, 27, 104-111.

Lester, D., & Wilson, C. Suicide in Zimbabwe. *Central African Journal of Medicine*, 1988, 34, 147-149.

Lester, D., & Wilson, C. Teenage suicide in Zimbabwe. *Adolescence*, 1990, 25, 807-809.

Mahy, G. Parasuicide in Barbados. *West Indian Medical Journal*, 1980, 29, 28-33.

Mahy, G. Attempted suicide in Barbados. *West Indian Medical Journal*, 1987a, 36, 31-34.

Mahy, G. Completed suicide in Barbados. *West Indian Medical Journal*, 1987b, 36, 91-94.

Mahy, G. Suicide behavior in the Caribbean. *International Review of Psychiatry*, 1993, 5, 261-269.

Mahy, G., & Griffith, E. E. H. Suicide and parasuicide in Barbados, 1974-1978. *Journal of the National Medical Association*, 1980, 72, 773-778.

Mugadza, W. Suicide attempts among young callers in Zimbabwe. Paper presented at the Befrienders Conference, Kuala Lumpur, Malaysia, July, 1996.

Naidoo, P., & Pillay, B. J. Parasuicide in a general hospital in South Africa. *Psychological Reports*, 1993, 72, 979-982.

Nhachi, C. F. B. An evaluation of organophosphate poisoning cases in an urban setting in Zimbabwe. *East African Medical Journal*, 1998, 65, 588-592.

Odejide, A., Williams, A., Ohaeri, J. U., & Ikuesan, B. A. The epidemiology of deliberate self-harm. *British Journal of Psychiatry*, 1986, 149, 734-737.

Ovuga, E. B. L., Buga, J. W., & Guwatudde, D. Risk-factors toward self-destructive behaviour among fresh students at Makerere University. *East African Medical Journal*, 1995, 72, 722-727.

Ovuga, E. B. L., Buga, J. W., & Guwatudde, D. Prediction of self-destructive behaviour among Makerere University students. *East African Medical Journal*, 1996, 73, 448-452.

Phillips, M. R., & Liu, H. Q. Suicide in China. Paper presented at the Befrienders Conference, Kuala Lumpur, Malaysia, July, 1996.

Rahaman, R., Poon-King, T. Paraquat as a cause of self-poisoning in South Trinidad (1972-1982). *West Indian Medical Journal*, 1983, 32, supplement, 37-38.

Rittey, D. A. W., & Castle, W. M. Suicides in Rhodesia. *Central African Journal of Medicine*, 1972, 18, 97-100.

Rwegellera, G. G. C. Suicide rates in Lusaka, Zambia. *Psychological Medicine*, 1978, 8, 424-432.

Salako, L. A. Self-poisoning by drugs. *Tropical & Geographical Medicine*, 1970, 22, 397-402.

Sefa-Dedeh, A., & Canetto, S. S. Women, family and suicidal behavior in Ghana. In V. P. Gielen, L. L. Adler & N. A. Milgram (Eds.) *Psychology in international perspective*, pp. 299-309. Amsterdam: Swets & Zeitlinger, 1992.

Singh, P. D. A., & West, P. Acute pesticide poisoning in the Caribbean. *West Indian Medical Journal*, 1985, 34, 75.

Spencer, D. Suicide in the Bahamas. *International Journal of Social Psychiatry*, 1972, 18, 110-113.

Stayt, H. A. The Bavenda. Oxford: Oxford University Press, 1931.

Steinmetz, S. R. Suicide among primitive peoples. American Anthropologist, 1894, 7, 53-60.

Thomson, I. G. Homicide and suicide in Africa and England. Medicine, Science & the Law, 1980, 20, 99-103.

Van Zyl, A. The role of depression and biochemical aspects in suicidal behaviour. In L. Schlebusch (Ed.) Suicidal behavior, pp. 44-60. Durban: University of Natal, 1988.

Vedder, H. The Herero. In C. H. L. Hahn (Ed.) The native tribes of South West Africa, pp. 153-211. Cape Town: Cape Times, 1928.

Walton, H. Attempted suicide in Cape Town. South African Medical Journal, 1950, 24, 933-935

Westermarck, E. Suicide. Sociological Review, 1908, 1, 12-33.

Wilson, D. A. B., & Wormald, P. J, Battery acid. South African Medical Journal, 1994, 84, 529-531.

Wilson, G. M. Homicide and suicide among the Joluo of Kenya. In P. Bohannan (Ed.) African homicide and suicide, pp. 179-213. New York: Atheneum, 1967.

Wyndham, C. H. Deaths from accidents, poisoning and violence. South African Medical Journal, 1986a, 69, 556-558.

Wyndham, C. H. Cause and age-specific mortality rates from accidents, poisoning and violence. South African Medical Journal, 1986b, 69, 559-562.

Yang, B., & Lester, D. Economic and social correlates of suicide in Caribbean nations. Psychological Reports, 1994, 75, 351-352.

Table 13.1
Suicide Rates around the World in 1990
(from the World Health Organization unless otherwise noted)

Hungary	39.9
Sri Lanka	33.2****
Finland	30.3
China	28.7 (Phillips & Liu, 1996)^
Slovenia	27.6
Estonia	27.1
Russian Federation	26.5
Lithuania	26.1
Latvia	26.0
Germany, East	24.4
Denmark	24.1
Austria	23.6
Belarus	23.6##
Switzerland	21.9
Ukraine	20.7
USSR	21.1
France	20.1
Belgium	19.3*
Czech Republic	19.3
Kazakhstan	19.1
Czechoslovakia	17.9
Luxembourg	17.8
Germany, West	17.5
Germany	17.5#
Sweden	17.2
Japan	16.4
Iceland	15.7
Norway	15.5
Yugoslavia	15.3
Bulgaria	14.7
Mauritius	14.2
Trinidad & Tobago	13.7

New Zealand	13.5
Singapore	13.1
Poland	13.0
Australia	12.9
Canada	12.7
Krygyzstan	12.5
USA	12.4
Hong Kong	11.7
Puerto Rico	10.5
Scotland	10.5
Uruguay	10.3
Northern Ireland	9.9
Netherlands	9.7
Ireland	9.5
Romania	9.0
Portugal	8.8
United Kingdom	8.1
Korea, South	8.0***
England & Wales	7.8
Liechtenstein	6.7
Uzbekistan	6.8#
Argentina	6.7
Taiwan	6.7 (Andrew Cheng)
Israel	6.5
Italy	7.6
Spain	7.5
Zimbabwe	7.4 (Mugadza, 1996)
Chile	5.6*
Costa Rica	5.2
Venezuela	4.8*
Barbados	4.7**
Ecuador	4.6**
Macao	4.4***
Panama	3.8***
Tadjikistan	3.8#
Greece	3.5

Bahrain	3.1**
Columbia	3.1#
Armenia	2.8
Malta	2.3
Mexico	2.3
St Lucia	2.3***
Albania	2.1*
Maldives	2.0***
Bahamas	1.2***
Kuwait	0.8***
Egypt	0.04***

* 1990 rates not available -- 1989 data
** 1990 rates not available -- 1988 data
*** 1990 rates not available -- 1987 data
**** 1990 rates not available -- 1986 data
# 1990 data not available -- 1991 data
1990 data not available -- 1992 data
^ 1990-1994

Table 13.2
Suicide Rates for Nations with a Significant Black Population

| | 1969-1971 | | | 1979-1981 | | |
	total	male	female	total	male	female
Angola	1.0	-	-	-	-	-
Kenya	0.2	0.2	0.2	-	-	-
Mozambique	0.8	1.1	0.3	-	-	-
Zimbabwe	6.0	9.5	2.4	6.1	9.9	2.6
Antigua	-	-	-	1.0	-	-
Bahamas	0.0	-	-	0.5	1.0	0.0
Barbados	1.9	-	-	1.5	2.6	0.5
Bermuda	6.0	-	-	2.8	-	-
Brit. Virg. I.	26.7	-	-	0.0	-	-
Cayman I.	10.0	-	-	6.0	12.3	0.0
Dominica	-	-	-	0.0	0.0	0.0
Grenada	1.0	-	-	-	-	-
Guadeloupe	3.4	-	-	9.5	-	-
Jamaica	1.4	2.7	0.2	-	-	-
Martinique	5.4	-	-	11.9	20.0	4.4
Montserrat	3.3	-	-	0.0	0.0	0.0
Nether. Ant.	-	-	-	2.0	3.2	0.8
St. Kitts	0.5	-	-	0.8	1.7	0.0
St. Lucia	-	-	-	0.8	1.7	0.0
St. Vincent	-	-	-	0.9	1.9	0.0
US Virg. I.	-	-	-	2.4	3.6	1.3

Table 13.3
Suicide Rates in Zimbabwe

	1969-1970			1983-1986		
	total	male	female	total	male	female
African	5.6	8.9	2.2	6.9	10.5	3.4
European	14.4	21.4	7.4	17.6	29.8	5.8
Asian/ Colored	0.8	-	-	9.7	18.0	1.4

Table 13.4
African Suicide Rates by Age and Gender in Zimbabwe

	1969-1970		1983-1986	
	male	female	male	female
10-19	3.2	1.4	3.2	2.7
20-29	9.5	3.4	22.2	6.2
30-39	22.5	2.6	25.5	5.3
40-49	24.9	5.3	21.3	5.8
50-59	16.8	5.8	23.4	9.7
60-69	29.7	21.1	33.4	10.2
70+	34.4	28.8	30.6	9.3

Table 13.5
Methods used for Suicide in Zimbabwe

	1969-1970		1983-1986	
	males	females	males	females
Africans				
hanging	94%	93%	76%	55%
poison	1%	2%	16%	35%
firearms	0%	0%	4%	0%
cutting	1%	2%	1%	0%
fire	0%	0%	0%	9%
other	4%	3%	3%	1%

	1969-1970		1983-1986	
	Africans	Europeans	Africans	Europeans
hanging	94%	4%	71%	14%
poison	1%	26%	21%	15%
CO gas	0%	22%	0%	26%
firearms	0%	42%	3%	34%
cutting	1%	1%	1%	5%
fire	0%	0%	2%	0%
other	4%	5%	2%	6%

CHAPTER 14

PREVENTING BLACK SUICIDE

In seeking to prevent suicide, we can divide our attack into three traditionally different goals: primary, secondary, and tertiary prevention. Let us look at each of these in turn.

PRIMARY PREVENTION

Primary prevention involves the prevention of the development of suicidal tendencies in the individual. If we were able to prevent suicide in this way, people in the society would never become suicidal. This is, of course, the most difficult kind of prevention. It presupposes that we know the causes of suicide, which is doubtful, even after many years of scientific study. However, some suggestions can be made.

Gibbs (1984) noted that black youth showed increases in a wide variety of problems from 1960 to 1980, including unemployment, delinquency, substance abuse, teenage pregnancy and suicide. Therefore, a variety of primary prevention programs are needed focusing on: (1) better secondary education, (2) employment, (3) sex education and family planning, (4) comprehensive services and child care programs for teenage parents, (5) delinquency prevention and early intervention, and (6) drug prevention and counseling.

Focusing on the poor social and economic conditions facing African Americans, Gibbs (1997) urged the establishment of programs to improve economic self-sufficiency and enhance family functioning. She noted that it was critical to increase life options for black youths, especially males. Graduation rates from high school should be raised, job training programs strengthened, and employment opportunities in good jobs increased. Clinics needs to be established in the inner cities (even in the schools) and in poor rural areas to address the physical and mental problems of African Americans, especially depression, post-traumatic stress, substance abuse and teenage pregnancy. In schools, youths at risk should be identified and steered into programs to lower their suicide risk.

Gibbs noted that, since black youth often are involved in negative educational and criminal justice experiences, efforts to identify black youth at risk should be located in educational and criminal justice institutions (Gibbs and Hines, 1989). Furthermore, the pattern of symptomatology differs for black versus white youth, and so suicide assessment scales should be modified to take this into account.^ Gibbs and Hines suggested assessing "depressive equivalents" such as conduct disorders, delinquency, school failure and violence, self-esteem and feelings of competence, experience of physical abuse and lack of nurturance, and involvement in risk-taking behaviors.

Gibbs (1988) suggested setting up comprehensive clinics in inner-city schools to provide physical and mental health resources. There have to be meaningful services, such as family counseling, for those who are identified as suicide risks, and a great deal needs to be done to improve police-community relations in inner cities. Gibbs, noting the lack of appropriate adult male role models for black youth, urged the development of programs such as Big Brothers and Big Sisters.

Frierson and Lippman (1990) proposed several recommendations for preventing black suicide. (1) Mental health workers need to appreciate the effects of racism on African Americans more, and to beware of "perceiving" paranoia or overreaction in African Americans, and thus (2) to avoid overdiagnosing schizophrenia in African Americans. (3) Psychiatric disorders should be diagnosed more accurately and treated appropriately. (4) Counselors need to become familiar with social agencies and resources in the community,

---

[1] As we saw in Chapter 8, there is no evidence that this is true.

(5) become acquainted with black culture and (6) involve black role models in the treatment of black suicidal patients, especially the young.

Baker (1984) made several recommendations for suicide prevention in the black community. (1) Consultation and education programs are necessary which focus on conflict resolution in families, and (2) these programs should be offered in schools, churches and adolescent drop-in centers. (3) Members of families in which one person is psychiatrically disturbed should be informed about the symptoms and warning signs of psychotic decompensation and suicidal risk. (4) When suicide attempters are treated, family or couple crisis intervention should also be available to enhance conflict resolution. Medical treatment alone is not sufficient. (5) Baker noted that only 22 percent of those referred for outpatient treatment attended consistently. He recommended that, if patients do not follow-up referrals to outpatient treatment, then they should be contacted and hospitalization considered.

PSYCHIATRIC DISORDER

Since a large proportion of suicides are psychiatrically disturbed, the primary prevention of psychiatric disturbance would go far toward preventing suicide. The same holds true for alcoholism and drug abuse. This, however, changes the problem to that of how can we prevent people from becoming psychiatrically disturbed or substance abusers.

EDUCATING PHYSICIANS

Rutz, et al. (1989) have shown that a program to educate physicians in the detection, evaluation and appropriate treatment of depression and suicide led to a reduction in the suicide rate on the island of Gotland (Sweden) as compared to the rest of Sweden.

Smith and Carter (1986) noted that physicians have a great deal of contact with members of the black community, and a training program to sensitize them to the recognition and treatment of depression and suicidal preoccupation might help reduce the incidence of suicide among African Americans. Earls, et al. (1990) found that African Americans were as likely to seek professional help when severely depressed; it was only for mild depression that they were less likely than whites to seek professional help.

Educating Students

One major tactic for preventing suicide has been to establish suicide education programs in schools. These programs are varied, but can include segments such as: (1) providing information about suicide in general, (2) teaching how to detect suicidal intent in peers, (3) simple crisis counseling techniques, and (4) information about the school and community resources for suicidal and distressed students.

Molock, et al. (1995) evaluated a suicide education program given to African American college students. Half of the sample attended the suicide education program while half attended a program on study habits. Both groups showed a decrease in depression scores and suicidal ideation scores after the programs, but the decline in suicidal ideation was greater in those students who attended the suicide education program.[2] Thus, Molock concluded that the suicide education program appeared to have no negative impact on the students, and it did not lead them to become more suicidal.

Survivors of Suicides

There are several groups at high risk for suicide, and early intervention with these groups might prevent suicide. For example, in the United States there has recently been a tremendous growth in groups for the relatives and loved-ones of those who have completed suicide. Work with these survivors of suicide promises to be a potentially powerful way of preventing suicide.

Alston (1994) noted that a survey of groups for those who have had a loved-one commit suicide (survivors) found that very few African Americans attended. Kirk, et al. (1994) found that only about seven percent of survivor group members and three percent of the group leaders were minorities. It may be that African Americans are unaware of these services, but it is also likely that African Americans feel uncomfortable with these formal organizations and in white-dominated groups. They may prefer the more traditional resources of family, friends and the church. However, the greater stigma attached to suicide in the black community may make these preferred resources less available to the black survivor.

---

[2] The men also showed a larger decrease in suicidal ideation than did the women.

SECONDARY PREVENTION

Secondary prevention is early intervention with persons who are on the verge of suicide. Several strategies have been developed for this.

SUICIDE PREVENTION CENTERS

Suicide prevention centers have been set up in many countries in the world, and some have extensive networks of centers so that an individual always has a center near at hand. Suicide prevention centers typically have a 24-hour telephone crisis counseling service staffed by paraprofessional volunteers. Some centers have, in addition, walk-in clinics and emergency out-reach teams who can visit distressed individuals in the community.

This type of suicide prevention has been oriented around a crisis model of the suicidal process. People who are suicidal are conceptualized as being in a time-limited crisis state. Immediate crisis counseling will help the suicidal individual through the suicidal crisis, whereupon a normal life may resume.

Suicide prevention centers are well equipped for secondary prevention. However, most of these suicide prevention efforts are essentially passive (Lester, 1989). A suicidal person has to contact the suicide prevention center. Active methods, such as seeking out discharged psychiatric patients, elderly males living alone, and other high risk groups could be undertaken. In addition, physicians as well as community workers such as police officers, clergymen, lawyers, and perhaps groups such as bartenders, prostitutes and hair dressers who also come into contact with the public, could be sensitized to the detection of depressed, disturbed and suicidal people and encouraged to refer them to appropriate resources.

Little has been written about the role of suicide prevention centers for preventing black suicide. Gibbs (1988) suggested that suicide prevention centers should also be established in inner-city neighborhoods with active outreach programs and minority staff members.

Dennis and Kirk (1976) surveyed six suicide prevention centers and found that only two had data on the clients by race. Black and white clients differed in characteristics. For example, the black female caller was most often a divorced or widowed person under the age of 30; the white female caller was most often married and under the age of 35. Both were likely to be calling about family or marital problems. The typical black male caller was typically under 35, unemployed, married or divorced and calling about drug, financial or mental problems; the white male caller was typically single, under the age of 30, and calling about family problems. The director of a suicide prevention center in Washington, DC, had the impression that white callers complain more about loss of prestige (jobs, grades, reputation, and social position) whereas black callers complain more about loss of a lover (Banks, 1970). Dennis and Kirk noted that black callers tended to be referred more often to publicly funded services and less often to private services than were whites.

One center felt that African Americans did not use the center as much as the white members of the community, while the other center did not report under-utilization. However, Dennis and Kirk urged that suicide prevention centers keep records which identify the callers by race so that the utilization of the suicide prevention centers by different ethnic groups can be monitored and efforts made to increase the use of the services by ethnic groups which may be less informed of the services or less willing to make use of them.

Green (1977) noted that 13 percent of the callers to the Los Angeles suicide prevention center were black, which was about their proportion in the city. Reingold (1975), however, reported that 91 percent of black suicide attempters in San Francisco did not consider calling the suicide prevention center.

RESTRICTING ACCESS TO LETHAL METHODS FOR SUICIDE

Clarke and Lester (1989) have argued that restricting access to lethal methods for suicide might well reduce the suicide rate. They noted that this idea first gained prominence after the reduction in the English suicide rate by about a third in the 1960s and 1970s when domestic gas was detoxified by switching from coal gas (which contains carbon monoxide) to natural gas (which does not). They conducted a number of studies to show that the availability of firearms, toxic car exhaust and toxic domestic gas appears to be strongly related to the use of those methods for suicide, and that reducing the easy availability of these methods for suicide often reduced the overall suicide rate since not everyone switches methods for suicide when their preferred method becomes less easily available.

Clarke and Lester urged the detoxification of domestic gas, limits on the sales and ownership of firearms, restricting the size of medication prescriptions, placing pills in plastic blisters which are hard to open, adding vomiting-inducing chemicals to medications so that an overdose will result in expulsion of the medication, prescription of suppositories rather than orally-taken tablets, prescribing the less toxic medications, cleaning up car emissions, changing the shape of the exhaust pipe to make it difficult to attach tubing, having an automatic engine turn-off mechanism if the car idles for more than a few minutes, fencing in bridges and high buildings from which people jump, and restricting the easy availability of herbicides and insecticides in developing countries.

As far as this strategy is concerned for black suicide, Gibbs (1988) stressed the need to reduce the ownership of firearms in the black community through gun control legislation. Baker (1984) also stressed that people should be encouraged to remove all unnecessary but dangerous methods for suicide from the home, such as unnecessary medications and firearms.

EMERGENCY MEDICAL SERVICES

Diggory (undated) has argued that we are preventing suicide with our emergency medical procedures. He estimated that in 1971, for example, the suicide rate in Pittsburgh was reduced from 15.2 to 12.5 (a reduction of 18 percent) simply by saving the lives of those who had attempted suicide. Thus, the improvement in emergency medical care in recent years has probably increased the extent to which those who might have died in the past from their suicidal actions now survive.

In recent years there have been problems in delivering good emergency medical care to many communities, including poor rural areas and inner cities. Current health care insurance programs and the need for hospitals to be profitable have led to the reduction and elimination of emergency medical care. This would be expected to increase the mortality from behaviors such as suicide.

TERTIARY PREVENTION

Tertiary prevention is the prevention of the recurrence of suicide in those who have already been suicidal. Strictly speaking there is no tertiary prevention for completed suicide. A completed suicide is dead. We can help only those who are not yet dead by their own hand. However, if we bear in mind that some people who seriously intend to kill themselves are thwarted by the intervention of others and by emergency medical treatment, then we can talk about preventing the recurrence of completed suicide in these individuals.

Such individuals constitute the group which we label attempted suicides. Tertiary prevention then would involve distinguishing carefully between those who are making suicidal gestures and those who would have died but for intervention. This latter group, once identified, could be made the target population for intensive tertiary prevention efforts, which in this case would resemble secondary prevention methods.

Available research shows that psychiatric treatment may be beneficial here. Several reviews of which medications appear to be best for suicidal clients have appeared (for example, Schifano and De Leo, 1991). With regard to counseling, Montgomery and Montgomery (1982) identified three methodologically sound studies of the effects of counseling on suicidal behavior and found that only one of these indicated that counseling had a significant impact on suicidal behavior. Recently, counseling strategies specifically oriented toward suicidal clients have been proposed, for example, Clum and Lerner (1990). Further research on tertiary prevention should focus on which medications and counseling techniques are most effective for treating seriously suicidal people who have made lethal attempts to kill themselves.

One other suggestion for tertiary prevention is to investigate the environments into which these serious attempters are released. Does their environment contain suicidogenic stresses, hostile significant others who increase the likelihood of self-destructive desires, or lethal means for suicide? One suicide prevention center in the United States used to search the homes of attempted suicides, removing all guns, large knives, poisons and lethal drugs. They were able to do this, of course, only for attempted suicides who contacted them, and they did it with the tolerance of the local police force. It is not a technique that is likely to be available to most preventers of suicide, but it does illustrate a technique for tertiary prevention.

COUNSELING SUICIDAL AFRICAN AMERICANS

In assessing suicidal African Americans, Gibbs (1988) noted that clinicians should be aware of the cultural differences in the expression of depression and suicidal intent in African Americans. Depressed African Americans, especially youths, are more likely to be verbally abusive, to report somatic symptoms of depression, to be hostile, to act out in school, and to have conflicted relationships with peers.

Gibbs noted that other self-destructive and risk-taking behaviors may indicate suicidal intent in African Americans, behaviors such as sexual promiscuity, substance abuse and delinquency. Clinicians should also take care to note the social stressors to which the individuals have been subjected, such as loss of parents, poverty, residential mobility, health problems, child abuse, and parent characteristics (unemployment, psychiatric disorder, substance abuse, and criminal behavior).

The suicidal indications, especially in black youth, will be evident in institutional settings, such as schools, health facilities, welfare agencies and criminal justice agencies, and so the personnel in these institutions should be trained in suicide prevention -- both in the identification of suicidal intent and in the appropriate referral of potentially suicidal individuals.

There are several general guidelines for counseling minorities in America, including African Americans, both for individual counseling (e.g., Sue 1981) and family therapy (e.g., Ho, 1987). However, very little has been written about counseling suicidal African Americans.

Gray (1987) noted that it was important for a counselor to deal with the racism and discrimination that black suicidal clients have experienced and are experiencing, and to distinguish carefully the stress from these experiences from stress caused by intrapsychic and interpersonal conflicts. Gray felt that it was important for the counselor to be familiar with the sociocultural background of the client. Earls, et al. (1990) have also stressed the importance of fostering an appreciation of and sensitivity to cultural differences in all mental health professionals, both white and black; Earls and Jemison (1986) felt that it was preferable to have black interviewers interviewing African Americans and to utilize black-administered institutions for both clinical and research purposes.

Drawing on books which have dealt with counseling minorities (Hendersen, 1979; Jones and Korchin, 1982; Marsella and Pedersen, 1981; Sue, 1981), McIntosh and Santos (1984) made several suggestions for suicide counseling with African Americans. They noted that counselors must take into account black history and experiences in the United States, since this is very important in the lives of African Americans. African Americans have feelings about these experiences, and they should be encouraged to express their thoughts about how these experiences have influenced their own lives.

McIntosh and Santos noted that African Americans use nonverbal communications (such as movements, facial expressions, and gestures) a great deal, and they also listen differently than do whites (for example, with less continuous eye contact and fewer head-nods and "uh-huhs" to indicate that they are paying attention). Counselors should not misinterpret these response patterns. Black clients often prefer being addressed by their surname. McIntosh and Santos also caution that, while knowledge of black slang may aid the counselor with black clients, counselors should not use this slang themselves. Counselors should also avoid clinical jargon.

Mental health agencies are typically seen as a last resort by African Americans, and they tend to distrust agencies in general. Going for counseling may be seen as a stigma by black clients. They are less likely to refer themselves to such agencies, but are referred instead by other agencies. These factors increase their apprehension, distrust, and lack of clear expectations about the services. Because they are less willing to visit agencies, African Americans who make use of suicide prevention services are likely to be at high risk for suicide.

For example, Sussman, et al. (1987) studied residents in St. Louis and found that depressed African Americans were much less likely to seek professional help than whites, especially if the depression was mild or moderate. The African Americans feared the stigma of mental illness, the treatment itself and the possibility of being hospitalized.

Because of their distrust of agencies, counselors must take care to establish good rapport with black clients initially. Counselor self-disclosure can be used with black clients to help put them at ease. If counselors probe too soon, black clients may not return for subsequent appointments. Black clients tend to minimize the crisis and to give the impression that they have things under control when, in fact, they do not.

Black clients prefer task-oriented and action-oriented counseling, and they expect specific advice and solutions for their problems. Outreach and home visits may be necessary with black clients, and counselors should be prepared to work with other agencies in finding solutions to some of the problems presented by black clients. Thus, counselors should familiarize themselves with the agencies and resources in the black community and refer clients only to those that will work effectively with the clients. Natural support systems, such as family, friends and the church, should also be assessed for the client, and efforts made to use these resources. The counselor should be prepared, therefore, to consult with these resources in order to find solutions for the client's problems.

OTHER ISSUES

THE ROLE OF THE CHURCH

Alston (1991) noted that church has traditionally played an important role in the African American community, providing affirmation, a sense of worth and emotional support. Alston felt that the church had recently become less involved in social problems, such as suicide, than it could be. She urged that the church become more willing to deal with such issues and to seek ways of gaining the experience and skills to do so. Earls, et al. (1990) noted, however, that the church may play less of a role in the lives of black youth than for older African Americans.

THE CRIMINAL JUSTICE SYSTEM

Earls, et al. (1990) noted that one way to motivate black youth, especially males, to seek professional help for depression and other psychiatric problems may be to form linkages with the criminal justice system. If staff in the criminal justice could be trained to recognize symptoms of depression and other disorders, they could refer the youths with such symptoms to mental health professionals, if they were available.

CONCLUSIONS

Commentary on the prevention of suicide in African Americans has not proposed new strategies, but rather has pointed out difficulties in applying the traditional strategies to African Americans. There are many aspects of these strategies that may impede their effectiveness in African Americans.

Reynolds, et al. (1975) surveyed adults in Los Angeles and found differences in the attitudes toward suicide between the ethnic groups.[3] African Americans and Mexican Americans were much more likely to view suicides as mentally ill whereas Japanese Americans and Anglo-Americans were more likely to see suicides as responding to psychological stress. Reynolds pointed out that this difference in attitudes would affect how you responded to a potential suicide and how you felt about yourself if you were suicidal. This difference in view also affects the focus for change in the situation -- the suicidal person versus the interpersonal situation -- and the prospects for change -- it is easier to change a situation than modify the psychiatric state of a person.

African Americans and Anglo-Americans were less likely to rely on family resources for suicidal crises and more likely to utilize personal and public resources than were Mexican Americans and Japanese Americans. The four ethnic groups did not differ in whether they had known someone who had committed suicide. African Americans were less likely to refer suicidal people to clergymen than were other groups, but more likely to contact the police and family members.

Reynolds noted that the newspapers serving the African American community were more likely to contain suicidal stories than the newspapers for the other ethnic groups; however, African Americans did not see suicide as a major concern for their ethnic group. Incidentally, the order for suicide rates were Anglo-Americans highest, Japanese Americans and African Americans tied for second, and Mexican Americans lowest.

Wyche and Rotheram-Borus (1990) also noted that African Americans may view suicides more as a sin or as a "crazy" act, attitudes which may inhibit their acting-out of their self-destructive impulses as suicidal behavior.

---

[3] For more general results about attitudes toward death in general in this sample, see Kalish and Reynolds (1976).

There has been concern in recent years with research into treatments of all kinds, medical, psychiatric and psychological, as to whether they have been adequately tested on females and on children and adolescents, since almost all research is conducted on adult white males. The same argument might be made for African Americans. Baker (1988) noted that pharmacological reactions, for example, are sometimes quite different in African Americans than in whites. Thus, psychiatric medications, and we might add psychotherapeutic techniques, need to be examined specifically for their effectiveness and drawbacks with African Americans.

Gibbs (1988), in her discussion of suicide prevention for African Americans, urged primary prevention, by which she meant eliminating poverty and racism, the strengthening of black families, employment policies to provide meaningful jobs and adequate incomes for African Americans, especially black men, and equal opportunities and equal administration of justice. These are fine recommendations for the society, but will they prevent suicide? It would seem that such policies would make the lives of African Americans in America more similar to the lives of whites; but whites have the higher suicide rates! So Gibbs's proposals would be expected to increase black suicide rates!

Perhaps America has to accept that suicide is a problem of modern society. It is more common in nations which have a higher quality of life, and improved living conditions have not been shown to lower the suicide rate. Improving the quality of life for African Americans is, obviously, a worthy goal, but it will not necessarily reduce their suicide rate.

REFERENCES

Alston, M. H. The African-American church in suicide prevention. In D. Lester (Ed.) *Suicide '91*, p. 138. Denver, CO: American Association of Suicidology, 1991.

Alston, M. African-American suicide survivors. *AAS Newslink*, 1994, 20(3), 16.

Baker, F. M. Black suicide attempters in 1980. *General Hospital Psychiatry*, 1984, 6, 131-137.

Baker, F. M. Afro-Americans. In L. Comas-Diaz & E. E. H. Griffith (Eds.) *Clinical guidelines in cross-cultural mental health*, pp. 151-181. New York: Wiley, 1988.

Banks, L. Black suicide. *Ebony*, 1970, 25(7), 76-84.

Clarke, R. V., & Lester, D. *Suicide: closing the exits*. New York: Springer-Verlag, 1989.

Clum, G. A., & Lerner, M. A problem solving approach to treating individuals at risk for suicide. In D. Lester (Ed.) *Current concepts of suicide*. Philadelphia: Charles Press, 1990, 194-202.

Dennis, R. E., & Kirk, A. Survey of the use of crisis intervention centers by the black population. *Suicide & Life-Threatening Behavior*, 1976, 6, 101-105.

Diggory, J. Empirical evidence for the improved prediction and prevention of suicide. Pittsburgh: Chatham College, undated.

Earls, F., Escobar, J., & Manson, S. M. Suicide in minority groups. In S. J. Blumenthal & D. J. Kupfer (Eds.) *Suicide over the life cycle*, pp. 571-598. Washington, DC: American Psychiatric Press, 1990.

Earls, F., & Jemison, A. Suicidal behavior in American blacks. In G. Klerman (Ed.) *Suicide and depression among adolescents and young adults*, pp. 133-145. Washington, DC: American Psychiatric Press, 1986.

Frierson, R. L., & Lippman, S. B. Attempted suicide by black men and women. *Journal of the Kentucky Medical Association*, 1990, 88, 287-292.

Gibbs, J. T. Black adolescents and youth. *American Journal of Orthopsychiatry*, 1984, 54, 6-21.

Gibbs, J. T. Conceptual, methodological, and sociocultural issues in black youth suicide. *Suicide & Life-Threatening Behavior*, 1988, 18, 73-89.

Gibbs, J. T. African-American suicide. *Suicide & Life-Threatening Behavior*, 1997, 27, 68-79.

Gibbs, J. T., & Hines, A. M. Factors related to sex differences in suicidal behavior among black youth. *Journal of Adolescent Research*, 1989, 4, 152-172.

Gray, B. Black clients. In P. Muehrer (Ed.) *Research perspectives on depression and suicide in minorities*, pp. 68-73. Washington, DC: Public Health Service, 1987.

Green, J. Ethnic aspects of suicide statistics. In C. L. Hatton, S. M. Valente & Rink, A. (Eds.) *Suicide*, pp. 138-143. New York: Appleton-Century-Crofts, 1977.

Hendersen, D. (Ed.) *Understanding and counseling ethnic minorities.* Springfield, IL: Charles Thomas, 1979.

Ho, M. K. *Family therapy with ethnic minorities.* Thousand Oaks, CA: Sage, 1987.

Jones, E. E., & Korchin, S. J. *Minority mental health.* New York: Praeger, 1982.

Kalish, R. A., & Reynolds, D. K. *Death and ethnicity.* Los Angeles: University of Southern California, 1976.

Kirk, A. R., Dennis, R. E., Reynolds, N. L., & Key, L. J. Black suicide victims and their survivors. In D. Lester (Ed.) *Suicide '94*, pp. 27-28. Denver, CO: American Association of Suicidology, 1994.

Lester, D. *Can we prevent suicide?* New York: AMS, 1989.

Marsella, A. J., & Pedersen, P. B. (Eds.) *Cross-cultural counseling and psychotherapy.* New York: Pergamon, 1981.

McIntosh, J. L., & Santos, J. F. Suicide counseling and intervention with racial/ethnic minorities. In C. L. Hatton & S. M. Valente (Eds.) *Suicide.*, pp. 175-194. Norwalk, CT: Appleton-Century-Crofts, 1984.

Molock, S. D., Williams, S., Blanton-Lacy, M., & Kimbrough, R. Werther effects in a black college sample. In D. Lester (Ed.) *Suicide '95*, pp. 115-116. Washington, DC: American Association of Suicidology, 1995.

Montgomery, S., & Montgomery, D. Drug treatment of suicidal behavior. *Advances in Biochemistry & Psychopharmacology*, 1982, 32, 347-355.

Reingold, E. Black suicide in San Francisco. In Anon, *Miniconsultations on the mental and physical health problems of black women*, pp. 111-120. Washington, DC: Black Women's Community Development Foundation, 1975.

Reynolds, D. K., Kalish, R. A., & Farberow, N. L. A cross-ethnic study of suicide attitudes and expectation in the United States. In N. L. Farberow (Ed.) *Suicide in different cultures*, 35-50, Baltimore: University Park Press, 1975.

Rutz, W., van Knorring, L., & Walinder, J. Frequency of suicide on Gotland after systematic postgraduate education of general practitioners. *Acta Psychiatrica Scandinavica*, 1989, 80, 151-154.

Schifano, F., & De Leo, D. Can pharmacological intervention aid in the prevention of suicidal behavior? *Pharmacopsychiatry*, 1991, 24, 113-117.

Smith, J. A., & Carter, J. H. Suicide and black adolescents. *Journal of the National Medical Association*, 1986, 78, 1061-1064.

Sue, D. W. (Ed.) *Counseling the culturally different.* New York: Wiley, 1981.

Sussman, L. K., Robins, L. N., & Earls, F. Treatment-seeking for depression by black and white Americans. *Social Science & Medicine,* 1987, 24, 187-196.

Wyche, K. F., & Rotheram-Borus, M. J. Suicidal behavior among minority youth in the United States. In A. R. Stiffman & L. E. Davis (Eds.) *Ethnic issues in adolescent mental health,* pp. 323-338. Newbury Park, CA: Sage, 1990.

CHAPTER 15

CONCLUSIONS

Although there has been a great deal of interest in suicide in African Americans, there has not been as much research into this problem as, for example, suicide in Native Americans (see Lester, 1997).

It is noteworthy how many commentators there have been on black suicide versus the small number of researchers. In Chapter 3, I printed a whole list of articles and chapters in books which were reporting the same phenomena about black suicide but which added little to our understanding of black suicide.

There have been only two major researchers in the field whose work has contributed to our understanding of black suicide, Robert Davis in the late 1970s and early 1980s and Sherry Molock and her colleagues at Howard University in the 1990s.

Added to this, there is an ethnic bias in the evaluation of research and theory given by the commentators. There is often a resentment expressed toward white writers in this field. For example, Miles (1979) notes his agreement with comments made by Wylie (no citation is given by Miles) that Hendin's theories about the relevance of the black family structure to black suicide is "platitudinist clap-trap" (p. 432). In contrast, Gibbs (1992) is permitted to speculate about the relevance of the black family structure, including the growth of female-headed households, without scornful contempt. If we are going to make progress in understanding and preventing black suicide, then the ideas and suggestions made must be evaluated on the basis of their usefulness and validity, not on the demographic characteristics of those proposing the ideas.

No Differences

This review has been based on all of the research studies and papers published on black suicide. However, there are many papers which include race as a variable in the study and which find race to have no effect on the results. These studies do not typically get indexed under "race" so that they can be easily identified. The result is, therefore, that there are probably many studies not cited in this book which find that race has little or no impact on the suicidal phenomena being studied.

For example, a study by Copeland (1985) on murder-suicide in Dade County, Florida, found that whereas men tend be the suicide victim and women the murder victim in these dyadic deaths, there was no racial difference here.[1] In one recent issue of *Suicide and Life-Threatening Behavior*, two studies reported no differences between African Americans and whites: Roberts, et al. (1997) found no black/white differences in the frequency of suicidality in the past two weeks or lifetime in 6th to 8th graders in Houston (TX), and Rohde, et al. (1977) found no black/white differences in the frequency of suicidality in adolescents in juvenile detention. There are undoubtedly many such reports, but it is difficult to locate them without re-reading all of the thousands of published research papers on suicide.

---

[1] Occasionally, however, racial differences are noticed and reported. For example, Rockett, et al. (1991) compared 16-18 year olds in Rhode Island who came to a trauma center for a suicide attempt or a motor vehicle injury in a car in which they were the driver. They noted that nonwhites were more likely than whites to be among the suicide attempters. It is very likely that such comments do not assume sufficient importance in the reports that the study is identified as pertinent to racial differences.

FACTS ABOUT BLACK SUICIDE

As a result of the effort made in this book to estimate black suicide rates by age and gender back to 1933 (when all states finally reported mortality statistics to the federal government), it can be seen that, at the national level, black suicides rates were and continue to be lower than white suicide rates, although the difference is getting less over time.

Contrary to most commentary (which has focused on black "youth"), the group which has been at most risk for suicide is black males aged 25-34, although the suicide rate of black males aged 15-24 is increasing (see Chapter 3). Black females of all ages have had consistently low suicide rates.

Research at the social level suggests that oppression has contributed to the low black suicide rate (as predicted by Henry and Short's theory of suicide), and the rising black suicide rate in recent years is consistent with the increasing number of African Americans moving into the middle class (see Chapter 10). However, a more in-depth analysis of individual black suicides might require this conclusion to be modified, for such an analysis would indicate more precisely to which social classes black suicides belong. There was also support for Holinger's cohort hypothesis for black male suicide rates (see Chapter 11).

There is also the suggestion that African American religious beliefs, perhaps influenced by the African cultures from which African Americans descend, beliefs which view suicidal behavior very negatively, may contribute to the relatively low black suicide rate, both here and in Africa (see Chapters 9 and 13).

At the individual level, the little research conducted so far indicates that the same risk factors which predict suicide in the general population also predict suicide in African Americans.

There has been much debate about whether African Americans and whites differ in the incidence of different psychiatric disorders and in the patterns of symptoms accompanying each psychiatric disorder. A recent review of the research on the incidence of depressive disorders in African Americans and whites revealed contradictory results -- some finding more depression in African Americans, some finding more depression in whites, and some finding no differences (Santos, et al., 1983). The research is also unclear about whether African Americans and whites differ, for example, in the symptoms manifested when they are depressed, aside from differences in relating to and responding to questions from a mental health professional. However, some studies do report clear differences between black and white patients, even on objective psychological assessment instruments (e.g., Nelson, et al., 1996).

What is needed is research which focuses on risk factors such as these and examines in detail whether African Americans and whites differ in their incidence and whether the risk factors predict suicide in the same way in African Americans and whites. If, for example, African Americans are less likely to have affective disorders than whites and if affective disorder predicts suicidal behavior in both African Americans and whites, then we would have a psychological theory for black/white differences in suicidal behavior.

As far as preventing suicide, it has been suggested, although not properly documented, that African Americans are less likely to use suicide prevention resources than are whites. However, no new ideas for preventing suicide have been proposed by those commenting on black suicide except that most commentators have stressed primary prevention, the improvement of the general social, economic, and psychological well-being of African Americans. However, it has been noted that such a social program might result in higher suicide rates as African Americans would then face more of the same suicidogenic factors that whites face.

REFERENCES

Copeland, A. R. Dyadic death. *Journal of the Forensic Science Society*, 1985, 25, 181-188.

Gibbs, J. T. Homicide and suicide in young black males. In C. D. Llewellyn & R. J. Brown (Eds.) *The African American male*, pp. 15-26. New York: National Urban League, 1992.

Lester, D. *Suicide in American Indians*. Commack, NY: Nova Science, 1997.

Miles, D. E. The growth of suicide among black Americans. *The Crisis*, 1979, 86, 430-433.

Nelson, D. V., Novy, D. M., Averill, P. M., & Berry, L. A. Ethnic comparability of the MMPI in pain patients. *Journal of Clinical Psychology*, 1996, 52, 485-497.

Roberts, R. E., Chen, Y. R., & Roberts, C. R. Ethnocultural differences in prevalence of adolescent suicidal behaviors. *Suicide & Life-Threatening Behavior*, 1997, 27, 208-217.

Rockett, I. R. H., Spirito, A., Fritz, G. K., Riggs, S., & Bond, A. Adolescent risk-takers. *International Journal of Social Psychiatry*, 1991, 37, 285-292.

Rohde, P., Seeley, J. R.,, & Mace, D. E. Correlates of suicidal behavior in a juvenile detention population. *Suicide & Life-Threatening Behavior*, 1997, 27, 164-175.

Santos, J. F., Hubbard, R. W., & McIntosh, J. L. Mental health and the minority elderly. In L. D. Breslau & M. R. Haug (Eds.) *Depression and aging*, pp. 51-70. New York: Springer, 1983.

INDEX